# Financial Services Anti-Fraud Risk and Control Workbook

PETER D. GOLDMANN

WILEY

JOHN WILEY & SONS, INC.

For general information on our other products and services or for technical support, please contact our Customer Care Department within the United States at (800) 762-2974, outside the United States at (317) 572-3993 or fax (317) 572-4002.

Wiley also publishes its books in a variety of electronic formats. Some content that appears in print may not be available in electronic books. For more information about Wiley products, visit our web site at www.wiley.com.

ISBN: 978-0-470-49899-6

Printed in the United States of America

10 9 8 7 6 5 4 3 2 1

# Contents

## Chapter 4 Employee-Level Embezzlement 51

## Chapter 5 Internal Fraud: Management Level 93

## Chapter 6 External Fraud against Financial Services Companies 123

## Chapter 7 Conducting a Successful Fraud Risk Assessment 175

## Chapter 8 Legal and Regulatory Compliance for Controlling Fraud Risk 185

## Chapter 9    Fraud Detection in Financial Services Companies

# Preface

*The man who is admired for the ingenuity of his larceny is almost always redis-covering some earlier form of FRAUD. The basic forms are all known, have all been practiced. The manners of capitalism improve. The morals may not.*

—John Kenneth Galbraith

This quote can be interpreted in different ways, depending on your view of the world and those who populate it. If you believe in the inherent good of those who make the financial markets what they are, you will take to heart the second-to-last sentence. If you are of a more cynical mind, the concluding sentence is the one that speaks most clearly to you.

This workbook is not designed to pass judgment on whether the ethical fabric of the financial services industry is more good than bad or vice versa. Rather, its pur-pose is to give internal auditors, accountants, and other financial professionals in financial services institutions a foundation of knowledge about fraud that affects their organization.

It is hoped that through the text, the interactive exercises, and chapter quizzes you will pick up some practical knowledge to help you mitigate fraud risks in your organization.

## ▶ About This Book

*How to use this workbook.* Read the text in each of the nine chapters. Each chapter contains one or more mini case studies of actual frauds. They are included to help illustrate key points in the chapter. At the end of the case studies, you will be asked how the fraud could have been prevented. Try to list as many preventive measures as you can. As you progress through the workbook, your list of measures will grow as you become more knowledgeable about the dynamics of how fraud is committed, detected, and prevented. Lists of sample preventive measures for each case study can be found in Appendix B.

At the end of each chapter, try to answer as many questions as you can in the Chapter Quiz and check them against the answer key found in Appendix A. These quizzes contain no trick questions. They are standard-format questions to help you complete the workbook and—most important—help you fight fraud and corruption at your organization.

---

### Remember

Throughout this workbook, you will see boxes titled "Remember." These are flags for key facts, concepts, or topics to pay particular attention to as you build your knowledge about fraud.

---

## ▶ About White-Collar Crime 101 LLC

White-Collar Crime 101 LLC (WCC 101) was founded in 1998 in Connecticut by Peter Goldmann, a graduate of the London School of Economics, an established business journalist who had reported for and edited many domestic and international business publications.

The company came into being as the result of Mr. Goldmann's acquisition of a monthly newsletter called *White-Collar Crime Fighter* directed primarily at law enforcement personnel.

After acquiring the publication, Mr. Goldmann redesigned it and reformulated its purpose and content, thus establishing it as the only monthly subscription-based publication designed to provide useful, actionable anti-fraud advice and insight to the private sector.

Over the following years, *White-Collar Crime Fighter* published articles based on interviews and contributions from hundreds of top U.S. and overseas anti-fraud experts from the fields of auditing, accounting, law, investigation, forensics, finance, compliance, and regulation.

Today, the publication enjoys a reputation as a leading source of reliable how-to information on detecting, preventing, investigating, and prosecuting fraud.

Thanks to *White-Collar Crime Fighter*'s success, several subscribers approached WCC 101 asking if the company provided employee fraud awareness training. At the time, 2001, the answer was no. However, Mr. Goldmann wondered why large corporations were coming to his publication for training. It must have meant, he reasoned, that no one else was offering such training, which to him seemed like a basic anti-fraud imperative for any organization, given the already serious and continuously growing threat of fraud.

After some digging, the WCC 101 team determined that, indeed, there was no such employee-friendly anti-fraud training on the market. There was plenty of training for "the profession"—for fraud examiners, accountants, auditors, and law enforcement investigators; but nothing taught employees how to recognize the red flags of fraudulent conduct in their organizations or how to report such incidents if they were detected.

Long story short, Mr. Goldmann resolved to fill this gap in the market for anti-fraud tools. He conceived and developed *FraudAware,* a customizable Web-based (e-learning) fraud awareness course designed for large companies. The basic, generic *FraudAware* program was completed in mid-2002—just around the time when Congress was dotting the *is* and crossing the *ts* of the Sarbanes-Oxley (SOX) Act.

As executives of public companies (*FraudAware's* initial targeted market) quickly learned that SOX compliance was going to cost them multiple millions of dollars and countless hours from the schedules of their internal auditors, accountants, senior financial executives, and attorneys, employee fraud awareness training was a decidedly low priority.

By 2005, as the financial and human resources burdens of SOX compliance had begun to decline, management at many organizations began to realize that despite its massive investments in SOX compliance, the problem was not getting better; in fact, it was getting worse.

*The result.* A growing number of organizations began to realize that they had to mobilize their greatest asset—their employees—to actively assist in the fight against fraud.

*FraudAware* training became a logical tool for accomplishing this. Indeed, in recent years, the team of *FraudAware* subject matter experts, instructional designers, and e-learning techies has been extremely busy, implementing customized training courses at organizations in all major industries in the United States and overseas.

Today, WCC 101 is the premier provider of published anti-fraud information and maintains the largest searchable Web-based archive of practical actionable fraud prevention information. It also has a reputation of being the only provider of customized anti-fraud training designed, developed, and implemented by a team of top subject matter experts *and* instructional professionals.

With the publication of *Financial Services Anti-Fraud Risk and Control Workbook,* WCC 101 adds another valuable source of practical anti-fraud training and guidance. This workbook will be followed by similar editions specifically for the not-for-profit and hospitality sectors.

# Acknowledgments

This workbook would not have been possible without the generous support and assistance of some outstanding thought leaders in fraud prevention, detection, and investigation.

Special thanks are owed to Paul McCormack, CFE, who generously shared his knowledge and experience in banking fraud. Paul, formerly Vice President of Fraud Detection for SunTrust Banks in Georgia, provided invaluable assistance in putting together segments of the book dealing with the many technical aspects of bank fraud and the various tactics that financial institutions have experimented with in the ongoing battle with both corrupt insiders and external criminals. Paul currently is a partner at Innovar, where he leads the firm's fraud practice. He is also a freelance author. His areas of expertise include fraud, commercial litigation, ethics, and compliance.

Thanks also to:

- LeAnn Bailey, CPA, former Vice President of Program Management at Washington Mutual and then JP Morgan Chase
- Christine Doxey, CAPP, CCS, Vice President of Business Development, Business Strategy Inc.

Thanks also to the many anti-fraud experts who generously shared their time and allowed me to interview them for articles published in *White-Collar Crime Fighter*, thereby enabling me to acquire valuable new knowledge for this project.

Appreciation also goes to John Wiley & Sons for choosing to add this new workbook format to its impressive array of anti-fraud titles.

# Introduction: Brief History of Fraud in the Financial Services Industry

The U.S. financial services industry has evolved in a relatively short 150 years from one defined by basic, unregulated lending and borrowing to one of ultra-sophistication and complexity that the average man or woman on the street finds incredibly difficult to fully understand.

What *is* understandable and equally incontrovertible is that fraud has "matured" in lockstep with the industry's evolution. No sooner has a new segment of the financial industry emerged than new ways to defraud it have been spawned. Indeed, each new product and each new service has been introduced only to unintentionally—but seemingly unavoidably—open a new door for fraudsters as well.

Unfortunately, thus far no regulatory control or legislative act has been able to fully close those doors again.

Before the Civil War, the United States had a banking and financial system that could be described as sketchy at best.

Until the Revolution, most of the colonies used tobacco as legal tender. Then came what came to be called specie money: currency made of material of value, such as silver and gold. But shortages of specie soon led to introduction by the states of paper money known initially as fiat money in that the paper was in theory backed by specie though in fact the states that issued the currency had no legal obligation to honor demands for redemption of the notes in gold or silver.

In any case, fiat money is what the Continental Congress used to finance the war against the British.

Following independence, the United States went through a brief period marked by the establishment of a primitive form of central bank known as the Bank of North America, which existed essentially for the sole purpose of financing federal operations. By 1782, after barely a year of operation, the federally sanctioned banking monopoly enjoyed by the Bank of North America proved untenable, as did its inflation-ravaged paper currency—and the institution was dissolved.[1]

This led to a congressional initiative—the Coinage Act of 1792—to reestablish the country's monetary foundations on "hard currency" (i.e., gold and silver).

The silver dollar was inaugurated and became the monetary standard of the federal government. Before long, however, numerous events combined to sabotage the coinage system, not least of which was a massive increase in the supply of silver from vast mining operations in Mexico. By 1820, following a financial panic induced by the checkerboard of state and federal rules regarding the use of gold and silver versus bank-backed paper notes as true currency, there were no more gold dollars in circulation, only silver coins. However, their value proved unstable, and it was not long before the coinage system collapsed.

In the interim, a second attempt at central banking was initiated, in the form of Alexander Hamilton's brainchild, the Second Bank of the United States. The bank operated alongside state banks, whose numbers increased rapidly in the early 1800s. Mandated by a Democratic-Republican political consensus, the bank was established in part to introduce a national paper currency.

A critical political lesson to be drawn from the 1816 establishment of the Second Bank of the United States is that the institution was born at the hands of influential New York merchants and traders, prominent among them the fur trader John Jacob Astor and financially powerful Philadelphia lawyer Stephen Girard, who had been instrumental in earlier federal banking initiatives.

Nonetheless, the culture of concentrated political and financial power as the driver of bank regulation was in full force as early as the beginning of the twentieth century. The influence peddling and horse trading that dominated federal banking policy only became more institutionalized in subsequent decades. That this had a direct influence on the rapid spread of financial institution fraud is not hard to ascertain. In fact, the Second Bank of the United States came to be characterized by one of the most massive management-level financial crimes in the country's short postindependence history.

The Second Bank of the United States owed its creation in large measure to the politically inescapable problem of inadequate financial resources to finance the War of 1812. However, political disagreements and power brokering over the rules governing the bank's capital requirements and lending guidelines dragged on for a full two years with as many as six failed attempts to agree on the legal terms of the bank's charter. Finally, in early 1816, a delicate compromise was reached and legislation was passed establishing the bank in Washington D.C. with $35 million in capital and limited federal government involvement.

The bank, however, was unique among American financial institutions in that it was mandated to have several branches—a structure that inadvertently laid the groundwork for the history-making fraud mentioned earlier. Specifically, the large Baltimore and Philadelphia branches were used as the staging area for an early version of a pump-and-dump stock scheme of immense proportions. As noted banking historian Murray N. Rothbart put it, "Outright fraud abounded at the Second Bank of the United States, especially at the Philadelphia and Baltimore branches, particularly the latter. It is no accident that three-fifths of all of the bank's loans were made at these two branches."[2]

Executives and directors of the Baltimore and Philadelphia branches of the bank perpetrated a massive stock manipulation and financial reporting scheme with bank shares. They were able to gain control of the bank and continue the fraud for several years, earning immense profits from their scheme.[3]

Unfortunately, as with earlier attempts at establishing a central federal bank, the Second Bank was also doomed. In large measure the failure was caused by the inflation that it fueled with the rapid expansion of the money supply through paper currency and a tangled set of rules regarding states' loans from the bank.

Beginning in the 1830s, the unregulated system of state banking saw individual states issuing their own currencies and wildcat bankers issuing currency and quickly going bankrupt as the currency depreciated to worthlessness almost as quickly as it was printed. This early form of bank fraud—in which the bank owners were the perpetrators—is explained by one scholar in this way:

> If the bond security [of a new bank] was valued at more than its market value, individuals had an incentive to buy bonds, issue notes, and abscond with the proceeds.
>
> For example, if someone could buy $80,000 worth of bonds at current market prices and the bonds were valued as security at their face value of, say, $100,000, and the notes could be passed for more than $80,000, say $90,000, there is a one-time gain of $10,000 in starting the bank. If the owner could avoid being sued for noteholders' losses, for example by leaving the court's jurisdiction, this difference between the amount received for the notes and the market value of the bonds created an incentive to start a bank and let it fail quickly.[4]

*Important.* Wildcat banking was an extreme form of what was called free banking. Beginning in the mid-1830s and reaching a crescendo in the 1850s, free banking was a considerably less chaotic system than wildcatting; in fact, as some historians have pointed out, the term was a misnomer in that financial institutions—primarily state banks—operating as free banks were anything but.

For example, as Rothbart put it:

> "[F]ree" banking, as it came to be known in the United States before the Civil War, was unrelated to the philosophic concept of free banking analyzed by economists. . . . Genuine free banking is a system where entry into banking is totally free, the banks are neither subsidized nor regulated, and at the first sign of failure to redeem in specie payments, a bank is forced to declare insolvency and close its doors.
>
> "Free" banking before the Civil War, on the other hand, was very different. . . . The government allowed periodic general suspensions of specie payments whenever the banks over expanded and got into trouble—the latest episode was in the panic of 1857. It is true that bank incorporation was now more liberal since any bank that met the legal regulations could become incorporated automatically without lobbying for special legislative charters, as had been the case before. But the banks were now subject to a myriad of regulations, including restrictive edicts by state banking commissioners and high minimum capital requirements that greatly impeded entry into the banking business.[5]

*Bottom line.* The problem from the late 1700s until the Civil War was the federal government's abject failure to stabilize the monetary system. As a result, the country lurched from inflationary periods to deflationary ones almost without respite as

INTRODUCTION

the federal government experimented with numerous "solutions" in the forms of revised federal bank charters to new specie standards and currencies and ever-changing rules on the issuance of credit.

This general state of chaos was ripe for fraud. As Republican Representative Elbridge Gerry Spaulding pointed out to a bankers' gathering in 1876, in reference to the early 1800s period of multiple currencies and unpredictable banking regulation:

> The various kinds of paper money in circulation made it necessary [for banks] to keep four separate ledger accounts in each . . . . [I]t was found impossible to maintain . . . continuous supervision of the revenues, and to exact those periodic settlements which constitute the only effectual safeguard against error, demoralization and fraud.[6]

## ▶ Banking the Civil War

As the Civil War began, the federal government suddenly had an insatiable appetite for funds to finance its military operations. This led to the next suspension of the untenable system of specie-based currency that had dogged the country throughout the preceding several decades. In 1862, Congress passed the Legal Tender Act and authorized the printing of $150 million in new paper currency dubbed "greenbacks."

Unfortunately, a by-product of this move was to throw the gold market into chaos with wild swings in gold's value as speculators bought and sold the commodity.

The volatility did not end until the final years of the Civil War, when Congress finally created the foundation of what ultimately emerged as the centralized banking system. Although the Federal Reserve Bank itself was not established until 1913, the decades following the end of the Civil War were marked by relative stability, except for a severe hiccup in 1873 that, until the 1930s, was known as the Great Depression. Triggered in part by excessive issuance of stock by railroad companies and speculation among stockbrokers, the economic contraction that spanned the next six years saw 30,000 businesses fail, wages plunge by 25 percent, and the price of oil decline to an incredibly cheap 48 cents per barrel.[7]

In the end, as a desperate effort to defeat inflation, the United States lurched back onto the gold standard in 1879.

Importantly, much of the country's financial activity during the post–Civil War period was conducted by the rapidly growing number of state banks, using combinations of individual state currency, greenbacks, and silver.

As for the formal banking industry itself, it came to be dominated in the late 1860s by railroad barons such as Jay Gould and Cornelius Vanderbilt, who exploited the underdeveloped and certainly unregulated businesses of borrowing and lending.

This state of financial chaos brought with it the landmark 1867 collapse of Credit Mobilier, a construction company turned financial institution indirectly owned by financial promoters of the Union Pacific Railroad, which at the time was controlled by the federal government. The bank—originally organized by one George Francis Train, existed for the prime purposes of financing the railroad's construction in exchange for ample "returns" generated by drawing down substantial loans that the government had earlier provided to the railroad. But shortly after Congressman Oake Ames took over the "bank," it was learned that Ames had generously spread Credit Mobilier shares among numerous congressional colleagues to secure votes for additional federal loans purportedly needed to complete the construction of the railroad. It took little time to discover that proceeds of the loans, to the tune of $23 million, had ended up in Credit Mobilier owners' pockets.

Credit Mobilier earned the dubious distinction of being the first major American financial institution failure. The event was a symbol of America's greatly underdeveloped financial and regulatory structure. It was soon followed by the first "real" stock market crash of 1892–93 and the era of the "Money Trust" of the early 1890s—a term that came to be synonymous with John Pierpont Morgan.[8]

Through the turn of the century and into the 1920s, Morgan built the London-based business partnership of his father, Junius, with American banker extraordinaire George Peabody into the first major U.S. investment banking firm.[9] During those years, Morgan managed to earn a reputation of what former banking executive turned economic history and financial writer Charles Morris defined as "absolute integrity and straight dealing."[10]

Morgan was the builder of modern securities markets, replacing the one-stop pseudomonopolistic financing approach of Jay Gould. Under Morgan, *shareholders* actually became living, breathing investors to be reckoned with.

This admirable achievement was the product of Morgan's recapitalizing of the railroads with fresh money, much of it originating in Europe, where Morgan commanded enormous admiration and respect. He simplified the capital structure of the railroads into no more than two layers of debt with interest rates that the railroads' cash flows could readily manage. Equity meanwhile was sold to a broad market of eager investors.

And then came the Great War, with the Allies' massive need for credit. Almost overnight the dollar became the "modernized" world's currency of choice. For help in raising funds for their war efforts, France and Britain turned to J. P. Morgan. In what was at the time the largest bond issue ever, Morgan's financial empire orchestrated a $500 million debt offer, being careful not to define the securities as "war bonds" to a public new to the securities game but more palatably as "trade finance."[11]

By the time the United States entered the war in 1917, demand for U.S.-issued bonds was so great that the U.S. Treasury was able to market some $17 billion of its own debt in the final year or so of the war.

By war's end, so many "average" Americans had bought government debt that demand for retail investment services was more than adequate to fuel the rapid emergence of a full-fledged retail securities industry.

## ▶ Twentieth-Century Fraud

Unsurprisingly, with the rapid growth of western capitalism in the nineteenth and twentieth centuries came great temptation for employees *and* outsiders to steal from the country's rapidly increasing number of banks and investment houses.

But in the end, it was naive individual would-be investors who suffered most at the hands of swindlers peddling bogus securities to a public red hot with visions of immediate wealth.

Things got progressively more precarious throughout the "Roaring" 1920s, which saw the frenzy over government debt spread to equities. And while only about 2 million Americans actually owned stock by the time the market crashed in October 1929, the spread of securities holdings among American investors was substantial enough to give rise to the widespread panic that broke out when the equities market ultimately crashed. In fact, as many historians have written, the market crash was *not* the cause of the Great Depression. Rather, the Depression was largely a by-product of misguided monetary policy and colossally misconceived foreign trade policies (in the form of the Smoot-Hawley Act of 1930, which effectively choked off the inflow of foreign goods through astronomical tariffs, causing an international economic slump and triggering rampant unemployment).

It is nonetheless undeniable that the spirit of speculation that gripped the U.S. stock market beginning in the mid-1920s had "imminent disaster" written all over it. And, indeed, fraud played a major role in bringing on the inevitable bursting of the bubble. Huge amounts of bogus stock was sold to investors, rich and poor, while legitimate issues of equities experienced stupendous price growth within very short periods of time.

As with the 2007–2008 bubble burst, the crash of 1929 was accompanied by a panoply of egregious frauds that helped to accelerate the country's plunge toward disaster.

*Examples.* According to the records of an aggressive investigation into the stock market crash and its aftermath by a subcommittee of the Senate Committee on Banking and Currency, led by Senate staffer Ferdinand Pecora between 1932 and 1934, major banks, investment houses, and even law firms had peddled hundreds of millions of dollars of worthless stock leading up to the fateful day in October 1929.

The Pecora Commission methodically examined—and exposed—the dirty laundry of virtually every big-name Wall Street firm, including Chase National Bank, J.P. Morgan & Co., Kuhn Loeb and Co., and National City Bank and its so-called securities affiliate, National City Co.

The latter two names are of particular interest. According to the Pecora Commission, one of the most brazen frauds of the 1920s was perpetrated by the large New York banks flogging off massive amounts of worthless securities to their securities affiliates, thereby applying copious layers of financial cosmetics to their own balance sheets.

Compared to the merciless grilling that Pecora and his staff gave to the banking lords of the 1920s, the questioning in February 2009 of the chiefs of Bank of America, JP Morgan Chase, and Wells Fargo about their actions following the late-2008 collapse of the credit markets should have caused American taxpayers to cringe. These modern-day titans of American banking were handled with kid gloves by the political elite.

And in yet another incident eerily similar to the self-enriching conduct of the captains of Lehman Brothers, Merrill Lynch, and other sinking Wall Street superships in late 2008, Pecora uncovered the fact that while the market was crashing in 1929, Chase's then boss, Albert Wiggin, made a $4 million profit as his bank's stock price rapidly tanked.[12]

In the end, the important but little-known fact is that the Pecora Commission's work to expose the criminal activities of financial institutions in the late 1920s led directly to the drafting and ultimate passage of the Securities Act of 1933, the Securities Exchange Act of 1934, and the Glass-Steagall Act of 1932.

## ▶ Savings and Loan Crisis

Between the country's painstaking emergence from the Depression and the mid-1980s, financial services fraud was relatively benign. Instead, the country was gripped by such mega-scandals as Watergate, allegations of political deception about U.S. activities in Vietnam and Cambodia, and other nonfinancial debacles. But then all hell broke loose when, due to the calamitous confluence of misguided federal regulatory measures, the entire savings and loan (S&L) industry was drop-kicked into insolvency.

But lest we get ahead of ourselves, we must first take a look at the origins of the S&L industry and the spectacular rise it experienced *before* the fall.

The Federal Home Loan Bank Act of 1932 established the Federal Home Loan Bank Board (FHLBB) with the laudable task of creating a reserve credit system to ensure that ample mortgage credit was available to facilitate home buying. It also became the principal regulatory agency for the S&L industry.[13]

In 1934, the second key S&L regulatory body—the Federal Savings and Loan Insurance Corporate (FSLIC)—was created. Its mandate: to insure S&L deposits.

Specifically, according to Bert Ely, head of the noted financial institution and monetary policy consulting firm Ely and Company, "Federal deposit insurance, which was extended to S&Ls in 1934, was the root cause of the S&L crisis."[14] As Ely explains it, the FSLIC was required by Congress to charge all S&Ls the same insurance premium, regardless of how risky the lending policies of individual thrifts were. As such, the entire S&L industry was effectively underinsured for decades, which made subsequent policy blunders more devastating than they might have been.

For example, from the mid-1930s on, the federal government required S&Ls to borrow short and lend long. In other words, because S&Ls were restricted to providing only fixed-rate 30-year mortgages but had to borrow from depositors on a short-term basis, they were inherently vulnerable to any unanticipated jump in short-term interest rates, which is exactly what happened in the 1970s. When, in the latter part of that decade, inflation reached the double-digit range, then Federal Reserve chairman Paul Volcker launched his famed "war on inflation" by severely restricting the money supply.

For the S&L industry, this was the equivalent of a nuclear attack. Until 1980, S&Ls were not permitted to pay more than 5 percent on deposit money. But when that restriction was lifted by the FHLBB, S&Ls could go after deposits without restriction—which they did with abandon.

*Problem.* When S&Ls still were collecting interest payments of only 5 percent on much of the 30-year fixed-rate mortgage debt on their books, their ability to turn a profit quickly evaporated.

The situation rapidly worsened in the 1980s, as the prime rate skyrocketed to 21.5 percent in December 1980. With thrifts now forced to pay depositors lofty rates on their short-term deposits, the immense gap between what the thrifts were paying depositors and the revenue they were receiving from fixed-rate mortgage holders spelled virtually instantaneous insolvency for the S&L industry—at least on paper.

What followed was a wild swing of the political pendulum to virtual *nonregulation* of the S&L industry. In 1982, Congress, for example, dropped the rule that S&Ls had to have a minimum of 400 shareholders. Now a sole entrepreneur could invest in an S&L. Thanks to the subsequent removal of other key regulatory constraints, he or she could charge whatever the market would bear for loans and pay whatever it took to attract deposits needed to fuel rapid growth. Going even further, the regulatory unshackling of S&Ls enabled would-be S&L owners to invest non-cash assets such as land in order to acquire an S&L, while allowing them to invest in any financial, real estate, or other opportunities they wanted, regardless of how risky.

S&L owners clamored to pay top dollar for deposits and then turned around to invest those dollars in highly—sometimes absurdly—speculative real estate deals.

Predictably, many of these deals promptly went bust, thus severely exacerbating an already financially untenable situation in the thrift industry.

In the course of it all, several bank owners, including the most infamous S&L felon, Charles Keating, as well as others, were prosecuted on charges of embezzling depositors' funds, perpetrating fraudulent real estate deals, and other costly frauds.

To say that numerous types of fraud came to characterize the S&L debacle is an understatement. For example, according to a 1989 General Accounting Office (GAO) report on the demise of the thrift industry:

> Indications of "fraud and insider abuse," as defined by the [Federal Home Loan] Bank Board were evident at all the failed thrifts [examined by the GAO]. A majority of the allegations of criminal misconduct at both the failed and solvent thrifts involved officers or directors.[15]

According to the GAO, these abuses ranged from outright looting of depositors' cash, to filing fraudulent financial statements, to conspiracy to defraud federal agencies, wire and mail fraud, and fraudulent appraisal of assets—to name a few.[16]

The essence of the fraud and abuse elements of the complex and costly S&L debacle is captured in a useful but decidedly understated passage from the GAO's above-referenced report:

> The [Federal Home Loan] Bank Board had cited the majority of the failed thrifts we reviewed for violations of laws and regulations prohibiting conflicts of interest and transactions with affiliates. In 1988, the Bank Board defined these and other characteristics as "fraud and insider abuse." The presence of fraud and insider abuse indicates management's neglect of its fiduciary responsibility to ensure the safe and sound operation of the insured institution.

These characteristics, combined with passive boards of directors at many of the . . . failed thrifts, contributed to a pattern of risky business transactions often made to benefit insiders, related parties, or others to the detriment of the thrifts' financial health. In many cases, even as the health of the thrifts deteriorated, management compensated itself and made expenditures which federal regulators said were excessive, violated sound business practices and, at times, a federal regulation on compensation. Such practices indicate a lack or circumvention of effective internal controls, creating environments in which the thrifts were vulnerable to abuse from thrift insiders and others.[17]

This, together with the rest of the GAO report, makes the S&L debacle seem like a series of unfortunate financial and regulatory misdemeanors when compared to the *real* story of the scandal meticulously chronicled in the book by former deputy FSLIC director William Black, *The Best Way to Rob a Bank Is to Own One*. In it, Black describes the S&L "problem" as a massive Ponzi scheme facilitated by misguided regulators and corrupt outside auditors but perpetrated by a band of swashbuckling Texas and California financial zealots whom he aptly calls "control frauds."

Control frauds are, in Black's words, "financial superpredators" who cause "catastrophic business failures."[18] These miscreants, according to Black, systematically abused the S&L industry for personal gain by creating loan schemes cleverly designed to exploit unsophisticated real estate developers by extending loans to them on risky development projects and then self-funding the interest payments with depositors' savings. The bogus income was recorded as profit. Despite the loans' accompanying equity kickers of up to 49 percent, the "Big Eight" audit firms that were signing off on the books of these institutions looked the other way when these investments were recorded as loans rather than equity. Thus, the S&Ls were able to fraudulently show huge profits from the bogus income they were self-generating.

And of course, much of this "income" ended up in the pockets of the S&L owners who generously bestowed upon themselves bonuses, salary increases, and lavish perquisites.[19]

To illustrate what the GAO, rather benignly, and Black more unequivocally were describing, one example in particular tells it all. It involved the famed—or infamous—Don Dixon, aka Donnie Ray Dixon, who mastered the art of what are commonly referred to as *nominee* loans but which in the case of Dixon meant simply making fraudulent loans to himself. In a 1991 article, *New York Times* reporter N. R. Kleinfield wrote:

> The Vernon Savings and Loan Association had been founded in 1960 by R.B. Tanner, an erstwhile bank examiner, and it grew in a slumberous way. The only leather around the place was people's wallets. By 1981, Vernon was unmistakably robust, with $82 million in assets and $90,000 in delinquent loans, a mere hiccup.
>
> Mr. Tanner wished to retire. The mood struck Don Dixon to buy the place and he offered $5.8 million. You could see his reasoning. He was building a lot of housing and having his own savings and loan to support his projects was a wonderful prospect to contemplate. . . .
>
> By July 1982, Mr. Dixon had himself a savings and loan without much damage to his pocketbook. He put only 20 percent down; Mr. Tanner and other Vernon stockholders agreed to accept a note for the balance and to be paid quarterly.

Quickly, Mr. Dixon became steeped in the joy of his new purchase. He went haring after large deposits by dangling fat interest rates. With those funds, he began some slippery lending to condominium developments and costly commercial real estate projects. A good deal of the money entered the pockets of Mr. Dixon's cronies, and some of it, regulators charged, went to Mr. Dixon himself.[20]

In fact, according to numerous sources, Dixon used Vernon Savings to finance various commercial real estate projects of questionable financial soundness. It was alleged, among other things, that Dixon funneled millions in deposits into his "holding company," Dondi Financial Corporation, which in turn used some of the funds to finance risky real estate deals but also served as a source of funds for his personal lavish exploits, including opulent trips to Europe, purchase of an outsized yacht, and investments in at least one casino. Unfortunately, once the FSLIC came into the picture, 96 percent of Vernon's loans were in default—a dubious record recorded for posterity in the *Guinness Book of World Records*.

It cost U.S. taxpayers $1.3 billion to clean up Dixon's criminal mess at Vernon. Dixon ultimately was sentenced to two consecutive five-year terms but was released after serving a mere 39 months. However, he was also sued by the U.S. government for stealing over $540 million of depositors' money.

Adds Black:

> [T]he Bank Board believed that he [Dixon] ran the worst control fraud in the nation, Vernon Savings, known to its regulators as "Vermin." This . . . S&L . . . provided prostitutes to Texas S&L commissioner Linton Bowman. . . . Dixon personified greed, immorality, incompetence, and audacity. . . . Dixon did not limit his pimping to Bowman. He inherited a conservative board of elderly directors, many of them leaders in their very strict Baptist church. Not a problem! One of his first acts after the acquisition was to invite the board of directors along on an overnight trip. He tactfully told the female member of the board she wouldn't be comfortable on the boys' night out. Dixon flew the board members to California . . . took them and eight prostitutes on a romantic cruise in a very spiffy sailboat to an equally romantic island restaurant off San Diego, and brought them back to a fabulous beach house.[21]

## ▶ Cleanup

The government's takeover of Vernon Savings & Loan was a small example of the vast federal cleanup project that involved nearly 700 failed S&Ls. The legal vehicle for accomplishing this costly task was the Financial Institutions Reform, Recovery, and Enforcement Act of 1989, which put thrifts under the regulatory umbrella of the FDIC and other banking agencies. The minimum capital-to-asset ratio, which, at a mere 3 percent prior to the S&L debacle, and which ultimately enabled swashbuckling financial bosses to buy S&Ls with little or none of their own money, was bumped up to 8 percent. And of course the famed Resolution Trust Corporation was set up with $50 billion in proceeds from government-sanctioned bond offerings and a mandate to take over insolvent banks, pay off the depositors, and sell off any assets that were worth anything.

Interestingly, while the total bill for dispatching the S&L debacle ultimately topped out at around $150 billion—three times the RTC's original estimate—the amount seems trivial in the context of the $700 billion bank bailout slammed through Congress in September 2008 when the collapse of Bear Stearns, Lehman Brothers, Washington Mutual, and other big-name financial institutions appeared to mark the beginning of the end for the American financial system.

It should be noted that in the world of greed, risk, and fraud, the 1980s was not known for the S&L crisis alone. It was also the time of Michael Milken, leveraged buyouts, junk bonds, and insider trading schemes à la Ivan Boesky.

Importantly, Milken's name is to this day synonymous with corporate scandal. When he pleaded guilty to insider trading, filing false financial records, manipulating stock prices, and defrauding his own clients, the news was monumental. Today, the indictment of a Wall Street "player" for such crimes would seem almost routine.

The point is that since the collapse of Milken's firm, Drexel Burnham Lambert, in 1990, the amounts of money involved in financial services meltdowns has gone through the roof. The approximately $100 billion in junk bonds raised by Drexel between 1977 and 1989 seems paltry when compared to the $43 billion lost by Citicorp in 2008 *alone*.

## ▶ Booming 1990s

The Wild West culture that characterized the 1980s through the boom in leveraged financing, hostile takeovers, and the out-of-control S&L boom and bust gave way to a decade of consistent financial market gains.

That turned out to be great for average folks' 401(k)s and individual retirement accounts, but it was by no means a period devoid of financial crime. The culprit this time, though, was derivatives, whose unceremonious birth and explosive growth set the stage for big trouble again once the historic housing boom of the 1990s came to crashing halt starting in 2006–2007. The term "derivative" is defined by Prof. Campbell R. Harrey, of Duke University, as "a financial contract whose value is based on, or 'derived' from, a traditional security (such as a stock or bond), an asset, (such as a commodity), or a market index."

Left holding the short straw in the form of immense amounts of worthless mortgage-backed paper was virtually every financial institution in the developed world (and some in the not-so-developed one). The sudden realization that the securities backed by mortgages that were issued en masse by a vast army of avaricious and ethically challenged mortgage brokers, appraisers, and lenders were worth less than the digital bits and bytes that recorded their existence in far-flung databases plunged the entire global financial system into a tailspin.

What turned out to be the worst financial crisis since the early 1930s was caused largely by the head-on collision of unprecedented cutthroat competitiveness among banks and investment firms that had been building since 1999 when the Glass-Steagall

Act was repealed, thus removing the rules prohibiting banks from trading securities and investment banks from engaging in conventional banking.

The extent to which fraud played a role in bringing down the credit markets remains to be fully analyzed. But as these pages go to press, the class action suits against banks, investment firms, and insurance companies for fiduciary breaches, fraud, and mismanagement are already clogging the courts.

## ▶ What Does It All Mean?

This greatly abbreviated snapshot of the history of fraud and scandal among financial institutions merely scratches the surface of the issue of financial crime in the banking, investment banking, and insurance industries. But it gives us enough of a framework to conclude that financial services fraud seems to come in waves, to be followed by great clamoring for re-regulation ostensibly to prevent future calamities.

Deregulation of the S&L industry by the Reagan administration, for example, sparked a massive boom in fraud and abuse, only to be followed by the establishment of a litany of new banking laws and regulations meant to establish the long-term stability of the American financial system.

As this book goes to press, we are on the wrong side of the pendulum's arc again, with the federal government having taken huge stakes in the country's largest banks, the stock market having plunged by 40 to 45 percent between 2007 and early 2009, and American businesses fighting to access capital.

As Scott MacDonald and Jane Hughes wrote in their excellent 2007 book, *Separating Fools from Their Money,* "Wherever there is a whiff of scandal in the air, we think of apples. Are the scandals the result of a few bad apples or is the entire orchard afflicted with blight? The historical record suggests that there are a few bad apples, but they keep coming back."[22]

The chapters of this book analyze the fraud risks currently facing the still-substantial community of well-run, financially healthy financial institutions and provide practical steps for avoiding being sucker-punched by the inevitable assaults on the financial services industries by the ethical deviants—both insiders *and* criminally minded customers—in future apple harvests.

# Why No Financial Services Institution Is Immune to Fraud

The introduction to this book painted a less-than-rosy picture of the ethical fabric of the American financial services industry. It is true that the industry has been wracked by colossal incidents of fraud and abuse and sometimes multiyear scandals that threatened its very survival.

In reality, despite what you read in the newspapers, which thrive on bad news, there are still plenty of financial institutions that run a tight ship, take care of their customers, invest depositors' cash prudently, and show a profit almost every quarter.

It is to the managers of *these* institutions, as well as those in institutions that have experienced fraud and who wish to prevent further incidents, that this book will be most useful. For, as stated earlier, even those institutions with the best of intentions and the highest of ethical standards cannot fully protect themselves from the large and growing population of financial fraudsters and the continuously evolving methods to their criminal modus operandi.

## ▶ Statistical Perspective

It cannot be denied that fraud is becoming an increasingly serious and costly problem in American business—especially in the financial services industry. The statistics that follow will demonstrate that. Despite this threat, the important thing to remember is that it is still possible to manage a bank or other financial institution in a relatively fraud-free manner. The upcoming chapters of this workbook will provide you with practical, actionable techniques for doing exactly that.

The next statistics will provide you with perspectives on the big picture of organizational fraud in America and on the seriousness of the fraud problem in the financial services industry in particular.

Starting with the big picture, did you know that:

- Organizations of all kinds collectively lose an average of 7 percent of gross revenue to fraud every year? In 2008, that represented approximately $994 billion.[1]

- The most common method by which fraud is detected is tips? Over 46 percent of cases that are detected are reported via a tip from an employee, vendor, or other whistleblower.[2]

- Billing schemes—the most common form of employee-level fraud—are twice as common in organizations as fraudulent financial reporting, which is the main form of *management* fraud?[3]

- Organizations that implement entity-wide fraud awareness training cut fraud losses by 52 percent?[4]

- Seventy-four percent of employees report that they have observed or have firsthand knowledge of wrongdoing in their organization in the past 12 months?[5]

- The average fraudulent financial reporting fraud costs the victim organization $2 million, while the average loss per incident of billing fraud is only $100,000?[6]

- The majority of public companies investigated by the Securities and Exchange Commission (SEC) for fraud subsequently suffer a substantial (50 percent or more) decline in stock price?[7]

- It takes an average of 24 months for a fraud to be detected?[8]

- One-third of large-organization executives say they have no documented investigative policies or procedures for fraud and one-half have no incident response plan?[9]

- The most common type of fraud affecting organizations—by far—is theft of assets, which can include money, services, or physical assets?[10]

**Financial Institution Fraud in Statistics**

- All financial institutions insured by the Federal Deposit Insurance Corporation (FDIC) together held $80.3 billion in asset-backed securities on December 31, 2005. By the same date in 2008, that number had ballooned to $129.2 billion.[11]

- Between 2005 and early 2009, the percentage of nonperforming real estate loans on the books of FDIC-insured institutions exploded from approximately 0.6 percent to 2.8 percent. See Exhibit 1.1.

- Seventy-one percent of financial institutions experienced attempted or actual payments fraud in 2007 (check fraud, Automated Clearing House [ACH] fraud, or credit card fraud).[12]

- Ninety-three percent of all financial institutions that were targets of payments fraud reported attempted check fraud in 2007.[13]

- Although electronic payments are steadily gaining on checks as the preferred payment method by many organizations, the incidence of check fraud remains far greater than that of ACH fraud.[14]

- Twenty-six percent of organizations that were targets of payments fraud in 2007 were hit by at least one incident of ACH debit fraud—down from 35 percent in the previous year.[15]

- Of 21 industries surveyed by the Association of Certified Fraud Examiners for its *2008 Report to the Nation on Occupational Fraud,* "Banking/Financial Services" topped the list in the percentage of total fraud cases, with 14.6 percent.[16]

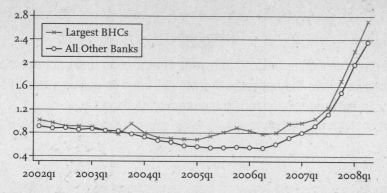

Exhibit 1.1: Nonperforming Real Estate Loans (Percent of Real Estate Loans)
Source: Federal Reserve Bank of New York, *Quarterly Report on Banking Statistics* (November 2008), p. 4.

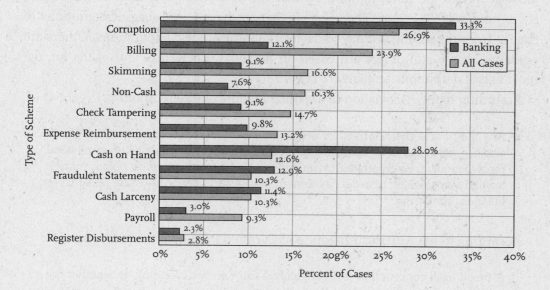

Exhibit 1.2: Occupational Fraud Schemes in Banking and Financial Services Industry
Note: Based on 132 cases. The sum of percentages in this chart exceeds 100 percent because several cases involved multiple schemes from more than one category.
Source: Association of Certified Fraud Examiners, *2008 Report to the Nation on Occupational Fraud and Abuse*, p. 29.

- The most common types of internal fraud affecting the financial services industries (see Exhibit 1.2) are corruption (primarily bribery and kickbacks), theft of cash, fraudulent financial statements, and expense reimbursement schemes.[17]

- In 2008, financial services companies were defendants in 103 class action filings, representing 49 percent of *all* securities-related class actions across nine industries represented in the Standard & Poor's (S&P) 500. Of the 103 filings in which financial services firms were defendants, 91 were related to the subprime credit crisis.[18]

- In 2008, 32 percent of the financial services companies in the S&P 500 were defendants in securities class actions, up from 9.4 percent the year before.[19]

- Reported incidents of mortgage fraud were up by a startling 45 percent in the second quarter of 2008 compared with the same period in 2007.[20]

- The number of reported mortgage fraud incidents represented by fraudulent appraisals jumped by 21 percent between the second quarter of 2008 and the same quarter of the previous year.[21]

## Remember

If you hear from a colleague or boss that your organization does not experience much fraud, the statistics prove the opposite. If anything, fraud is getting worse. For that reason, everyone in the organization must be more alert to it than ever.

## ▶ What Is Fraud?

Most people in the fraud-fighting business have their own concept of what fraud is . . . and what it is not. The result is that we have a grab bag of definitions to choose from in guiding our day-to-day work. Some are legal definitions. Others are academic, while still others are based on personal experience. Out of the lot, the most useful definitions boil down to two.

According to the Association of Certified Fraud Examiners, fraud is:

> Any illegal acts characterized by deceit, concealment, or violation of trust. These acts are not dependent upon the application of threat of violence or of physical force. Frauds are perpetrated by individuals and organizations to obtain money, property, or services; to avoid payment or loss of services; or to secure personal or business advantage.[22]

According to the American Institute of Certified Public Accountants, fraud is:

> A broad legal concept that is distinguished from error depending on whether the action is intentional or unintentional.[23]

Regardless of whose definition of fraud you accept, you will find that nearly all incidents of fraudulent activity—also called white-collar crime—fall into one or both of two categories: theft and deception. Exhibit 1.3 is a graphic illustration formulated by White-Collar Crime 101 of this dual-category definition of fraud.

In attempting to narrow down the definition of fraud to criminal conduct specific to the financial services industry, it is fair to say that the same division between theft and deception holds true. However, as you will learn in upcoming chapters, the *types* of fraud scheme that this definition applies to differ in many instances from those in other industries. For example, in financial services companies, mortgage fraud is a significant subcategory of the overall fraud definition, whereas this type of fraud would obviously *not* be represented in the definition of fraud in, say, the food and beverage industry.

For now, keep in mind the broad definition of fraud as a combination of theft and deception (both of which, by the way, apply to many forms of mortgage fraud, as you will soon find out).

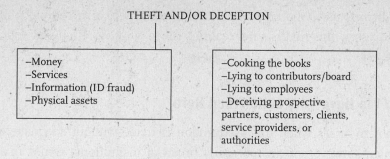

THEFT AND/OR DECEPTION

| |
|---|
| –Money |
| –Services |
| –Information (ID fraud) |
| –Physical assets |

| |
|---|
| –Cooking the books |
| –Lying to contributors/board |
| –Lying to employees |
| –Deceiving prospective partners, customers, clients, service providers, or authorities |

**Exhibit 1.3:** White-Collar Crime 101 Definition

## Remember

There are various definitions of the term "fraud," but the bottom line is that all fraudulent activities fall into the category of either theft or deception—or a combination of both.

### ▶ Myths and Realities about Financial Services Fraud

According to research by the anti-fraud consulting firm Protiviti, released just prior to the full-blown meltdown of the financial markets, management at a majority of organizations is still surprisingly complacent about the threat of fraud.

For example, the Protiviti study determined that only 49 percent of executives believe their organizations' strategies for addressing fraud risk are "very well defined."[24]

Less than half of organizations proactively identify fraud risk and have anti-fraud programs, policies, and controls in place that are monitored and enforced by the board and senior management.

Similarly, a Deloitte Forensic Center survey concluded that only 41 percent of executives considered their companies to be "more effective" in the area of fraud control, compared with the remaining 59 percent who described their organizations' fraud control efforts as "less effective."[25]

While Deloitte notes that companies overall have in recent years enhanced their anti-fraud measures, a substantial "fraud control gap" is still glaringly evident from the data collected.

These findings suggest that six-plus years into the Sarbanes-Oxley era, and in the throes of the worst financial and economic catastrophe since the 1930s, most companies—including financial services firms—still are highly vulnerable to fraud of all kinds, and management appears to show little intention of tightening up its anti-fraud defenses. In fact, as recession-phobic executives slash budgets for anti-fraud training, internal audit, and security, the opportunities for fraudsters to exploit softened anti-fraud defenses naturally multiply. As a result, new forms of fraud targeting financial services organizations are cropping up all the time.

This fact brings us to the critical psychological aspect of corporate fraud, which squarely addresses the myths and realities as to why no financial institution is immune.

## ■ Myth #1: We Have Very Little Fraud Here

A costly problem arises when this assumption is made without adequate and unimpeachable quantitative proof. In too many financial institutions, senior management believes there is little fraud because it *wants* to believe that. Meanwhile, employees, vendors, or customers could be stealing huge amounts of money.

Conveniently, one of the best examples of the we-have-no-fraud-here myth is the case of subprime mortgage fraud. Banks were lending dollars to unqualified mortgage borrowers by the billions in the 1990s and leading up to the housing crash that began in early 2007. Top executives at large mortgage lenders were making money hand over fist as their salespeople, underwriters, and independent mortgage brokers essentially threw every standard for loan qualification out the window, confident that if a borrower ultimately defaulted, the bank could foreclose and sell the property at a profit because housing prices were on a seemingly endless upward trend.

What the bankers failed to address was the issue of how much fraud was being perpetrated by brokers, appraisers, attorneys, and even their own underwriters in order to meet increasingly challenging volume quotas for loan closings.

The truth was that throughout the country, lenders were approving more and more so-called liar's loans, a colloquialism for "stated income" loans—which are approved by lenders without checking tax returns, employment history, credit history, or any other pertinent financial documentation on the applicant.

Moreover, leading up to the subprime crisis, prospective borrowers were directly *encouraged* by mortgage brokers to defraud lenders by filling out mortgage applications with completely fictitious income figures, made-up numbers reflecting their assets and liabilities, and so forth. But to shareholders, regulators, and the general public, bank executives claimed that their lending operations were completely professional and that no fraud was involved.

The truth came out only after the crash—when regulators, lenders' attorneys, and politicians started digging into the matter and discovered that as much as 90 percent of stated income loans were approved despite the existence of at least *some* fraudulent application information.

This example is only one of many that you could find to debunk the no-fraud-here myth that many senior executives throughout the U.S. financial services industry continue to embrace.

In reality, financial services organizations experience less fraud than others. But anyone in the anti-fraud profession will tell you that if a financial company says it has *no* fraud, it is either outright lying or hopelessly naive.

## Alleged Mortgage Fraud of Massive Proportions

Washington Mutual, or "WaMu" as it was affectionately called until its dramatic and unceremonious demise in late 2008, was for decades one of the country's top home mortgage lenders.

It amassed huge profits through the 1980s and 1990s as its aggressive home mortgage juggernaut pressed into more and more local markets, ultimately becoming active in nearly every state in the country.

Not until late 2008 did the truth about WaMu's real financial condition and, more important, how it got there start coming to light.

The real story of WaMu's collapse appears in a 400-plus-page federal class action complaint against WaMu and its former chief executive, Kerry Killinger, in which numerous former employees offer gory details about highly questionable—possibly fraudulent—lending practices as well as alleged securities fraud.

In one exceptionally vivid account, a former WaMu employee explained how the illegal practice of inflating appraised values of homes whose prospective buyers were applying for mortgages was a common practice among appraisers working for WaMu. The experience of this particular "Confidential Witness" (CW)—one of 89 former WaMu employees and others who, on condition that their names not be revealed in the class action filing, provided firsthand accounts of their experiences to the class action attorneys—was described in the filing in this way:

> [I]n-house appraisers received kickbacks from loan consultants to "hit" value on appraisals. Despite CW 25's complaints to management about the appraisal process at WaMu, WaMu management did nothing to change the situation. Indeed, CW 25's job was threatened on many occasions in response to CW 25's complaints of appraisal corruption.
>
> CW 31, who was a contract appraiser with eAppraiseIT after leaving WaMu as an in-house appraiser, also confirmed that WaMu pressured appraisers to inflate appraisal values.
>
> Specifically, CW 31 stated that WaMu dictated appraisal values that it needed to satisfy the LTV [Loan-to-Value] ratios it desired. CW 31 explained that WaMu pressured the third-party appraisers by (i) badgering them to meet the Company's desired appraisal values, and (ii) ceased to hire appraisers who did not bring in the inflated appraisal value that WaMu desired.[26]

***How could this fraud have been prevented?*** List as many controls as you can. Compare yours with those listed in Appendix B.

1. _____

2. _____

3. _____

*The bottom line.* Even as WaMu was on its way down, its top executives were publicly stating that "everything was okay." Whether the C suite knew that alleged appraisal fraud and other potential forms of mortgage fraud were being systematically perpetrated by its employees may never be known for sure.

Chapter 3 addresses the thorny issue of subprime mortgage fraud in greater detail. However, the key lesson here is that even widespread financial wrongdoing can exist in an organization with or without top management's knowledge. This finding teaches us to be skeptical at all times when evaluating the ethical and legal activities of financial services institutions, since *none* is without its fair share of fraud.

## ■ Myth #2: Ethics and Compliance Training "Has Us Covered"

The Sarbanes-Oxley Act of 2002 requires all publicly traded companies to inform the Securities and Exchange Commission if they have a code of conduct in place. If they do not, they are required to explain why. For better or worse, most publicly traded financial services firms do have such codes in place. And along with them, most have over the past several years offered ethics and compliance training.

The ethics and compliance training myth assumes that such training addresses key issues about fraud and instructs employees how to detect the red flags of fraud and how to report it.

The problem is that compliance and ethics typically have little to do with fraud. Most of the codes of ethics that companies now have in place do not even contain the word "fraud."

In most organizations, such a code informs employees about issues like sexual harassment, antitrust issues, accepting gifts from vendors, and other ethical issues that are important—but are not related to fraud.

The important thing to remember is that while all fraud is unethical, not all unethical conduct is fraudulent. For example, accepting a generous gift from a vendor—such as a free vacation, tickets to professional sporting events, or other such items—is unethical and most likely in violation of your organization's ethics policy. However, such gifts are *not* necessarily illegal, and hence they often do not represent fraud.

In any case, the statistics indicating an ongoing increase in the incidence of fraud suggest that ethics training is definitely *not* deterring many employees from breaking the law.

## ■ Myth #3: Fraud Is an Unavoidable Cost of Doing Business

This is a concept often heard in reference to credit card fraud: It is commonly believed that when credit card fraud occurs, the credit card companies have already accounted for it, so they do not go after the perpetrators aggressively.

As for credit card companies, it may be true that fraud is a fact of business life, but it certainly does not mean the card companies are doing nothing to reduce their risk of fraud.

As for other financial services institutions, the cost-of-doing-business mind-set is equally false. An extreme example would be Enron, where fraud cost thousands of employees their jobs and retirement savings. In less serious instances, fraud can damage the bottom line and do considerable harm to the organization's viability. This was illustrated in the massive Tyco International fraud case of the early 2000s, when the company's former chief executive, Dennis Kozlowski, was convicted of looting the company and committing securities fraud and other major crimes. The company's survival was seriously threatened; it took several years to restructure Tyco and return it to long-term viability.

In the financial services sector, the 2007 collapse of two major hedge funds run by Bear Stearns employees after they had assured investors that their investments were safe was enough to trigger the firm's demise just before its acquisition by JPMorgan Chase. The two fund managers, whose investors lost $1.6 billion due to the collapse of the subprime mortgage securities market, were indicted for mail fraud and conspiracy.

---

## Remember

Fraud, while usually not serious enough to destory a financial services firm, often is much more than just a necessary cost of doing business.

---

## ▶ Review Points

- Statistical picture of fraud. The numbers do not lie: Fraud is a *huge* worldwide problem—for all organizations.

- Financial services fraud. Seventy-one percent of financial institutions experienced attempted payments fraud (check fraud, ACH fraud, or credit card fraud).

- Definitions of fraud. The broad definition of fraud is illegal activity representing either theft or deception or a combination of both.

- Myths about fraud. It is easy to become complacent about fraud, but doing so can be very costly. Fraud *does* occur in every organization, and it *is* potentially serious enough to cause major long-term damage.

- Main types of fraud. Countless varieties of fraud threaten financial institutions. Fraudsters are constantly thinking up new ways to target financial services institutions.

## ▶ Chapter Quiz

True or False:

1. The majority of public companies investigated by the Securities and Exchange Commission (SEC) for fraud subsequently suffer a substantial (50 percent or more) decline in stock price.

    ❑ True     ❑ False

2. It takes an average of 36 months for a fraud to be detected.

    ❑ True     ❑ False

**3.** Only 5 percent of large-organization executives say they have no documented investigative policies or procedures for fraud, and 50 percent have no incident response plan.

❑ True ❑ False

**4.** Organizations that implement entity-wide fraud awareness training cut fraud losses by 52 percent.

❑ True ❑ False

Circle the correct answer to the following questions:

**5.** Between 2005 and early 2009, the percentage of nonperforming real estate loans on FDIC-insured institutions' books exploded from approximately:

    **a.** 0.1 percent to 0.9 percent

    **b.** 0.6 percent to 1.4 percent

    **c.** 0.6 percent to 2.8 percent

    **d.** 0.4 percent to 3.2 percent

**6.** In the mortgage industry, "stated-income" loans are synonymous with:

    **a.** Adjustable-rate mortgages

    **b.** Liar's loans

    **c.** Brokerage loans

    **d.** Teaser rate mortgages

**7.** A major reason mortgage lenders in the 1990s lowered the standards for approving mortgage applications was that:

    **a.** Borrowers had high credit scores

    **b.** Unemployment was very low

    **c.** Home prices were expected to continue rising indefinitely

    **d.** Interest rates were extremely low

**8.** The most common types of fraud affecting the financial services industries include all EXCEPT:

    **a.** Corruption

    **b.** Theft of cash

    **c.** Fraudulent financial statements

    **d.** Ponzi schemes

Fill in the blank:

**9.** Regardless of whose definition of fraud you accept, all incidents of financial wrongdoing fall into one or both of the following categories: theft and _____.

**10.** In the area of payments transactions, the incidence of check fraud is much greater than that of _____ fraud.

**11.** The most common form of employee-level fraud is _____.

*For the answers, please turn to Appendix A.*

# The Human Element of Fraud

Chapter 1 provided an abundant array of statistics illustrating the nature and magnitude of the fraud problem. One critical set of data *not* included was defining *who* commits fraud. There is some disparity in the findings of several research studies on how much of total fraud is committed by insiders compared with external perpetrators.

Some data put the ratio at 60–40;[1] others come in closer to 80–20. In any case, while most research shows that on average, a majority of fraud committed against *all* U.S. organizations is internal, the ratio varies from one industry to the next.

Due to the absence of reliable statistics, it is difficult to determine the percentages of fraud committed specifically against financial institutions by outsiders as compared with insiders. However, by virtue of the fact that they are in the money business, the banking and finance industries provide more opportunities for outsiders to perpetrate (or at least attempt to perpetrate) fraud than do most other industries. This is especially true in light of the rapid growth of Internet-based fraud attacks against banks. As such, many financial institutions report that external frauds are considerably more costly in aggregate than internally perpetrated crimes.

What we do know is that financial institutions of all kinds are constant targets of fraud perpetrators from inside *and* outside and that management must devote substantial financial, human, and technological resources to detection, prevention, and deterrence of frauds of all types and origins.

## ▶ Who *Are* the Bad Guys?

When it comes to external fraudsters, financial services institutions have a dizzying variety of perpetrators to worry about.

Most serious, in terms of the dollars involved (although not necessarily dollars lost) are money launderers. This group includes the far-flung global population of drug traffickers as well as members of organized crime, illegal gambling operators, terrorists, and others.

*Note.* Although financial institutions are directly responsible for monitoring and reporting money-laundering activity to federal regulators, because they typically are not victims of such activity, this book does not address the money-laundering problem in great detail.

However, plenty of external fraudsters besides money launderers cause massive losses to financial services companies. Their illegal exploits and how to detect and prevent them are discussed in coming chapters. This band of ethically challenged outsiders includes:

- Dishonest customers (retail and commercial)
- Identity thieves/fraudsters
- Check forgers and counterfeiters
- Dishonest vendors
- Ex-employees
- Internet fraudsters (including phishing attackers, hackers, malicious code programmers)
- Credit card fraudsters
- Crooked mortgage brokers, appraisers, and attorneys

Because external fraudsters are so varied in terms of both the business and social environments in which they operate, as well as their geographical location, it is difficult to identify common personal, behavioral, or demographic characteristics. Some are hardened career criminals; others are occasional opportunists; others target financial institutions for the "thrill of it"; still others do what they do out of desperation (which is increasingly the case during economic downturns, when banks regularly experience spikes in credit card fraud, identity-related frauds, and Internet crime).

The bottom line is that there are few if any behavioral or demographic characteristics common to external fraudsters. For that reason, we will need to focus on the varieties of crimes they perpetrate and learn to spot the red flags, *regardless* of who the perpetrators are.

## ▶ Insider Threat

Fortunately for fraud fighters, the same is not true with regard to internal fraudsters. Employees who commit fraud do have common personality and behavioral traits. They are also prone to scientifically proven psychological influences that help fraud prevention experts to identify them.

In general, research on internal fraud shows that about 80 percent of employees in any financial services institution are fundamentally honest.

If that is the case, you may wonder, how can internal fraud be such a costly threat to financial institutions? Many fraud prevention experts use the so-called 20–60–20 rule to illustrate the human component of fraud:

- Twenty percent of the people in any organization will never steal—no matter what. They are individuals whose character and integrity are so incorruptible that nothing could pressure or tempt them to do anything dishonest.

- Sixty percent of the people in the organization are "fence sitters." They are basically honest people. But if given the *opportunity* to commit fraud and they perceive the risk to be minimal, they might cross the line.

- The remaining 20 percent are inherently dishonest. They will always commit fraud when the opportunity arises. In fact, they often will seek out or even *create* opportunities to steal or deceive if they think it will result in personal financial gain.

To understand the insider fraud threat, it is helpful to divide it into two key categories:

1. Employee-level fraud. This type of fraud is committed by people who are neither supervisors nor managers or executives. They may be salaried professionals or hourly employees.

2. Management-level fraud. These crimes are committed by managers at all levels, including the most senior levels. Many of the frauds committed by these individuals are the same as those committed by employees lower down the organization chart.

Although committed with less frequency than employee-level fraud, virtually all management-level frauds result in much greater losses than those perpetrated at lower levels.

The reason is clear: Managers have more authority and therefore more opportunity to cheat than those who work under them.

These statistics do not include fraud by business owners and top executives. Although such frauds are committed with less frequency than those committed by managers and employees, frauds by the "top dogs" result in losses 5 times greater than those committed by managers and 11 times greater than those by employees.[2]

### Remember

There is an inverse ratio between the level of the organization at which fraud is committed and the amount of financial loss resulting from frauds at each level. Thus, while management-level frauds are committed less frequently than employee-level frauds, the financial loss resulting from these crimes is almost always significantly greater than the amount lost to frauds committed by "regular" employees.

## ▶ The Fraud Triangle

One set of factors common to internal fraudsters *at all levels in any financial services organization* is the Fraud Triangle. The theory behind the Fraud Triangle was developed in the 1940s by a leading criminologist, Donald Cressey, who conducted extensive research with convicted embezzlers to determine what motivated seemingly honest people to commit fraud.

His research led him to coin the term "trust violators" to describe people who embezzle. According to Cressey's research:

> Trusted persons become trust violators when they conceive of themselves as having a financial problem which is "nonsharable," are aware this problem can be secretly resolved by violation of the position of financial trust, and are able to apply to their own conduct in that situation verbalizations which enable them to adjust their conceptions of themselves as trusted persons with their conceptions of themselves as users of the entrusted fund or property.[3]

This somewhat convoluted language essentially means that people who are experiencing severe financial problems about which they are embarrassed (or for other reasons cannot discuss with others) find ways to commit fraud—thinking that they will not get caught while convincing themselves that they are doing nothing wrong.

Eventually, Cressey's findings came to be summed up in what is now widely referred to as the Fraud Triangle. The three components of the Fraud Triangle are—just as Cressey suggests in more complex wording—Pressure, Opportunity, and Rationalization. See Exhibit 2.1.

Pressure in the context of Cressey's Fraud Triangle relates specifically to financial difficulties, such as large amounts of credit card debt, an overwhelming burden of unpaid healthcare bills, large gambling debts, extended unemployment, or similar financial difficulties.

Opportunity exists when an employee discovers a weakness in the organization's anti-fraud controls. Such a weakness might exist, for example, if an employee is able to set up a phony vendor and have fraudulent invoices paid and mailed to an address that he or she controls.

Rationalization—the third element of the Fraud Triangle—is a psychological process whereby persons who have committed fraud convince themselves either that the act is not wrong or that even though it *may* be wrong, it will be corrected because they will eventually return the money. Another, often more damaging form of rationalization occurs when employees justify the fraud by taking the attitude that they *deserve* the stolen money—because the company was unfair by denying them a raise or promotion, or that some other form of mistreatment made them "victims."

Cressey's theory teaches that when all three of these elements are in place in people's lives, they are very likely to commit fraud (or already have).

**Exhibit 2.1:** Fraud Triangle

## ▶ The Fraud Triangle in Financial Services

It is important to note that Cressey's research was based on the activities of internal embezzlers and was designed to analyze the motives behind this specific type of fraud. As such, it certainly applies in assessing the motives behind attempts by financial services employees to steal money or other assets from their employers.

However, over the decades since he first published his findings in 1953, use of the Fraud Triangle has been greatly expanded to help anti-fraud professionals understand the conduct of many types of white-collar criminals, including dishonest senior executives of leading financial institutions.

In the context of financial services, for example, *pressure* has frequently manifested itself in the form of a perceived imperative on the part of top banking executives to win at all costs. This is dramatically illustrated by the cutthroat mind-set that drove major financial services institutions to push the envelope of legal and regulatory constraints on the securities business in the 1990s and early 2000s. Some examples include:

- A series of investigations from 2003 to 2005 by New York State and the federal government into alleged bid rigging and accounting fraud by insurance giants AIG, Marsh & McLennan, Aon, and others, resulting in multimillion-dollar settlement payments by these firms.

- The 2008 meltdown and subsequent buyout by Merrill Lynch of Bear Stearns after two hedge fund managers were found to have committed a massive fraud by misleading investors about the true financial condition of their operations. (See also Chapter 1.)

- The near-overnight demise of Lehman Brothers under the weight of a huge portfolio stuffed with risky commercial real estate loans and toxic derivatives, most of them related to the subprime mortgage debacle. This (so far) has not been shown to have involved any fraud, although the outcome of numerous legal and regulatory actions may prove otherwise in coming years.

## ▶ Pressure at Lehman: An Extreme Example

In the wake of the implosion of the 160-year-old investment firm he had run for 15 years, Lehman Brothers' last chief executive officer (CEO), Richard Fuld, told Congress that he never regretted any of the decisions he had made in his final months at Lehman.

Fuld, who has been characterized by numerous Wall Street experts as ferociously competitive and dead set on victory in every business challenge he takes on, proved to have exercised excessive hubris during the heyday of the subprime mortgage frenzy.

"He exuded hostility," said New York author and critic Ken Auletta, in an interview with ABC News.[4]

That quality apparently served him well over the 40 years he was employed by Lehman. But in his final years as CEO, Lehman amassed a reported $650 billion in assets, much of which was represented by risky commercial real estate loans, subprime mortgage-backed securities and other assets, with only 3 percent in shareholder equity. This earned Fuld widespread criticism for having made over-the-top bets with far too much borrowed money.

No doubt, had Fuld read the tea leaves accurately and continued to grow the firm's profits as he had done by astounding leaps during his 15 years at the helm, he would have been the hero of Wall Street.

This is a dramatic example of Cressey's concept of pressure in the context of the Fraud Triangle. In the 1990s and early years of the twenty-first century, pressure, either self-imposed or a product of the financial services culture, drove some of the best and the brightest of Wall Street to take risks that would have been unheard of 10 or 20 years earlier. Their actions poured tankloads of fuel on the financial wildfire that threw the entire global financial system into unprecedented panic and distress.

Richard Fuld was the archetypical tragic figure in this calamity.

It is important to note that the Fraud Triangle's element of *pressure* can take many other forms at both the executive and employee levels of financial institutions.

For example, exorbitant executive compensation packages took center stage in the debate over whether and how much federal bailout money should be given to the likes of Merrill Lynch, Citigroup, AIG, and JPMorgan Chase in 2008. Many analysts, politicians, and pundits argued that the pressure on these executives to boost their companies' financial performance in order to "earn" bigger bonuses induced them to cut legal and ethical corners.

Although this issue is complex, there is little dispute that the culture of short-term earnings performance that swept through not only the financial services industry but American business in general in the 1990s and early 2000s, and which was linked directly to executive compensation, did create intense pressure on many top executives to break rules governing accounting and securities matters. According to numerous analyses, this was done specifically in order to obtain the performance goals they felt compelled to attain and in the process fatten their bonuses . . . or, in some cases, to preserve their jobs.

## ▶ Opportunity and Rationalization

In the arcane and often complex world of financial services, the Fraud Triangle's elements of *opportunity* and *rationalization* have characteristics that at times overlap with those conceived by Cressey in his analysis of embezzlers. But they also have their unique traits, given the hypercompetitive and sketchily regulated nature of these markets.

As discussed earlier, at the employee level, opportunity can resemble the absence of internal operational controls that constitute the way in for embezzlers at organizations of all kinds. Poor controls can enable employees to move funds from customer accounts to their own, process fraudulent loans for their own benefit, or pay personal expenses from bank funds.

In financial services, opportunity to commit fraud may exist when employees are able to trade securities without adequate supervision or controls and can execute transactions for their own benefit. While this is not an uncommon occurrence, as mentioned in Chapter 1, this trap was spotlighted dramatically in early 2008 when "rogue" trader Jerome Kerviel of Société Générale was found to have lost the bank $7 billion by taking a number of large, unauthorized but highly risky trading positions.

At middle-management levels, poor controls or lack of oversight can enable dishonest insiders to falsify loan applications and other financial documents, authorize and/or approve phony appraisals of property for which financing is sought, or collude with dishonest mortgage brokers.

However, the big-time, headline-grabbing financial institution frauds are those committed by top executives. In the context of *opportunity*, these crimes typically involve falsifying financial statements and records in response to the pressure discussed earlier.

Opportunities to commit these potentially costly financial crimes exist when there is lack of board oversight or weak or nonexistent internal controls over financial reporting (ICFR), or when illegal transactions are unusually complex and therefore cannot be readily understood let alone stopped before being carried out.

A commonly cited case of executive-level financial statement fraud attributed to inadequate ICFR involved the $500 million financial statement fraud perpetrated by the giant insurance company General Re.

Four former General Re executives and one from former General Re client, AIG, were convicted on charges related to fraudulent transactions between the two insurance giants. In early 2008, a federal jury found them guilty on all 16 counts in their indictment, including conspiracy, securities fraud, mail fraud, and making false statements.

Specifically, prosecutors had accused the executives of inflating AIG's reserves by $500 million in 2000 and 2001 through fraudulent reinsurance deals that made AIG—Gen Re's largest client—look financially stronger than it was, thereby artificially boosting its stock price.

During the trial, former AIG CEO Maurice ("Hank") R. Greenberg, who led the company for nearly four decades and is credited with much of its growth, and General Re's then CEO, Joseph Brandon, were identified as unindicted co-conspirators.

The General Re frauds were perpetrated because the five executives felt pressure to embellish AIG's financials and saw an opportunity to manipulate the company's records without getting caught.

The internal controls *and regulatory oversight* that might have prevented this blatant violation of securities laws and other federal criminal statutes were clearly not in place. The case was one in a string of financial reporting frauds, beginning with Enron, that prompted Congress ultimately to pass the Sarbanes-Oxley Act.

## Remember

The opportunity element of the Fraud Triangle helps to explain the ways in which many frauds are committed by employees, middle managers, and executives of financial services organizations.

## The Amazing Tale of How Arson Tipped Off Investigators to Massive Financial Statement Fraud

Herman Jacobowitz, former CEO of the now-bankrupt Allou Healthcare Inc., pleaded guilty to conspiracy to commit bank fraud, securities fraud, mail fraud, and filing a false annual report with the Securities and Exchange Commission (SEC) in connection with the multimillion-dollar looting of his pharmaceuticals, health, and beauty products distribution company.

In addition, Herman's brother Jacob, Allou's former executive vice president, pleaded guilty to filing a false annual report with the SEC, while another brother, Aaron, who ran several Allou-controlled shell companies, pleaded guilty to money laundering. The guilty pleas relate to charges involving what prosecutors called "a staggering, decade-long bank fraud and securities fraud scheme," involving hundreds of millions of dollars of phony sales and inflated inventory that ultimately drove the company into bankruptcy.

*Background.* Prosecutors say that over a period of more than 10 years ending in March 2003, the Jacobowitzes fabricated financial statements by inflating sales by falsifying invoices and reporting millions of dollars of nonexistent inventory in order to increase the amount of money Allou could borrow under lines of credit with several banks. It is estimated that Allou's lenders lost approximately $130 million through the scheme.

*Key.* The frauds were facilitated in part by the fact that the terms of the revolving credit line that the banks had with Allou allowed it to borrow based on accounts receivable. Allou's executives manipulated the company's receivables records to make millions of dollars of aged receivables appear current. In fiscal years 2002 and 2003 alone, some $4 million of aged receivables were falsely included among the company's total $121 million in current receivables.

Because the banks allowed Allou to borrow up to 85 percent of current receivables, the company was able to fraudulently borrow approximately $3.4 million in additional funds in each of these two fiscal years.

*Added example of fraudulent financial reporting.* According to court documents, for one nine-month period in 2002, the company reported revenues of $471 million, of which $158 million was represented by falsified invoices. At around the same time, the company falsely reported $60 million in nonexistent inventory.

While the company was misrepresenting its financial condition and drawing down tens of millions of dollars from bank lines of credit, much of the "borrowed" cash was being siphoned off to companies controlled by the Jacobowitz family. Between January 2002 and March 2003 alone, approximately $180 million was siphoned off to shell corporations owned by the Jacobowitz family.

***How they got caught.*** A fire at an Allou warehouse in Brooklyn led to charges of bribery and insurance fraud. As a result of the fire, Allou included an insurance claim of $87 million in its third-quarter 10-Q for fiscal year 2003. Suspicions were raised because investigators believed the amount of claimed inventory loss was overstated. Following an investigation, the fire was deemed to have been the result of arson, and Allou's insurance carriers withheld payment on the claim.

Prosecutors claim that Herman and Aaron Jacobowitz offered $100,000 to bribe an unidentified insurance official to obtain a falsified report classifying the blaze as accidental. Ultimately, $50,000 was handed to an undercover fire marshal who was working for the prosecution. Allou filed for bankruptcy in April 2003.

***How could this fraud have been prevented?*** List as many controls as you can. Compare yours with those listed in Appendix B.

1. _____

2. _____

3. _____

## ▶ Rationalizing High-Level Fraud

With regard to rationalization, the most common psychological justification for committing fraud at the top levels of financial services companies is, in crude terms, "Whatever it takes."

Richard Girgenti, national leader for KPMG's Forensic Practice, used this exact term to describe the mind-set that in recent years has overtaken U.S. business as a result of misguided performance reward systems. He added: "Restoring trust and confidence in the integrity of our capital markets and institutions will require business leaders to build corporate cultures that reward 'doing the right thing,'"[5] implying that the ethical culture of U.S. business has been severely compromised by the pressures that "give rise to fraud risks."

Although there is no scientific or academic research to explain the rise of the rationalizing attitude of "Whatever it takes," the timeline appears consistent with the steady fragmentation of the financial services industry.

Recent history bears out Girgenti's assessment. Whereas Wall Street firms and banks throughout America (excluding perhaps savings and loan institutions) had acquired an image of integrity, financial conservatism, stability, and unshakable profitability in the early decades of the post–World War II era, this all came apart once the steamroller of industry acquisitions, mergers, and divestitures that populated the business news headlines shifted into high gear in the late 1980s, 1990s, and early 2000s.

The list of such changes in financial institution ownership is lengthy. A helpful snapshot comprises these milestones:

- Lehman sold itself in 1984 to Shearson, an American Express–backed electronic transaction company. Later the same year, the combined firms became Shearson Lehman/American Express.

- In 1988, Shearson Lehman/American Express and E.F. Hutton & Co. merged as Shearson Lehman Hutton Inc.

- In 1993, under newly appointed CEO Harvey Golub, American Express began to divest itself of its banking and brokerage operations. It sold its retail brokerage and asset management operations to Primerica, and in 1994, it spun off Lehman Brothers Kuhn Loeb in an initial public offering, as Lehman Brothers Holdings, Inc.

- Citicorp merged with Travelers Insurance in 1998. (The previous year, Travelers had absorbed Salomon Smith Barney.) In 2001, Citi bought European-American Bank.

- In 2002, Citi acquired Golden State Bancorp, parent company of First Nationwide Mortgage and Cal Fed, the second-largest U.S. thrift.

- Between 2002 and 2005, Citi spun off Travelers.

These and scores of other takeovers, mergers, divestitures, and partnerships between and among Wall Street firms essentially eradicated employee, management, and executive loyalty to any given institution. Replacing the old-school purposefulness of long-term business builders such as John Reed of Citibank, Harvey Golub of American Express, Sanford Weill of Citicorp, and even Richard Fuld of Lehman Brothers was a new brigade of short-term "money tacticians" who seemed to care little about the prestige, financial soundness, and long-term prosperity of their employers. The only thing that motivated them was making money *for themselves*—quickly, any way they could.

The likes of Stan O'Neal of Merrill Lynch, Angelo Mozilo of Countrywide, and Kerry Killinger of Washington Mutual set the stage for a new way of doing business in the financial markets, one defined by a credo of "Take no prisoners."

The questionable ethics governing the "rules" for approving and underwriting subprime home mortgages in the years leading up to the financial crisis of 2007 to 2009 encapsulates this myopic "make-the-numbers" driver of precrisis financial services management.

This mind-set was rather astoundingly summed up by James LaLiberte, former chief operating officer of People's Choice Bank, a California-based subprime lender that filed for bankruptcy protection in 2007 and court-administered liquidation in 2008. LaLiberte told NBC News that People's Choice's chief appraiser had stated to him, "Fraud is what we do," referring to the bank's reported practice of approving loans based on fictitious home appraisals as well as egregiously falsified mortgage applications.

People's Choice is a perfect example of how mortgage lending became a vast playground for unscrupulous loan brokers, lenders, appraisers, underwriters, and executives. Another People's Choice employee—an underwriter—told NBC News that she was actually bribed by loan salespeople with cars, cash, and even breast implants in exchange for approving loan applications that were clearly doctored and were for borrowers who had no way of making the loan payments. (She said she declined these offers.)[6]

Unsurprisingly, People's Choice's founder and former CEO Neil Kornsweit denied any knowledge of such nefarious activity, but hundreds of top executives of failed or struggling subprime lenders at least tacitly sanctioned out-of-control sales conduct by loan officers, appraisers, and underwriters.

## ▶ A Fraud Diamond?

The People's Choice example, as well as the transformation of Wall Street from venerated standard bearer of international financial integrity to hotbed of numbers-chasing mayhem, reveals a fourth side to the Fraud Triangle.

It cannot be denied that in the period from 1999 until the onset of the financial crisis in mid-2007, unadorned lust for money became a root cause of the debacle.

The cycle fueled by Wall Street securitization of billions of dollars of fraudulently processed and default-prone loans that generated outlandish paydays for everyone from top Wall Street executives to Main Street subprime mortgage brokers brought a fog of avarice over the entire financial system, ultimately dooming it to its inevitable crash and burn.

Thus, by the mid-2000s, the Fraud Triangle, as it applied to the financial services industry, had morphed into a Fraud Diamond with *personal greed* forming the fourth side and creating new characteristics of the already deeply engrained fraud problem in the financial services industry.

## ▶ Review Points

- External fraudsters are a varied and demographically diverse group, which makes it difficult for fraud fighters to profile these criminals. The best approach to detecting and preventing external fraud against financial institutions is to understand the red flags of these crimes.

- Internal fraudsters do have common behavioral and personality traits, which helps to detect suspicious activity before it is too late.

- Up to 80 percent of employees are either totally honest or honest to the point that they will not steal except in situations in which the opportunity to do so presents itself. And even then, these "fence sitters" may err on the side of honesty. The remaining 20 percent of your organization's employees are fundamentally dishonest and will go out of their way to commit fraud.

- Internal fraud can be divided into two categories: employee level and management level. There is an inverse ratio between the level of the organization at which fraud is committed and the amount of financial loss resulting from frauds at each level. Thus, while management-level frauds are committed less frequently than employee-level frauds, the financial loss resulting from the former is almost always significantly greater than the amount lost from the latter.

■ The Fraud Triangle (Pressure, Opportunity, and Rationalization) helps fraud fighters identify and stop potential fraudsters from carrying out crimes that could result in financial losses to the organization.

■ The elements of the Fraud Triangle have their own unique meaning in the context of the financial services industry.

■ The Fraud Triangle can arguably be reinterpreted as a Fraud Diamond when the element of greed is included as a key motivator for fraud in the financial services sector.

## ▶ Chapter Quiz

True or False:

1. External fraudsters cannot be profiled easily because of their diverse demographics, varied social and business environments, and varied geographical locations.

   ❏ True    ❏ False

2. Twenty percent of the employees in your organization will commit fraud only if provided with the opportunity to do so.

   ❏ True    ❏ False

3. Although committed with less frequency than employee-level fraud, virtually all management-level frauds result in much greater losses than those perpetrated at lower levels.

   ❏ True    ❏ False

Circle the correct answer to the following questions:

4. Management-level fraud is:

   a. Committed more frequently than employee-level fraud.

   b. Committed less frequently than employee-level fraud.

   c. Results in lower financial losses than employee-level fraud.

   d. Results in about the same degree of losses as employee-level fraud.

5. Which of the following is NOT an element of the fraud triangle:

   a. Opportunity

   b. Greed

   c. Rationalization

   d. Pressure

**6.** Which of the following choices best fits the description of how high-level Wall Street executives justify potentially fraudulent activity:

    **a.** "Doing the right thing."

    **b.** "The ends justify the means."

    **c,** "Whatever it takes."

    **d.** "Greed is good."

**7.** The rash of Wall Street mergers, acquisitions, and divestitures in the 1980s, 1990s, and early 2000s resulted in a shift away from:

    **a.** Executive commitment to long-term building of a business they were loyal to.

    **b.** Excessive concentration of financial power in the hands of too few Wall Street leaders.

    **c.** Intensive competitiveness among Wall Street firms.

    **d.** Focus on short-term financial success among investment firms.

Fill in the blank:

**8.** The element that transforms the fraud triangle into a fraud diamond in the context of financial services is _____.

**9.** During the trial of General Re insurance company for allegedly inflating insurance giant AIG's reserves by $500 million, former AIG chief Maurice "Hank" Greenberg was named a(n) _____.

**10.** There is a(n) _____ between the level of the organization at which fraud is committed and the amount of financial loss resulting from frauds at each level.

**11.** People's Choice Bank was a prime example of a _____.

*For the answers, please turn to Appendix A.*

# CHAPTER THREE

# Internal Fraud: Loan and Mortgage Fraud

As discussed in Chapter 2, internal fraud is committed at two main levels of the organization: the employee level and the management level. There is some overlap in the *types* of fraud perpetrated by each group; however, in those crimes, the degree of loss is almost always much greater at the management level than it is at lower levels.

This chapter addresses employee-level loan and mortgage fraud. Chapter 9 addresses how to detect the ones that are not readily identifiable. In this chapter and Chapter 4, we provide red flags of specific frauds.

## ► Loan Fraud (Nonresidential Mortgage)

According to the Association of Certified Fraud Examiners (ACFE), "Loan fraud represents the highest risk area for financial institutions. Although the number of occurrences may be small, the dollar amount per occurrence tends to be large."[1]

The ACFE is referring here to loan frauds *in general*, including real estate loans of all kinds, personal loans, home equity lines of credit, and so on.

This section discusses key loan frauds excluding home mortgage loans (which are addressed later in this chapter).

### ■ Loans to "Phantom" Borrowers

In banks with poor internal controls and compliance monitoring, an employee may be able to submit a completely fictitious loan application using a phony name, a post office (PO) box address, and phony Social Security number (SSN), employment information, and so on to a loan officer of the same institution who approves the application—either knowingly, as a co-conspirator, or unknowingly because the submitted documentation appears legitimate.

To create a fictitious loan that will be booked on the financial institution's loan system and resemble a legitimate loan on which interest will accrue and payments must be paid, the dishonest lender or employee usually must control all correspondence with the "borrower." To conceal the fraud, the perpetrator simply gives the borrower an address that he or she controls, such as that of a friend or a PO box. Alternatively, this problem is resolved by having correspondence addressed to a legitimate individual who is unaware of the fraud and then intercepting the loan-related mail.

Often, once the loan proceeds are obtained, the perpetrator will make no payments and let the financial institution deal with the bad loan according to its established policies. This can take time, and the perpetrator may be long gone by the time the fraud is detected.

## ■ Loan Lapping

Sometimes, however, the fraudster will make loan payments from funds received from subsequently closed fraudulent loans in a form of loan lapping scheme.[2]

It is important to note that there are numerous ways that insiders can commit lapping frauds, also referred to at times as accounts receivable fraud. For example, instead of crediting payments to existing loans with the proceeds from new ones, as Ibell Abellon did, in the following case study, a financial institution employee could simply use *existing* accounts to perpetrate the crime. By diverting a loan payment from Customer A's account to his or her own, the employee typically would have a day or

### ◄ Case Study #3

## Lapping All the Way from the Bank

Ibell Abellon, who worked as a loan officer at a Southern California credit union, pleaded guilty to four counts of bank fraud and was sentenced to two years in jail in connection with 17 bogus loans resulting in losses of $267,000.

*Details.* According to court documents and the Federal Bureau of Investigation, Abellon orchestrated a scheme that induced Southland Credit Union to fund auto loans that appeared to be obtained by legitimate credit union customers but in reality were requested and obtained by Abellon. She admitted to using a series of stolen Social Security numbers (SSNs) and vehicle identification numbers obtained from legitimately funded loans. Some of the personal identification information belonged to legitimate Southland customers.

Abellon perpetuated the scheme by using the proceeds of newer loans to make payments on older loans—thus conducting a "loan lapping" scheme.[3]

*How could this fraud have been prevented?* List as many controls as you can. Compare yours with those listed in Appendix B.

1. _____

2. _____

3. _____

two less than a month to find the money to cover the next payment on the account. The employee would simply wait for Customer B's monthly payment to come in (knowing that it is due well before the time that Customer A's account would be past due) and credit Customer A's account with the payment from Customer B. If the payment from Customer B is in excess of what is needed to cover A's payment, the employee could divert the excess to a personal account. The fraud is further perpetuated by having Customer C's loan payment credited to B's account and so on, until the fraudster either leaves the bank or gets caught.

## ■ Nominee or "Straw Borrower" Loans

As discussed later in this chapter, nominee or "straw borrower" schemes are initiated most often by dishonest mortgage fraudsters without the knowledge (at least immediately) of bank employees. However, bank insiders such as loan officers also can initiate such schemes or collude with an outsider to process a fraudulent loan application for the outside collaborator. Alternatively, the outside party can be a sham entity or fictitious individual for whom the insider has the authority to approve a loan. Either way, the proceeds of the loan end up in a bank account controlled by the perpetrator.

In some cases, where regulation limits the amounts that bank employees can borrow from their employer, nominee loan fraud is perpetrated to circumvent such restrictions. According to the Federal Financial Institutions Examination Council, "Nominee loans and similar transactions . . . are constructed to circumvent laws, regulations, and institutions' internal limits or internal policies."[4]

## ■ Kickbacks on Illegal Loans

In kickback schemes, a bank insider is induced to approve a personal loan or line of credit to a noncreditworthy borrower or to an accomplice. In either instance, the borrower agrees to pay a substantial "loan fee" (or something else of value) to the bank.

In reality, the loan fee is never paid to the bank; instead, it goes to the dishonest employee, as a kickback for making the loan.

To conceal this type of fraud, the dishonest employee may arrange for the "bad loan" to be written off. (This may require collusion with other insiders if the financial institution has segregation-of-duties controls in place to mitigate the risk of fraudulent write-offs.)

Alternatively, the fraudulent loan may be concealed with a lapping tactic, using proceeds from future loans to make payments on the illegally generated one.

## ■ Reciprocal Loans

With reciprocal loans, a dishonest loan officer or bank manager agrees to authorize loans to one or more crooked bank colleagues or to dishonest counterparts in *other* financial institutions.

*How the scheme works.* During the savings and loan (S&L) crime spree of the 1980s, bank owners lent to each other in order to avoid drawing regulators' attention by issuing loans to themselves. Each loan made to an accomplice was made with the understanding that a comparable, reciprocal loan would be made in return.

Similarly, multiple S&Ls would agree to swap their bad loans back and forth to each other in a daisy chain of fraudulent transactions.[5]

In what the authors of the seminal work on the S&L crisis, *Big Money Crime,* call a "macabre variation on reciprocal lending," multiple banking institutions trade their nonperforming loans back and forth to each other to remove them from their books temporarily in order to make their financial statements look less rotten than they actually are. The practice, according to the authors, is perpetrated to fool regulators and to buy time for the owners or executives to continue looting their own banks.[6]

For example, according to documents from an actual 1987 federal investigation:

> The Defendants in this case are alleged to have controlled one bank in Wyoming and, as a result of borrowing from this bank and a bank located in Nebraska, the insiders obtained control of a second bank and a savings and loan. The insiders then caused the transfer of millions of dollars from the savings and loan in a series of transactions, including causing the savings and loan to "invest" in subordinated debentures and preferred shares issued by bank holding companies owned by the insiders, with the funds eventually being funneled into the pockets of the insiders. In addition, the thrift made multi-million dollar loans to one of the insiders based upon false financial information and invested in real property transactions, at the direction of [the] insiders, in which the insiders had direct ownership and for which one of the insiders received a "finder's fee" of several hundred thousand dollars.
>
> In a separate series of transactions, the insiders are alleged to have caused several million dollars in loans to be made to an un-creditworthy corporation and received back some stock in the corporation in return for causing the loans to be made. All of the foregoing loans and transactions were in default prior to the closure of the institution.[7]

## ■ Linked Financing

Somewhat similar to reciprocal lending, linked financing is a form of loan fraud in which a large depositor or a deposit broker agrees to give a bank its business in exchange for a loan that it might otherwise not qualify for or that is used to perpetrate a real estate fraud.

As the Federal Deposit Insurance Corporation describes:

> Linked financing and brokered deposit transactions have contributed to the failure of several banks and savings associations. Offers of large deposits in return for favorable treatment on loans to out-of-area borrowers or to other borrowers previously unknown to the institution should be handled with caution.
>
> Where the brokered deposits are not pledged to secure the associated loans, the institution is exposed to substantial risk since it must refund the deposits regardless of the collectability of the loans.[8]

## ■ Fraudulent Commercial Loans

Loans to businesses sometimes can take the form of mortgages, but financial institutions make numerous other forms of credit available to businesses, such as equipment loans, franchise loans, and commercial construction loans.

Unfortunately, in all areas of commercial lending, fraud is a potentially serious threat. The next section discusses some of the most common forms of these crimes.

### Construction Loan Fraud

The commercial construction industry traditionally has been a breeding ground for fraud and corruption. The majority of these crimes are perpetrated by external fraudsters—usually the construction company seeking financing—or by building inspectors and other regulators taking bribes from construction companies to overlook building code or other violations.

Other common external construction frauds involve falsification of documentation to obtain unqualified "draws" on the loan as well as bidding schemes.

The details of external construction and commercial loan fraud are discussed in Chapter 5.

### Asset-Based or Working Capital Loan Fraud

Asset-based commercial loans typically are made by committing the borrower's receivables, inventory, or other assets as collateral.

According to the prominent banking industry consortium BITS, commercial loan fraud is committed most often by companies experiencing financial difficulties. Typically, the borrowing organization is cash strapped and is having trouble paying vendors, making payroll, or covering payroll taxes.

If the company has a working capital line of credit with funds availability based on a minimum percentage of qualified receivables and inventory, the owner or senior executive may attempt to increase the company's borrowing power by falsely overstating the values on the certifications submitted to the bank.

One variation on this fraud occurs when business borrowers create false invoices to document bogus receivables and obtain funding or otherwise cook the books to appear financially sound.[9] They may also accelerate revenue recognition by double-counting contracts.

In addition, borrowers may use lines of credit for unapproved purposes. For example, a business borrower may use the line for personal or other purposes but generate a phony invoice for the purchase of a piece of equipment to mislead the loan officer into thinking that the loan proceeds were used for that purchase.[10]

Alternatively, if the lending institution's loan officer or manager is in collusion with a prospective borrower with assets worth less than the amount of credit sought, the borrower may pay kickbacks in order to circumvent the necessary due diligence required to verify the true value of the pledged assets.

Since these loans typically do not meet the institution's lending standards, there is a good chance that such a fraud would lead to eventual default, leaving the lender with an unsecured loan balance.

A related fraud involves financing high-value in-stock merchandise—such as automobiles, boats, or furniture—that is pledged as collateral for a loan. This is sometimes called floor plan lending. In a legitimate transaction, the loan is repaid as the merchandise is sold. In a loan fraud, the merchant sells an asset but fails to use the proceeds to repay the loan. Instead, the merchant pays a kickback to the loan officer or manager, who ensures that the appropriate due diligence procedures to verify the value of the merchandise are ignored and that any false documentation required to conceal the loan is taken care of. As with asset-based lending, a fraudulent floor-plan loan ultimately becomes nonperforming, and the bank is left holding the bag.[11]

### ■ Disguised Transactions

Disguised transactions are collusive schemes involving a lending institution employee and an existing or a new customer.

*How the scheme works.* The lending institution employee's objective is to sidestep the institution's rules requiring recording of additional loan loss reserves in connection with a specific nonperforming loan. The lending employee may "sell" such "other real estate owned" (OREO)—real estate owned by the lender as a result of foreclosure or other special circumstances—to an existing or prospective new customer in exchange for approving a new loan to the customer or an unrelated property.[12]

### ■ Suspense Account Fraud

"Suspense" or "pass-through" accounts are special accounts held by the bank in which funds are temporarily held for various reasons, such as insufficient loan documentation, pending closing of a loan, or interdepartmental transfers or wire transfers. It is easy for bank employees with authority to credit and debit these accounts to move funds from such accounts to one that they control (such as a personal checking account).

Such frauds are concealed by falsifying the general ledger entries. Unfortunately, without specific anti-fraud controls and oversight, suspense accounts are extremely vulnerable to fraud by employees with authority to move funds into and out of them.

---

#### ◄ Case Study #4

#### "It Was the Bank's Fault"

Cynthia Reynolds was an employee of North Island Federal Credit Union (NIFCU) in Chula Vista, California. As part of her responsibilities, she was authorized to move funds in and out of the NIFCU real estate suspense account.

Reynolds pleaded guilty to embezzling about $917,000 from that account by transferring money from the suspense account into a relative's personal account at NIFCU without the credit union's knowledge.

Reynolds also generated official NIFCU checks drawn on the suspense account and used the funds to buy vehicles and to pay various individuals and businesses for her own benefit and that of her relatives.

*Important.* Reynolds concealed her activity by making false entries into NIFCU's general ledger system. Despite having little if any experience in banking, she was able to conceal the fraud for over two and a half years.

*Outcome.* Reynolds received a 33-month jail sentence and an order to forfeit four late-model cars allegedly purchased with the proceeds of the fraud plus repayment of the $917,000 in stolen funds.

*Amusing twist.* Cynthia's father, Don Reynolds, wrote a letter to the judge in his daughter's case, essentially claiming that she was not guilty because the bank made a bad hiring decision and failed to train her properly. In his own words: "The bank that hired her in my opinion is equally responsible for what has happened. They chose to hire her from a temp service no previous bank experience or monies experience. They gave her no training, policy & procedures or guidelines to follow and abide by."

*How could this fraud have been prevented?* List as many controls as you can. Compare yours with those listed in Appendix B.

1. _____

2. _____

3. _____

## Remember

There are seemingly countless ways for financial institution employees to exploit their positions and weaknesses in anti-fraud controls to perpetrate loan fraud. The first step to preventing these crimes is understanding how they work.

## ▶ Mortgage Fraud

Home mortgage fraud started making front-page news in mid-2007 when so-called subprime mortgage lending, which had become a booming business for numerous banks, began showing signs of having been grossly mismanaged or abused by criminally minded "players" in the home mortgage game. These players included mortgage brokers, builders, real estate appraisers, loan underwriters, and even senior bank executives. Adding to the overall financial frenzy in subprime lending was a small army of securities professionals who packaged the growing number of risky loans into marketable investment products.

It is important to note that mortgage fraud in general did not begin with the subprime crisis. It has been a problem since the birth of the American Dream. But such fraud shifted into overdrive during the years after the savings and loan crisis of the late 1980s. Ironically, the deregulation of the S&L industry was intended to make it easier for prospective home buyers to obtain mortgages at affordable rates. What happened was something far different. Instead, the loosening of S&L deposit and lending rules attracted a cadre of nonbanker entrepreneurs who saw opportunities to exploit the S&L business for personal—and decidedly fraudulent—gain.

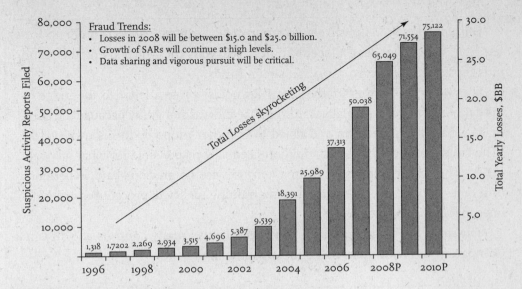

**Exhibit 3.1:** Mortgage Fraud Is Causing Massive Losses

Source:   Mortgage Asset Research Institute, *Eleventh Periodic Mortgage Fraud Case Report to Mortgage Bankers Association*, March 2009, p. 7.

As discussed earlier, instead of lending to home buyers, owners and senior executives of S&Ls made loans to themselves, to unscrupulous real estate developers, and to friends, neighbors, and anyone else, that were clearly in violation of thrift rules and blatantly criminal.

Ultimately, the S&L industry collapsed, and the federal government was forced to bail out depositors who had lost money, ultimately costing the taxpayers some $150 billion.

So rare was mortgage fraud before the S&L debacle that it was not until 1989 that Freddie Mac (one of the two government-sponsored enterprises, together with Fannie Mae), created in the 1970s to purchase loans from banks and thereby expand the mortgage lending market), established its fraud investigation unit.[13]

Mortgage fraud remained under control in the aftermath of the S&L crisis due in large measure to a swing of the political pendulum back toward *re*-regulation of banking. Fortunately for bank executives, the tighter regulatory climate did not prevent them from building their loan portfolios with new types of loan "products." Thus, in the early 1990s, the subprime lending business established its roots.

But it did not take long for fraud to become a permanent and increasingly costly fixture of the mortgage business. In a rather stunning perspective on the past 14 years or so of mortgage fraud, the Mortgage Asset Research Institute (MARI, a unit of Lexis-Nexis), reported that in 1996, a mere $1.3 billion was lost to mortgage fraud (see Exhibit 3.1). In 2008, the total approached $25 billion.

## ▶ Types of Internal Mortgage Fraud to Beware Of

Importantly, while the S&L debacle was characterized by widespread mortgage fraud perpetrated by bank executives themselves, much of the mortgage fraud that has occurred *since* the late 1980s has been perpetrated by dishonest outsiders—primarily unscrupulous buyers, sellers, builders, appraisers, brokers, and agents.

However, as is discussed in Chapter 6, the subprime mortgage crisis did involve widespread dishonesty and fraud on the part of many bank employees and executives without whose encouragement (and often collaboration) the crisis could not have grown to its staggering dimensions.

"Straw buyer" frauds, for example, are commonly linked to so-called flipping schemes. As discussed in detail in Chapter 6, these crimes usually are initiated by dishonest outsiders. However, with the collusion of a senior banking official, an internally perpetrated fraud with sizable illegal proceeds can occur. Thus, the 1990s and early 2000s saw an increase in the incidence of straw buyer schemes initiated by dishonest insiders.

*How the scheme works.* Straw buyers are loan applicants who are used by fraudsters to obtain home loans but have no intention of occupying the home being purchased. Straw buyers are chosen—and compensated—for their good credit rating. They may be active participants in the scheme; they also may believe they are simply investors, not knowing the true nature of the scheme; or they may be led to believe they are helping people with poor credit who, without the straw buyer's personal information, would not be able to qualify for a mortgage.

In the case of internally perpetrated fraud, straw buyers are approached by a dishonest banker with an offer of generous loan terms to buy a property the bank owns and wishes to sell. Straw buyers may be offered a flat fee to use their credit or a percentage of the sale proceeds.

In one form of straw buyer scheme, borrowers are instructed by the banker or the banker's "agent" to represent their intention to live in the home on the loan application even though the banker and the "buyers" agree that the property will be resold shortly after it is bought—at a profit that the banker and borrowers will split.

Buyers enter into contracts stipulating the purchase price, the terms of the sale, and other basic contractual elements. The dishonest banker rubber-stamps the loan.

The banker then retains a dishonest appraiser who values the home at, say, $50,000 more than it was just sold for, and then the banker recruits a *second* straw buyer. The same process is followed, and once the deal is closed, the $50,000 profit is split between the crooked banker and the first straw buyer. This scheme can be repeated again and again until an audit detects it or until a coworker or colleague of the dishonest banker blows the whistle.[14]

## ▶ Red Flags of Employee-Level Loan and Mortgage Fraud

Now that you have a good understanding of the main kinds of employee-level fraud that can hurt your organization, it is time to learn how to spot the red flags of these crimes.

Your familiarity with the key indicators of major forms of employee fraud will enable you to blow the whistle on wrongdoers before fraud losses become excessive.

It is important to know that there are two key categories of indicators of potential or actual employee fraud: soft indicators and hard indicators.

## ■ Soft Indicators

Soft indicators are intangible behavioral signs displayed by dishonest employees or employees with an intention to commit fraud. Unlike hard indicators, soft indicators do not point to a specific type of fraud. They are simply behavioral signals that someone may be up to no good. The main ones include:

- Weak sense of ethics. A coworker whose behavior clearly indicates a lack of respect for "doing the right thing"—by constantly lying, deceiving, or maliciously undermining others for no apparent reason—may be equally willing to commit fraud.

- Excessive risk taking. People who act in ways that could get them into trouble—by, for example, borrowing heavily to finance a lavish lifestyle, investing in speculative ventures, or engaging in insubordinate conduct at work—also may find it easy to steal from their employer.

    This behavior is similar to a dislike for working within the system. People who think the rules do not apply to them or who enjoy beating the system may be prone to exploiting opportunities to steal or commit other types of fraud.

- Refusal to take time off. Someone who is committing fraud at work typically fears being caught if he or she is away from the office for too long. Doing so gives others the opportunity to tamper with the fraudster's work space, thus creating the risk of discovering evidence of fraud. This is one reason that more and more companies are implementing policies of *mandatory* vacation—specifically to examine employees' computer records and files for potential signs of misconduct.

- Coming in early and/or staying late. This can be a sign that someone is trying to hide incriminating evidence or needs privacy to commit fraud.

- Abuse of drugs or alcohol. These are expensive habits that create financial pressures that could lead an employee to steal.

- Sudden or unusual mood swings. Normally cheerful, relaxed individuals who suddenly show signs of impatience, tension, or irritability may be suffering from guilt related to illegal conduct that they have or are about to engage in. Or they may be dealing poorly with mounting financial pressures that eventually could drive them to commit fraud.

- Showing off possessions beyond their financial means. People earning modest salaries who start driving to work in a luxury sports car may have inherited money from a relative. But more often than not, they are stealing to support an excessive lifestyle.

## ■ Hard Indicators

In contrast, hard indicators are pieces of evidence that are *tangible*. Often they are signs represented by numerical oddities or by physical evidence. The remainder of this section on red flags lists the major hard indicators of specific internal financial institution frauds.

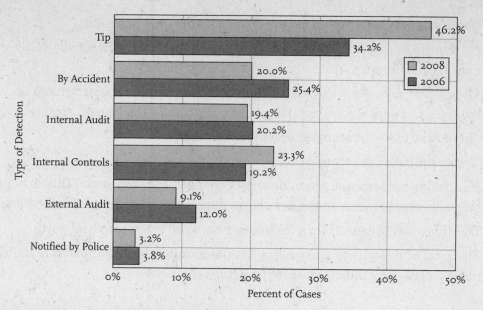

**Exhibit 3.2:** Initial Detection of Occupational Frauds

Note: The sum of percentages in this chart exceeds 100 percent because in some cases respondents identified more than one detection method.

Source: Association of Certified Fraud Examiners, *2008 Report to the Nation on Occupational Fraud.*

To help you remember the many red flags of employee-level fraud, we break them down into the categories that you learned about in this chapter.

There are several ways to spot and report the red flags of employee-level fraud. In fact, for many financial services organizations, the most common way that fraud is brought to management's attention is by employee tip (see Exhibit 3.2). That is because a growing number of financial services companies provide training such as that contained in this workbook—aimed specifically at improving employees' familiarity with the red flags of fraud.

---

## Remember

Without clear familiarity with the red flags of internal fraud, there is little hope of being able to find ways to prevent or stop it.

---

The next lists of red flags of employee fraud are not all-inclusive. Others may apply in your organization. However, the red flags listed here do represent those found most frequently in connection with the frauds discussed in this chapter.

### Red Flags of Loan Fraud

- Short-term volatile deposits are used to fund long-term loans of questionable credit quality.
- An unusually large point spread exists between the loan interest rate and the interest rate on deposits.

- Out-of-territory loans are made to previously unknown borrowers.

- Loan employees personally deliver disbursement of loan proceeds. (This may indicate an attempt to conceal a fictitious loan scheme.)

- Large-dollar deposits are offered in consideration for favorable treatment on loan requests, but deposits are not pledged as collateral for the loans.

- There is an excessive number of nonperforming loans.

- There is missing documentation.

- An insider randomly suggests or resists changes in appraisers. (This may indicate collusion between an insider and an appraiser in fraudulent property loans.)

- The "borrower" requests loan disbursements to be made to a third party.

- The ratio of deposits to outstanding loan amounts is high compared to industry norms. (This may indicate linked financing schemes.)

## ▶ Preventing Employee-Level Loan and Mortgage Fraud

This is where the proverbial rubber meets the road with regard to fighting back against the army of fraudsters out to steal from your financial institution. The red flags just listed should serve as clues to help in identifying weaknesses in the organization's anti-fraud controls. With a clear picture of where these vulnerabilities lie, it is possible for management to devise and implement new or improved preventive measures to stop many of the frauds discussed in the early sections of this chapter.

To aid in formulating these controls, the red flags should be used in conjunction with the findings of a fraud risk assessment (FRA), which is designed to pinpoint areas of weakness that may expose your organization to specific types of fraud. Chapter 7 lays out the formula for conducting an effective FRA. For now, keep in mind the red flags you have just learned about to understand the list of basic fraud prevention measures that should be in place at *all* financial institutions.

First, however, it is critical for your organization to set the cultural and policy-based backdrop for developing an anti-fraud mind-set. This mind-set is what was conspicuously lacking in so many financial institutions during the subprime lending spree of the 1990s and early 2000s. The driving forces behind lending in those years were greed and excessive competitiveness. These forces pushed lending decision makers to effectively eliminate most lending standards, opening the door to irresponsible risk taking and fraud on the part of both insiders and outsiders. To avoid this destructive environment, consider the next set of preventive measures.

### ■ Implement and Enforce Official Written Anti-Fraud Policies and Procedures

Official anti-fraud policies and procedures are brief but clear descriptions of the categories of internal fraud with management's policies of zero tolerance and disciplinary actions for employees who violate the rules prohibiting such illegal conduct.

## ■ Implement a Code of Conduct

As discussed in Chapter 2, a code of conduct lays the cultural foundation of effective fraud prevention. The Federal Financial Institution Examination Council further points out:

> A code of conduct, which is expressed strongly and applied vigorously, gives all employees a way to resolve ethical conflicts and positions the institution as one that does business fairly and honestly. . . . The code of conduct should be impartially enforced and include sanctions.[15]

## ■ Implement Thorough Employee Fraud Awareness Training

Your code of conduct is a good starting point for implementing *detailed* fraud training for all bank employees. Well-informed and trained employees are the first line of defense against loan fraud. All employees should be able to recognize the red flags of fraud—at least the types of fraud that could occur in their area of the bank—and know the procedure for reporting suspicious activity.

Moreover, early detection and prevention by employees can reduce the financial institution's risk of increased operating costs and reduce financial and reputational risk. Solid employee training and awareness programs and a written code of conduct policy will greatly reduce financial losses to both the institution and its shareholders.

If an employee fails to adhere to these standards and a crime is committed, the associate *and the institution* may be held criminally liable or suffer reputationally. Therefore, any questionable, fraudulent, or illegal event should be reported to management promptly. Any associate who has knowledge or information about inappropriate conduct by another employee, director, or agent of the financial institution should report that conduct.

Review your existing anonymous whistleblower hotline to determine if it is receiving employee tips about fraudulent or suspicious activity. If few such tips are coming through the hotline compared to institutions of comparable size and structure, investigate reasons for this and consider replacing the existing service with one better suited to your organization's needs.

---

### Remember

Incorporate loan fraud awareness training into your new-employee or department orientation programs. A growing number of financial institutions use annual Web-based awareness training and certification programs or formal classroom training to ensure that awareness training content is up to date.

---

Additionally, fraud awareness newsletters and brief fraud alerts disseminated via the company intranet help employees stay abreast of new fraud scams and schemes. Training should be extended to areas such as loan servicing and collections.

Detection of early fraud indicators, such as failed change-of-address or check-reorder attempts and first-payment defaults, help reduce loss exposure. Providing employees with adequate tools to verify information about an applicant's identity, income, credit, and other information is imperative for detecting falsified information.[16]

Educate employees on all internal audit and/or compliance rules and all state and federal laws and regulations to enhance overall awareness and thereby reduce fraud risk.

## ■ Enforce Rigorous Hiring Practices

To reduce the risk of insider fraud, financial institutions must go beyond basic background checks on prospective employees to include evaluation of fingerprint samples by law enforcement forensic specialists, verification of educational transcripts, and interviewing of references to determine potential involvement by the candidate in unlawful activity.

A personnel procedure for monitoring changes in *existing* employees' lifestyles, behavior, or actions is also important.

## ■ Enforce Strict Segregation of Duties

"Segregation of duties" (SoD) refers to separating job functions in a way that no single employee is in a position with sufficient authority to perpetrate a fraud single-handedly or with a collusive vendor, customer, or ex-employee.

SoD is undoubtedly one of the most important internal controls for many key lending processes. It is also a control likely to be identified as a necessity by your fraud risk assessment.

### Remember

It should never be possible for a single loan officer to complete all elements of a loan application review. Nor should loans above a specified amount be approved without the review of at least two if not more bank officials.

Similarly, when applied to the bank's due diligence procedures, SoD can be instrumental in uncovering internal loan fraud. Dividing the due diligence functions among independent staff members reduces the opportunities for dishonest senior bank officials to doctor borrower or loan application information.

That is because proper due diligence involves a list of critical research and verification exercises that should be conducted at some point prior to closing the loan. It is important to note that there is no one-size-fits-all due diligence formula for all loan applications. The level or depth of due diligence will be decided by the degree of potential risk inherent in a particular loan request.

For example, with commercial loans, the loan relationship manager is usually responsible for prefunding due diligence. In many institutions, that individual has sales quotas to meet as well as a portfolio to service and numerous other duties to perform. There is an inherent conflict associated with the relationship manager's sales goals and his or her responsibility to perform adequate due diligence. While relationship managers may not intentionally avoid or disregard serious issues, lenders who are under pressure to perform up to expectations may overlook ambiguous financial or character details in a potential borrower's past.

To resolve this, consider moving the formal due diligence process from the sales and loan processing area to another function, such as loan or credit administration. Commentary in the loan approval memorandum by this separate group should be part of each new borrowing relationship over a specified dollar threshold. The group should note any additional significant credit requests as well as line-of-credit renewals.

Similarly, in the postfunding period, loan administration techniques often are the responsibility of the relationship manager.

Documentation requirements, facility tours and inspections, and level of detailed review of receivables and payable agings generally are subjective and depend on the competence, integrity, and time availability of relationship managers and/or their perception of the customer. Requirements such as frequency of financial statements, certifications, and field exams, as well as quantification of covenants and type of financial statements, generally are contained in the loan approval document and are subject to minimal individual interpretation.

These are all responsibilities that should be separated from the loan relationship manager and carefully and consistently managed by a different area of the organization.[7]

### ■ Enforce Clear-Cut Delegation of Authority

"Delegation of authority" (DoA) refers to having specific levels of authority indicating who is permitted to approve particular components of the lending process, performing postfunding review functions and other key credit-related activities.

This is critical for preventing most forms of internal loan fraud. For loans over a certain amount, consider requiring a review by a loan committee that is populated at least partially by independent outsiders, or by a second senior loan officer.

### ■ Separate Bad Credit from Loan Fraud

It is impossible to prevent all loan frauds, primarily because there are so many opportunities to falsify the numerous documents involved in these transactions and because many financial institutions have neglected to assess their specific loan fraud risks, making it unlikely that they have formulated and enforced effective anti-fraud controls.

This problem is exacerbated, according to BITS, by the fact that many financial institutions fail to distinguish between "bad loans" resulting from credit risk and actual loan fraud. This further hampers the task of pinpointing the causes of a fraud loss, in turn creating added challenges for fraud prevention professionals charged with eliminating weaknesses in the bank's anti-fraud controls. In addition, according to BITS, separating fraud losses from credit-related losses helps management mitigate fraud risks by facilitating:

- Improved fraud awareness training. This training should be focused in areas where internal fraud risk or losses are greatest.

- More effective anti-fraud spending. Without a clear picture about loan fraud losses, it is difficult to achieve optimal resource allocation for targeted fraud prevention (e.g., electronic check fraud detection tools or automated prefunding screening tools for specific types of loans).

- Identification of loan fraud trends. Financial institutions should regularly compare fraud losses among business units to facilitate analysis of the effectiveness of fraud reduction projects.

- Budgeting for fraud losses. Separating internally perpetrated loan fraud losses from bad credit and applying the specific losses to the department that originated the fraud losses helps to estimate future losses in specific areas of the organization.

- Loan fraud investigations. To avoid investigating cases of bad debt, separating it from loan fraud improves investigator productivity and better identifies investigative expertise requirements (credit versus noncredit).[18]

With a method in place for identifying the causes or origins of loan fraud, the bank can formulate anti-fraud controls much more efficiently.

## ■ Conduct Rigorous Due Diligence

Conducting rigorous due diligence involves a list of critical research and verification exercises that should be conducted at some point prior to any loan closing. As mentioned, there is no one-size-fits-all due diligence formula for all loan applications. According to BITS, the essentials of prefunding due diligence, however, typically include knowing your customer and knowing your documents.[19]

### Know Your Customer

- For consumer loans *and* commercial loans, obtain character references, trade references, credit references, or an association review of borrowers, including company principals and/or guarantors.

- Confirm the existence of a legal commercial entity by verifying registration with the applicable state department of corporations, secretary of state, and licensing, bonding, or insurance agency. Searches also can be conducted through the Better Business Bureau, which can provide complaint information that may be helpful in evaluating the entity.

- Use investigative search engines, such as LexisNexis, to locate additional information available from public records (judgments, tax liens, etc.).

- Conduct more extensive background checks for large or risky transactions using an external investigative company (or internal resources if you have them and they provide results equal to, or greater than, those available through a vendor).

- Subscribe to and review credit repository alerts, which can identify nonresidential addresses, such as post office boxes, and incorrect, deceased, or newly issued Social Security numbers.

- Review credit reports for inquiries from other lenders, multiple new trade credit lines, and other red flags.

- Validate the borrower's SSN. Several vendors offer SSN validation directly with the Social Security Administration for a nominal fee.

- Verify applicant identities by positive identification (e.g., driver's license, passport, or other government-issued identification containing a photo, signature, and expiration date). The identification should be documented in the loan file for future reference.

### Know Your Documents

Responsible financial institutions rely on the integrity of the documents provided by customers and third-party entities to make sound underwriting decisions. Therefore, as BITS aptly suggests, close inspection of the documents for errors, omissions, and—especially— misrepresentations, as well as an *independent* verification of the information contained in the documents, is essential.

Again, segregating the duties in this important function is critical to fraud prevention. If a single loan officer is allowed to manage the know-your-documents (KYD) process, the opportunity to falsify documentation is likely to be exploited sooner or later. Some specific KYD controls recommended by BITS include:

- If a credit report was submitted by a broker/dealer, independently obtain a credit report and ensure that it is identical to the one submitted. If inexplicable discrepancies exist, terminate the broker/dealer or, at a minimum, place him or her on watch.

- Review all customer or third party–supplied documents for red flags. Ideally, have two or more independent reviewers check the documentation to deter internally perpetrated loan schemes.

- Perform an oral verification of employment (VOE). Obtain a phone number for a loan applicant's employer using directory assistance, the phone book, or the Internet.

     Do not rely on the phone number provided on the loan application as it may be a staged or dummy phone number set up by a perpetrator.

     Perform reverification as close to the closing as possible, since fraudsters expect the call during the processing phase of the loan and are prepared with the appropriate VOE responses. In addition, the borrower's employment status may change during the processing of the loan.

- Complete an IRS Form 4506-T to request a copy of tax transcripts or W-2s, which can serve as hard evidence of fraudulent income information on applications.
- Use reverse phone directories to confirm that addresses and phone numbers match the information on the loan application.
- Review the appraisal report for potentially fraudulent details.
- For mortgages over a specified amount (typically $1 million), obtain an independent verification of the subject property value by having an independent appraisal review specialist examine the appraisal for accuracy and/or order an automated valuation model—a computer-generated home appraisal.
- Verify that the funds to close the loan have been available for at least 60 days.
- Compare the owner/seller on the title binder (commitment), purchase contract, and appraisal to ensure they are the same.
- Compare the applicant name on the loan application, credit report, purchase contract, and tax returns. Ensure they are the same, and check to see that any alerts on the credit report have been researched and resolved.

    Research any "hawk" alerts on an applicant's credit report. These are generated by credit bureaus and provide alerts about SSNs that were not issued by the Social Security Administration; if the SSN or phone number has been used in suspected fraud; and if a commercial address appears on the application for a residential mortgage.[20]

- Research any discrepancies between the applicant's addresses on the application and the supporting documents (e.g., tax returns, bank statements, W-2s).
- Prior to disbursing funds, perform a review of the Housing and Urban Development-1/Settlement Statement to identify uncommon contributions and/or unusual payouts. Review both the borrower's and seller's side of the settlement.[21]

### ■ Implement and Enforce Detailed Postclosing Quality Controls

Postclosing quality controls are designed to monitor the effectiveness of your loan production process in generating loans of investment quality in accordance with internal, investor, and industry guidelines. The controls also ensure that loans are in compliance with applicable state and federal laws, rules, and regulations.

During postfunding reviews, your bank's quality control or quality assurance department reaffirms the authenticity, completeness, and accuracy of legal documents, credit documentation, collateral documentation, and the underwriting decision. Although the quality control department may review only a sample of the institution's loans, it is an opportunity to discover misrepresentation or suspicious activity.

Postfunding reviews to detect fraud should include:

- Reverification of income, employment, rental history, mortgage history, bank statements, gift funds, and down payment assistance programs (including independent verification of receipt of down payment assistance funds by the settlement agent).
- An in-depth review of appraisal or other collateral documents.

- Examination of signatures on loan documents for consistency.

- Occupancy certification when there is any indication on an owner-occupied loan that the borrower may not be occupying the property. Specifically, look for a mailing address that is different from the property address, public records that fail to show a connection between the borrower and the property address, or borrower's phone numbers that are in an area code other than the property location's area code.

- Detailed loan file review to screen for concealment of noncompliance with lending standards; loan amounts that exceed a loan official's authorized limit; missing collateral valuations; altered or missing borrower identification documentation; altered or forged loan documents.

- Mailing confirmation letters to borrowers to verify loan ownership, address, payment terms, collateral, and so on. This is a common practice by internal and external auditors to validate loan assets on an annual basis. It is conducted by selecting a sample of loans and mailing a letter to the borrower to verify key loan elements. The borrower is asked to sign and notify the bank of any discrepancies.

- Mailing confirmation letters to the appraiser to verify that he or she did in fact complete the appraisal report in the file and the value assigned is correct. The appraiser is asked to sign and confirm that he or she completed the appraisal report and assigned value. This process helps identify appraisal report forgeries or alterations.

## ■ Conduct Regular Internal Monitoring and Loan Portfolio Reviews

Even the most in-depth prefunding loan review process and a thorough postfunding quality control audit cannot guarantee that fraud will be detected. However, by monitoring portfolio trends and implementing internal checks and balances, financial institutions can detect many signs of potential fraud.

If fraud is indicated, the institution may need to expand its basic review process to determine whether irregularities are isolated or reveal a pattern with a broker, dealer, appraiser, title company, loan officer, underwriter, or another affiliated party.

To monitor for suspicious activity in a loan portfolio:

- Review monthly production to identify multiple properties purchased or refinanced by a common party. For example, duplicate loans to the same borrower in the same ZIP code may indicate that a loan is intended as an investor property rather than owner occupied.

- Screen for loan concentrations in specific geographic areas. Identifying average property values in a geographic area and comparing them to your financial institution's portfolio may help to identify pockets of higher-risk loans. Properties with substantially higher-than-average values in a concentrated area could indicate possible fraud. In addition, monitor ZIP codes by loan amount and appraised value to detect unusual variances.

- Periodically review high-volume producers. This may include high-producing geographic markets, an unusually successful internal loan officer or branch associate, or a broker or dealer. A higher-than-average production rate may indicate fraud, especially if the increase is significant.

  To avoid embarrassment, this step is particularly important prior to making employee-of-the-month awards or announcing similar recognition.

- Develop a report to search for duplicate home and business phone numbers in the loan origination or loan servicing system to identify different borrowers with the same phone numbers. This may be an indication of an employment verification scam or could identify investment property or the existence of a straw buyer instead of an owner-occupied property as indicated on the loan application. Verification can be accomplished through a duplicative phone number report with parameters set for the number of times it is acceptable to have multiple numbers.

- Review production for suspension and resubmission under new loan programs.

- Monitor exception reports. Screen for loans that were approved outside of normal guidelines, lists of suspect items, or loan document exceptions. Also determine who approved loans with these irregularities and inquire about the reasons for the errors.

- Monitor early delinquency, early payoff, or investor repurchase and charge-off trends to identify recurring brokers, originators, underwriters, or other parties.

- Monitor documents and reports from internal departments, business partners, and other organizations that could include contract compliance, outstanding final documents, mortgage insurance premium payments, and quality control exception reports. Make management responsible for reviewing and approving or rejecting all exceptions.

- Review insurance code changes. Use monthly reports identifying loans with origination dates within the last six months for which the status of the property was changed from owner occupied to investment.

- Monitor change-of-address requests. Address changes for loans on properties within six months of origination can indicate investor versus owner occupied or straw buyer frauds.

- Track addresses of declined applications for three months to check for new applications that can point to instances of straw buyers or multiple loans.

- Track "stale" dealer titles to determine whether a dealer is stealing identities or providing false collateral.

- Examine commercial floor plan lines of credit to identify out-of-trust situations.

- Form an asset review committee or problem loan committee that meets monthly to review problem assets, trends, and problematic relationships.[22]

## LOAN FRAUD DEPARTMENT POLICIES

According to BITS, Internal fraud department policies should outline internal risk management processes and provide a service-level agreement to business partners. The loan fraud department should be responsible for investigating all suspicious activity and suspected fraud-related activities related to lending. This includes tracking and accumulating data to identify suspicious trends involving brokers, appraisers, lending branches, loan officers, underwriters, and others.

Loan fraud department policies should include:

- An outline of the escalation process in response to suspicious activity incidents. This process should be clearly communicated to all employees, regardless of their role in the company.

- Communication and reporting requirements for management, legal, internal audit, human resources, and each business line. Escalation thresholds should be defined.

- A definition of the escalation process in response to law enforcement and legal inquiries. The fraud department should maintain close contact with the institution's legal department and function as its investigative resource for customer/attorney complaints and law enforcement inquiries.

- Suspicious activity report procedures, if applicable.

- Secondary marketing requirements for investor notifications, if required. The parameters for notification and a definition of the process should be determined internally.

- A process for terminating or suspending third-party relationships. The fraud department should establish collaborative business relationships with the departments responsible for maintaining third-party relationships.

- Reporting requirements for outside parties, such as the Mortgage Industry Data Exchange (MIDEX) database maintained by the Mortgage Asset Research Institute (MARI), credit bureaus, law enforcement agencies, licensing bureaus, and so on.

- Protocols for responding to hotline reports. Hotline complaints should be investigated and resolved quickly and thoroughly. The hotline also should be available to customers and the public to report misconduct.

The loan fraud department also should stay abreast of news related to recent fraud incidents by subscribing to industry periodicals and regularly searching the Internet for relevant articles and alerts.[23]

## BITS ON CONDUCTING PREFUNDING FIELD EXAMINATIONS

Field examinations on working capital lines of credit often are performed by inexperienced financial institution personnel, such as lenders in training or recent college graduates employed by local accounting firms. While this system seems to function properly on the surface, the substantial incidents of fraud due to an overstated borrowing base (receivables and inventory) highlight serious weaknesses in the field examination status quo.

*Key.* A properly conducted prefunding field examination provides a critical opportunity to uncover fraud or other unknown significant borrowing base or accounting issues. Not closing a loan is, at times, the necessary result.

Field auditors must apply both professional skepticism and technical skills to identify fraud and uncover critical accounting policies or other problems. Hiring outside field examiners and scheduling audits should be centralized within the bank's loan administration area.

Disseminating audit reports to the line officers and the credit administration sides of the corporate lending bank is also critical. Almost always, hiring highly qualified employees and vendors will pay for itself in reduced fraud and credit losses.[24]

### ■ Specific Loan Fraud Prevention Checklist

With the preceding policies and procedures in place as a framework for general loan fraud prevention, the next *detailed* controls will have optimal impact in catching many of the fraud types discussed at the beginning of this chapter:

■ Enforce a policy prohibiting any loan address from being coded "hold mail."[25]

■ If "hold mail" coding is unavoidable, require all mail directed to the borrower to be directed to an individual who is independent of the borrower. Then require the independent person to sign an authorization form for retrieving the mail. Any mail not retrieved within 30 days should be forwarded directly to the borrower. If the borrower cannot be contacted by mail, chances are the loan is fictitious.[26]

■ Have your internal audit or loan operations department run periodic computer reports to screen for multiple loans with no apparent legitimate connection but with the same mailing address—usually a PO box. (Possible fraudulent straw buyer schemes.)

■ Require appraisals for all loan applications over a specified amount to be conducted by a certified, nonbank appraiser. (Possible nominee/straw buyer/asset-based loan fraud.)

■ Regularly monitor for loans with partial charge-offs that do not appear on the bank's problem loan list. This may indicate a nominee loan where the bank employee charged off a certain amount to keep the loan balance below the minimum that would trigger increased scrutiny.[27]

- Establish automated systems that flag loans with addresses that match those of existing loans in the bank's portfolio. (Possible straw buyer or fictitious loans.)

- Ensure proper separation of duties with regard to loan disbursements and loan payments. No single employee should have access to computer systems that manage general ledger activity and ones dedicated to disbursements.

- Regularly review board minutes and interview senior management to screen for possible requests or attempts to change appraisers. (May indicate collusion between insider and appraiser to perpetrate nominee/phantom borrower schemes or asset-based loan fraud.)[28]

- Establish a loan committee, including members of the board, to review all large loans after they have been approved by a loan official—to screen for irregularities that may point to insider fraud.

- Conduct periodic background checks on loan officials, underwriters, bank appraisers, and brokers. Look for unusual changes in credit reports, such as sudden spikes in outstanding consumer debt or unusually high past-due accounts. This may indicate involvement in straw buyer schemes that are generating fraudulent income, which is in turn being spent excessively. Be particularly thorough in examining financial information of employees displaying possessions of value that appear to be beyond their means.

- Review loan officers' personal financial disclosures to screen for conflicts of interest with borrowers who may not be legitimate.

## ▶ Review Points

- While mortgage fraud was instrumental in bringing about the subprime mortgage crisis, it is important for anti-fraud professionals to remember that non-mortgage loan frauds and numerous forms of other internal white-collar crime also can be very costly.

- Mortgage fraud, while sometimes perpetrated by dishonest insiders, is *primarily* an externally initiated fraud. The criminals typically include dishonest mortgage brokers, appraisers, borrowers, and builders.

- The first step toward preventing employee-level fraud is understanding and detecting the numerous red flags of such schemes.

- With a solid understanding of red flags, an organization can conduct detailed risk assessments to gather evidence of suspected frauds and put into place effective controls to minimize its vulnerability to most employee-level frauds.

- A virtually limitless variety of anti-fraud controls can be implemented to minimize the organization's fraud risk. The choice of which controls to put into place is best determined by conducting a fraud risk assessment that pinpoints signs of specific fraud vulnerabilities.

True or False:

1. The savings and loan crisis resulted in deregulation of the banking industry.

   ❏ True ❏ False

2. A "straw buyer" in a fraudulent mortgage scheme is not a real person at all—just a name.

   ❏ True ❏ False

3. Straw buyer schemes are perpetrated by outside criminals, dishonest bankers, or both.

   ❏ True ❏ False

4. A dormant account is one that has been closed by the bank.

   ❏ True ❏ False

Circle the correct answer to the following questions:

5. A reciprocal loan is one where:

   a. Two banks cooperate in making a loan to a mutual client.

   b. A lender has the borrower commit to referring a friend or relative to the bank.

   c. One bank makes a loan to another in exchange for a similar transaction in reverse.

   d. Two loan officers swap clients to help each other earn commissions.

6. Linked financing involves:

   a. Making a loan to a customer in exchange for the customer depositing a large sum of money at the bank.

   b. A loan linked to a specific interest rate.

   c. Lending to a customer who has used other services the bank offers.

   d. Providing a line of credit linked to a customer's checking account.

7. Asset-based loans typically are made using any of the following for collateral EXCEPT:

   a. Inventory

   b. Receivables

   c. Floor-plan assets

   d. Payroll account balances

8. A suspense account is one that:

   a. Is controlled by the bank for special reasons.

   b. Is controlled by federal regulators.

   c. Has been frozen due to suspected fraud.

   d. Is pledged to the bank by a borrower until a loan is closed.

Fill in the blank:

9. Loans made to nonexistent or fictitious borrowers are called _____ loans.

10. Special accounts held by the bank in which funds are held temporarily due to insufficient documentation, pending closing of a loan, interdepartmental transfers, or wire transfers are referred to as _____ accounts.

11. Loan applicants who are used by fraudsters to obtain home loans but who have no intention of occupying the home being "purchased" are known as _____.

12. Separating job functions in a way that no single employee has sufficient authority to perpetrate a fraud single-handedly or with a collusive vendor, customer, or ex-employee is called _____.

*For the answers, please turn to Appendix A.*

◄ **CHAPTER FOUR** ►

# Employee-Level Embezzlement

Financial services is like any other industry in the sense that the theft of funds—generally understood to be synonymous with embezzlement—represents one of the costliest categories of employee fraud.[1] Although financial institution employees do have numerous other ways to steal (such as engaging in illegal lending practices like those discussed in Chapter 3), embezzlement remains high on the list.

Two categories of embezzlement are pertinent to financial services institutions. The first involves looting of customer accounts, such as checking or savings accounts, certificates of deposit (CDs), and money market accounts, and the common problem of teller skimming of bank funds.

The second category covers embezzlement by exploiting control weaknesses in the bank's business operations, such as accounts payable, travel and entertainment (T&E), procurement, and similar activities. We will start with the first category.

## ► Looting Customer Accounts

More delicately defined as "making unauthorized withdrawals," looting crimes occur when financial institution employees with access to customer accounts engineer schemes to divert funds from those accounts and conceal their frauds with false records, as in the next example.

---

### ◄ Case Study #5

### When Bank Employees Have Too Much Control over Customer Accounts

Milton Pereira, the former manager of two branches of Hudson Savings Bank, was convicted on charges of embezzling more than $650,000 from his former employer.

*Details.* U.S. Attorney Michael J. Sullivan, together with agents of the Federal Bureau of Investigation (FBI) and the Office of Inspector General of the

*(Continued)*

---

Federal Deposit Insurance Corporation, said that Pereira pleaded to two counts of misapplication and embezzlement of funds from Hudson Savings Bank in connection with a seven-year scheme perpetrated through the bank's Marlborough and Hudson, Massachusetts branch offices. During this period, Pereira tampered with more than 60 customer accounts by executing or authorizing hundreds of fraudulent credits and debits.

*The modus operandi.* Pereira repeatedly withdrew funds from existing customers' deposit accounts and from active or inactive home equity lines of credit and transferred them to accounts he had created and controlled and from which he illegally withdrew funds. He evaded detection by repaying credit lines from other customers' accounts, preventing customers from receiving account statements for extended periods of time, creating phony loan statements that were sent to customers, and changing the mailing addresses on loan accounts to addresses he controlled.

*The undoing.* When a few customers became aware of unauthorized activity in their accounts, Pereira corrected the "errors" by depositing funds from other customers' accounts. Then he sent letters to the customers reporting that there had been an error in their accounts and falsely noted in the bank's data system that the accounts had been "corrected" and the customers notified.

An ensuing investigation uncovered details of Pereira's scheme. He was ultimately sentenced to two years in prison, to be followed by three years of supervised release. He was also ordered to pay restitution.

*How could this fraud have been prevented?* List as many controls as you can. Compare yours with those listed in Appendix B.

1. _____

2. _____

3. _____

## ■ Dormant Account Fraud

A deposit account is considered dormant when it has been inactive for a long period of time—often for more than 12 months—and the bank's contact with the account owner is lost (i.e., the account statements are undeliverable, usually indicating that the account holder has moved and neglected to close out the account).

Although most dormant accounts have small balances, those with larger balances are tempting targets for dishonest employees. A teller or other bank insider authorized to access these accounts simply needs to make entries into the deposit system and steal the money. Because the legitimate account holder is not monitoring the account's activity, there is little chance that the fraud will be detected.

A similar version of this crime involves external fraudsters who intercept the bank statements that arrive at the address from which the legitimate account holder has moved. If funds are in the account, the fraudsters can use the account information to commit identity fraud by posing as the legitimate customer and withdrawing the funds.

## ■ CD Fraud

Certificates of deposit are potential targets of fraud by insiders who may sell these widely used interest-bearing bank savings instruments and pocket the funds provided by customers to pay for them. To conceal the crime, the bank employee never actually records the transaction in the bank's books.

Because most customers leave their CDs untouched until maturity, and because of the high rate of branch employee turnover, there is usually little risk of detection prior to maturity. When the customer does come in to either roll over the CD to a new one or cash it out, if the employee still works at the bank, he or she uses funds from another customer's account to transact the CD redemption, thus committing a second fraud.

### ◄ Case Study #6

## The Case of the Phony CD Sales Scheme Using Forged Bank Documentation

Charlene Pickhinke, the former branch manager of the Lake View office of South Dakota–based MetaBank, allegedly stole $4 million over 13 years by selling bogus CDs to unsuspecting bank customers.

According to the indictment, Pickhinke established relationships with individuals who referred customers to her specifically for the purpose of purchasing CDs, which they were led to believe were being issued by Pickhinke's employer, MetaBank. In reality, Pickhinke was operating solely on her own behalf, falsely informing her "customers" that the CDs she was selling were MetaBank CDs. She was able to perpetrate this fraud by forging documents using MetaBank CD forms or forms fraudulently created on a personal computer.

To launder the ill-gotten proceeds of the phony sales, Pickhinke allegedly set up two bank accounts using the Social Security numbers and other personal information of deceased individuals. She had the proceeds of the fraudulent CD sales deposited in those accounts and allegedly further manipulated various bank accounts to conceal the fraud. According to the indictment, Pickhinke issued some 40 fraudulent CDs over the 13-year period. The scheme

*(Continued)*

was able to continue for so long in part because of Pickhinke's payments of interest and redemption checks to individual "customers" on CDs they thought they owned but actually didn't.

*How could this fraud have been prevented?* List as many controls as you can. Compare yours with those listed in Appendix B.

1. _____

2. _____

3. _____

## ■ Fraudulent Fee Reversal

Banks have been widely criticized for "nickel and diming" their customers with fees for everything from purchasing a money order, to writing checks over a maximum monthly limit, to making a mortgage payment over the phone.

In addition, in the wake of the financial meltdown of 2008, many banks increased their fees for nonsufficient funds, late payments on credit cards, and overdraft protection.

Naturally, customers who themselves tightened their belts as they lost their jobs or began fearing for their livelihoods responded with increased outrage over these perceived rip-offs.

The result was a substantial increase in calls to customer service centers asking for reversal of fees that customers felt had been unfairly debited from their accounts. This in turn created a big opportunity for customer service representatives (themselves worried about bank layoffs when the economy is weak) to divert approved fee reversals to their own accounts.

Specifically, customer service reps with the authority to grant indignant customers a "courtesy" credit for a fee that was applied to their account often can credit these refunds to their own accounts or to those of coworkers rather than to the legitimate customers. The reps are then able to process the transactions through fraudulent entries. They bet on the low odds that customers will remember to check their bank statement to verify that the credit was actually made to their account. If they do remember and later complain that the promised fee reversal was never credited to their account, the customer service rep (who can verify from the bank's computer records that the reversal was "mistakenly" credited to the wrong account) apologizes and processes the refund.

Similarly, dishonest call center reps may be able to falsify fee reversals simply by creating fictitious reversals that are credited to accounts they control—without any involvement of a customer's legitimate account.

The second category of embezzlement, as mentioned, involves abuse of bank business processes and procedures that are unrelated to customer funds.

## ■ Teller Theft of Cash, or "Skimming"

Not surprisingly, many experts say that at the branch level, teller theft of cash is the most common and costly form of financial institution fraud.

There are two main types of theft of teller cash: One involves theft of cash assigned by the branch to a specific teller *by that teller*; the other is theft of the same cash by another bank employee.

*How the scheme works.* Most branches assign a specified amount of cash each day to each teller on duty. The amount may be $20,000 or more, depending on the size and location of the branch and its volume of customer activity. Typically, the head teller has access to significantly more cash in order to fill cash needs of tellers on an as-needed basis throughout the business day. The head teller thus also has considerably more custodial authority over the branch's daily cash activity. This naturally makes it much easier for head tellers to steal than it is for their subordinates at the teller windows.

For example, at the end of the day, a head teller could bag a certain amount of currency to be transferred, label it as containing more than it actually contains, and pocket the deficit. Alternatively, the head teller could create what fraud investigator Mike Thomas refers to as "Fed-wrapped packages"—plastic-wrapped packs of paper currency, but with, say a $20 bill on either end of the pack, with 4,000 singles in between.[2]

Or, similar to the next case study, a teller could make an entry into the branch's daily records indicating that cash he or she stole was transferred to another teller or to another branch.

## ◄ Case Study #7

### Teller's $1 Million Six-Year Theft Scheme Shows How Easy It Can Be to Rob a Bank

Karen L. Baer pleaded guilty to bank fraud in connection with a scheme to steal what the FBI reported to be over $1 million from the bank where she worked.

According to her guilty plea, from 1998 until her termination on October 25, 2007, Baer was a teller at PNC Bank or one of its predecessors, Westminster Union Bank or Westminster Bank, which had both been acquired by Mercantile Bankshares in 1972. PNC acquired Mercantile in 2007. Baer was the teller supervisor of one of PNC's shopping center branches at the time of her termination.

*(Continued)*

### ◄ Case Study #7 (*Continued*)

Beginning in June 2002, Baer stole cash from the branch on a monthly basis in amounts of $10,000 at a time. To conceal her thefts, she made false entries in an account named "Due from Mercantile" by creating false debit and credit tickets designed to document cash shipments sent from her branch to the Federal Reserve and cash shipments received by the branch *from* the Federal Reserve.

According to court documents, Baer made at least several hundred bogus debits and corresponding credits in order to make her initial theft difficult to detect and to hide additional thefts. The FBI, which investigated the case, stated that over the course of her scheme, the debits and credits totaled $1,050,000.

Amazingly, Baer's conduct was not uncovered until nearly *six years* after she started stealing, when PNC began an audit in September 2007 in connection with its acquisition of Mercantile. Had the merger been blocked by regulators, chances are the scheme would have continued indefinitely.

Fortunately, however, PNC's auditors finally did discover the $1,050,000 in missing cash. Further investigation revealed the pattern of suspect debit and credit tickets signed by Baer.

In October 2007, when a PNC investigator confronted Baer concerning these allegations, she admitted that she had been stealing cash from her teller drawer since 2002.

As part of her plea agreement, Baer agreed to forfeit her interest in a home she had acquired, nine bank accounts, a 2004 Hummer, a Chevrolet Corvette, and several snowmobiles and all-terrain vehicles.

***Outcome.*** Baer was sentenced to 33 months in prison and ordered to pay $890,000 in restitution.

***How could this fraud have been prevented?*** List as many controls as you can. Compare yours with those listed in Appendix B.

1. _____

2. _____

3. _____

## ■ Theft of Consignment Items

Consignment items are traveler's checks, cashier's checks, and money orders. Dishonest insiders can steal these instruments and cash them. Then they may quit their jobs or, if the job market is unfavorable, they often attempt to conceal the frauds by making false entries to bank records, indicating that the items had been legitimately sold.

## ■ Accounts Payable or Billing Fraud

To further complicate the embezzlement picture, several varieties of accounts payable (AP) fraud, while not limited to financial institutions, are potentially just as costly to them as they are to organizations in other industries.

The perpetrators are typically employees who:

- Have access to the organization's checks.
- Have the authority to approve invoices.
- Can authorize additions or changes to the vendor master file (VMF).
- Can intercept disbursement checks before they are sent out.
- Have authorization for various check-related processes.

Internally perpetrated billing schemes represent one of the most common and costly forms of fraud in financial institutions. Chief among them are shell company frauds and phony invoices as well as making unauthorized purchases.

### Shell Company Frauds and Submitting Phony Invoices

Setting up phony vendors and generating false invoices to be paid by the organization is among the most common and varied categories of billing fraud. The payees are not companies at all but rather businesses in name only. They are created by employees with the intention of generating bogus invoices in the "vendor's" name and submitting them to the bank for payment. These perpetrators often are procurement or accounts payable staffers or more senior managers who have the authority to approve payments to third-party payees.

The perpetrators usually set up a bank account in the entity's name, using fraudulent incorporation documents that they obtain for as little as $80, depending on which state they are located in. (Some may simply create counterfeit incorporation documents to open a business bank account.) After that, it is a simple matter of producing fraudulent invoices in the "vendor's" name using a basic personal computer and an inexpensive printer.

But what if an employee is not in a job with the authority to approve phony invoices and get them routed through the payments process? Sometimes criminals get around this problem by entering into a collusive scheme with a coworker who does have the necessary authority.

Others generate phony purchase orders (POs) for goods or services that the bank purchases on a regular basis—such as office supplies, catering services, maintenance services, and so on—and forge an authorized manager's signature. They then generate the phony invoices for the shell company and await payment. Of course, no goods or services are ever delivered.

Another common form of phony vendor fraud involves creating a shell company with a name very similar to a legitimate vendor that the financial institution regularly makes payments to—but with a different address. For example, a sham vendor with the name of Central Office Maintenance, Inc. may be completely phony but its bogus invoices may get paid and credited to the bank's legitimate vendor, Central Office Maintenance *Corp.*, despite the latter's different address.

### Making Unauthorized Purchases

Schemes involving making unauthorized purchases generally take the form of initiating improper transactions to acquire goods for personal use, rather than cash, as is the objective of most sham vendor frauds.

These schemes are easiest to pull off when the perpetrator is the authorized approver of purchase orders or invoices. He or she may, for example, tack-on items to legitimate company orders that are for personal use. This is easily done by over-ordering legitimately purchased goods and physically stealing or diverting the excess to a home or other address.

Similarly, a dishonest employee simply may authorize the purchase of goods he or she wants or needs, having the orders delivered to a home address and putting the invoice through accounts payable as if it were a routine business-related order.[3]

Such schemes are especially easy to pull off if the offender is a professional in a special area, such as computers or telecommunications, and the manager approving purchase requests is not sufficiently familiar with the nature of the goods or services being ordered—or is the perpetrator.

An example of this occurred at Boeing Corp. when an employee of the company's photocopier vendor, Xerox, was able to pose as a Boeing worker and initiate a unique unauthorized purchasing scam. While the victim company was not a bank or other financial services firm, the same scheme could have occurred at one just as easily.

### ◄ Case Study #8

## Industrial-Strength Copier Toner Ends Up on eBay

Asdrubal Sampayo, a five-year employee of Xerox, pleaded guilty to fraud in connection with a scheme involving theft of Xerox toner cartridges worth at least $300,000. The scheme was hatched when Sampayo, a customer service engineer for Xerox, was assigned to Boeing Corp.'s Tukwila, Washington, facility, where several leased Xerox photocopy machines were located.

Over a period of six months, he posed as a Boeing employee, going by the names of John Riards, Tom Riards, and John Lards, among others, and placed at least 18 fraudulent orders for Xerox toner, ostensibly for use in the Xerox copying machines located at the Boeing facility.

Unfortunately for Sampayo, his fraudulent purchase orders had several suspicious details, some of which a fellow Xerox customer service engineer, Dan Knuth, noticed and reported to Xerox's regional office.

Specifically, Knuth first noticed that the toner products ordered by Sampayo were not compatible with the Xerox machines located at Boeing's Tukwila facility.

Once Knuth reported this suspicious detail to local Xerox management, the company began looking into the Sampayo orders and soon discovered a number of additional red flags, such as:w

- None of the individuals who appeared to have ordered the toner supplies was a Boeing employee.

- The shipping code indicating the origin of the order was inconsistent with proper Xerox ordering procedure.

- The serial numbers of photocopy machines at Boeing for which the toner orders were supposedly ordered were not entered on the order documents, as required by standard Xerox procedure.

- Return phone numbers of the people placing the orders were inaccurate.

- Orders being placed were inordinately large compared with normal ordering patterns.

Sampayo was caught when local Xerox management informed James Hughes, Xerox's manager of Western Security Operations & Investigations, about the suspicious orders. Hughes determined that three of the suspicious orders for which paperwork had been discovered had yet to be delivered. He informed the Tukwila Police Department of his investigation and explained that Xerox and Boeing investigative personnel planned to put the scheduled deliveries under surveillance in the expectation of catching Sampayo red-handed.

Boeing security personnel videotaped delivery of a toner order to Boeing's loading dock. Hughes informed Tukwila Police of the events, upon which Tukwila officers placed Sampayo under arrest.

Further investigation by federal officers determined the toner shipments had been diverted from the Boeing facility. It was also learned that Sampayo had sold approximately $135,000 of the stolen toner cartridges on eBay.[4]

Sampayo ultimately pleaded guilty to mail fraud.

*How could this fraud have been prevented?* List as many controls as you can. Compare yours with those listed in Appendix B.

1. _____

2. _____

3. _____

As with shell company schemes, in unauthorized purchasing crimes, not all fraudsters who attempt them are authorized to approve purchases. In these instances, resourceful and determined employee-fraudsters may create bogus purchase orders. In these instances, once the PO is approved, the fraudster must make arrangements either to have the delivery rerouted to a personal address or to intercept the delivery at his or her place of work and physically remove the merchandise.

For example, when employees who lack the authority to approve purchase orders and invoices find a loophole in the organization's purchasing system, they may orchestrate schemes like the one that victimized a community college system in Spokane, Washington. In that case, a heating, ventilating, and air-conditioning control technician abused the system's purchase order system to fraudulently approve purchase orders for material and equipment that he diverted for his personal benefit. The maintenance manager of the department failed to monitor the approval of these purchases for almost eight years.[5]

### Vendor Master File Fraud

Employees who work in the organization's accounts payable or vendor management department and are authorized to access the vendor master file (VMF) can wreak criminal havoc in numerous ways.

For starters, dishonest employees with VMF access can enter bogus vendors, generate fraudulent invoices, and obtain approval of fraudulent transactions.

*How the scheme works.* An employee who has authorization to add new vendors to the VMF or make changes to existing ones can:

- Add completely bogus vendors and submit invoices as if the vendors were legitimate.
- Alter the mailing address of an inactive vendor and generate bogus invoices with his or her own address or that of an accomplice.

### Remember

As the bank's business changes, so do the vendors it uses. However, too many financial organizations fail to purge their VMF of inactive vendors regularly.

When no-longer-used vendors remain on your VMF, dishonest employees can abuse these dormant accounts to add fictitious vendors whose names are similar to a legitimate one—such as XYZ Company Inc. instead of XYZ Company LLC—and submit invoices for the phony vendor listing an address that the fraudster controls.[6]

### Collusion with Vendors

Collusion with vendors typically involves a bribery or kickback scheme jointly perpetrated by a dishonest bank employee and a crooked vendor, customer, or regulator.

The most widely reported type of collusive frauds are those between insiders and vendors. In a typical collusive scheme, a vendor seeking to do business with the financial institution may offer a bribe or a kickback to a procurement employee in exchange for awarding a specific contract or piece of business to the vendor. If the deal involves circumventing the organization's competitive bidding rules, the crime usually requires the dishonest purchasing employee to rig the bidding process by using one of several techniques such as those described below.

These frauds are technically not AP schemes but are included here because the payment process triggered by them *does* involve AP staff, who are often the employees best positioned to detect the red flags of such collusion.

As Joseph Wells aptly describes in *Corporate Fraud Handbook: Prevention and Detection,* the technique chosen typically is dictated by the stage of the bidding process in which the two parties decide to commit the crime. There are, according to Wells, three such stages: presolicitation, solicitation, and submission.[7]

In the presolicitation phase, collusive acts may include:

- Purchasing of unnecessary goods. In these schemes, dishonest insiders accept bribes or kickbacks from a specific vendor in exchange for recognizing the need for the vendor's product or services by his or her organization. Often the corrupt vendor is one who has little or no competition, thereby justifying the purchase of its goods or services without competitive bidding.

- Specification schemes. In these frauds, vendors pay corrupt procurement employees to write contract specifications that favor their particular goods or services.

    One of the best definitions of this type of fraud actually comes from the U.S. Federal Highway Commission: "[Accepting bribes to write] specifications . . . that appear to favor the services and materials of certain contractors, subcontractors, suppliers, sole sources, etc."[8]

- Bid splitting. This fraud is possible when competitive bidding is required only for contracts or purchases over a minimum amount. For example, if a contract is for a project costing over $100,000 and $100,000 is the threshold requiring competitive bidding, a corrupt procurement employee may accept a bribe from a vendor to split the contracts so that the amounts fall below the competitive bidding threshold. Then the procurement employee can direct the business to the corrupt vendor without being questioned about failure to comply with bidding rules.

In the solicitation phase of a competitive bidding project, bribery or kickbacks can come into play through:

- Creating phony suppliers. Here, a dishonest procurement employee may be paid off to permit a collusive vendor to create nonexistent "competitors" who submit phony bids with pricing that ensures that the actual vendor wins the business.

- Pay-per-view schemes. A dishonest purchasing employee may accept a corrupt vendor's offer for payment in exchange for advance access to the contract specifications. The obvious result is that the crooked vendor obtains a competitive (and illegal) advantage over rival bidders and essentially is guaranteed to win the business.

- Early-start schemes. A dishonest buyer accepts something of value from a crooked vendor in exchange for receiving advance access to the contract specifications. The preferred vendor gains extra time to prepare its bid, thereby putting the competition at a disadvantage.

In the submission phase, according to Wells, the principal form of corruption is providing a preferred (i.e., bribe-paying) vendor with the details of already-submitted bids in order to give the corrupt vendor a leg up in tailoring a bid in a way that ensures he or she will win the business. Alternatively, the bribe-accepting procurement employee simply may allow the bribe *payer* to see the actual bids submitted by the competition.[9]

Another form of bid rigging in the solicitation phase is bid pooling. Although this form of fraud does not involve collusion with a dishonest insider, it is illegal under the federal Sherman Antitrust Act and should be readily detectable by your organization's financial professionals.

Interestingly, it is a technique used not only in business but in the world of art auctioning as well, where bidders collaborate to submit bids in amounts agreed on by consensus in order to secure a portion of a contract (or in the case of auctions, a desired work of art) by agreeing not to bid against each other.

This activity too is a Sherman Act violation and can result in severe penalties.

A slight variation on this type of fraud is bid rigging to illegally fix prices. This too is a federal offense under antitrust laws. It simply involves vendors who wish to "compete" for a specific contract consensually setting prices in order to make more money on the deal. As it happens, one of the best illustrations of bid rigging involved several of the country's largest financial institutions.

### ◀ Case Study #9

## Multibank Collusion Victimizes Taxpayers

The City of Oakland, California, filed a federal antitrust lawsuit in April 2008 against some of the nation's most powerful financial institutions, including AIG Financial Products, Bank of America, Bear Stearns, JPMorgan Chase, Wachovia Bank, and others.

*Details.* The financial companies and brokers allegedly agreed among themselves to give cities artificially low bids for guaranteed investment contracts (GICs), which cities buy with the proceeds of municipal bond issuings that are spent immediately on such projects as new school construction, sewer and highway development, and so on.

By conspiring to eliminate competitive bidding, the financial companies allegedly gave cities abnormally low interest rates, thereby cheating taxpayers out of a legitimate rate of return on their municipal bond money.

*Background.* Oakland had previously purchased hundreds of millions of dollars' worth of GICs from the financial firms named in the suit. Damages to the City of Oakland were projected to be hundreds of thousands of dollars. Across the country, cities, counties, school districts, and other public entities have been overcharged in the tens of millions of dollars, if not more. (Similar lawsuits have been filed against financial firms by the State of Mississippi, the Charlestown County School District, and other local governments in southern states.)

Oakland's lawsuit was filed as the Department of Justice, the Securities and Exchange Commission, and the Internal Revenue Service were conducting a vast investigation into massive bid rigging in the overall U.S. municipal bond market.

Bank of America announced that it would cooperate with the Department of Justice investigation in return for amnesty from antitrust prosecution. Bank of America also agreed to a $14.7 million settlement with the Internal Revenue Service relating to the company's role in providing GICs.

*How could this fraud have been prevented?* List as many controls as you can. Compare yours with those listed in Appendix B.

1. _____

2. _____

3. _____

### Travel and Entertainment Fraud

As any seasoned accounts payable manager will tell you, employee spending on travel and entertainment is extremely vulnerable to embezzlement. Unfortunately, T&E frauds are also among the toughest to detect.

For some statistical perspective on the dimension of the T&E fraud problem, in a 2008 study, the Association of Certified Fraud Examiners (ACFE) reported that 22.1 percent of all fraud schemes are related to expense reimbursement. That is a disturbing statistic when you consider there are thousands of internal frauds going on every day that have nothing to do with T&E. The key lesson is that regardless of who or which department is responsible for reviewing and approving expense reimbursement claims, travel and entertainment should not be taken lightly when it comes to the potential for fraud losses.

Some financial institutions find out the hard way that they have a serial T&E fraudster on their payroll. This is a fundamentally dishonest person who looks for any opportunity available to cheat on his or her expense account.

The motives for committing "average" T&E frauds often boil down to an attitude of entitlement. In many instances, financial services employees who travel for business feel that since they are being asked to endure the hassles of modern business travel and to sacrifice time away from home, they are entitled to "a little extra." Here are examples of the common fraudulent schemes that have been uncovered in organizations of all kinds over the years:

- Falsifying receipts. Receipts for transportation, hotel, restaurant, and other business travel expenses are easily obtained and "recycled" by employees either by forgery or by alteration. It is all too easy, for example, to alter the date or amount on a receipt before it is faxed or scanned.

- Making multiple expense submissions. When two or more employees dine together while on the road, each may submit a claim for reimbursement for his or her own meal even though a single member of the group paid the entire bill. Similar practices often occur with shared taxis, airport shuttle services, and other expenses.

- Claiming expenses just below the minimum documentation requirement. If receipts are required for all expenses over $25 for meals, an employee may fraudulently submit undocumented claims for amounts of $24.99 or $24.95.

- Falsifying expense approvals. In organizations with lax internal controls over expense reimbursement, employees may be able to get away with forging a supervisor's signature on the claim forms.

- Claiming for "out-of-policy" expenses. A dishonest employee may test your organization's anti-fraud controls by submitting a receipt for a personal expense incurred during a business trip. If the expense claim form is complicated, the reviewer or processor might overlook an improper expense and approve reimbursement for it.

### Purchasing Card Fraud

Banks that suspect purchasing card (P-card) fraud often make the mistake of assuming that the perpetrator is an employee. You might be surprised to know that, according to the Association for Financial Professionals (AFP):

> Seventy percent of organizations that were subject to fraud committed using an organization's own corporate/commercial card indicate that the fraud was perpetrated by an unknown external party, while 11 percent of such organizations report that the fraud was committed by a known third-party, such as a vendor, professional services provider or business trading partner.[10]

While so far no scientific research has been done to determine the reason for this, the voluminous body of statistical evidence regarding credit card fraud makes it easy to draw reliable conclusions. In recent years, computer and network system hackers have grown increasingly adept at breaching institutional information security systems; therefore, it is reasonable to assume that a significant portion of the hundreds of millions of credit card records stolen through such attacks are those of corporate P-cards. As such, stolen P-card data have undoubtedly been mixed in with the massive body of stolen consumer credit card records and made their way into the Internet-based black market for buying and selling stolen data. The end users of the data typically are overseas career criminals who use the purloined card data to manufacture counterfeit credit cards and sell them to other criminal groups who use them to initiate fraudulent online purchases with the victims' credit card information. Of course, the charges end up on the legitimate cardholders' monthly statements. This triggers the long and costly process of undoing the identity fraud that puts the cardholders' credit history at risk or, in the case of corporate P-cards, creates massive headaches in untangling the frauds committed with use of the stolen P-card data.

In addition, however, P-cards have a rich history of being abused by their legitimate holders who charge nonbusiness expenses to the employer and falsely document them as legitimate job-related charges. And the statistics bear this out. According to the AFP, 30 percent of organizations report that they have been victimized by internal abuse of P-cards.[11] As you might imagine, this type of fraud is easier to detect and stop than the identity fraud–related crimes associated with theft of the organization's P-card data. That is because it sometimes can take several months for fraudulent charges or other abuses of stolen P-card data to show up on card statements. With respect to cardholder abuse of P-cards, effective reviewing and monitoring for questionable charges can catch such activity quickly.

## ■ Check Fraud and Tampering

According to the AFP, 91 percent of all organizations were targets of check fraud in 2008. Exhibit 4.1 further indicates that 28 percent of all organizations were targets of Automated Clearing House (ACH) debit fraud, while P-card fraud targeted only 14 percent of organizations. As mentioned in Chapter 1, those data are down from 93 percent and 35 percent respectively in 2007.

Despite the gradual replacement of checks by ACH and other payment methods as the preferred method for settling business-to-business transactions, checks remain the preferred method by which payments fraudsters attempt to steal from organizations.[12]

The good news is that while most organizations continue to be targeted by internal *and* external check fraudsters, most sustain no significant fraud losses (see Exhibit 4.2). Thanks to the effectiveness of anti-fraud methods such as positive pay, payee positive pay, and ACH debit blocks and filters, only 37 percent of organizations actually lost money to payments fraud in 2008.[13]

The statistics shown in Exhibit 4.2 illustrate payments fraud patterns that incorporate both internal *and* external fraud. There are few reliable data illustrating the breakdown of various methods of payments fraud by internal and external perpetrators. It is, however, safe to assume that for most types of payments fraud, the majority of attempts are initiated by outsiders.

Digging a little deeper into the check fraud problem, the AFP data indicate that for those organizations victimized by payments fraudsters, checks were used in 60 percent of all loss incidents in 2008. Consumer credit or debit cards came in a distant 20 percent in the same year (see Exhibit 4.3).[14]

| Payment Methods | All Respondents (%) | Revenues over $1 billion (%) | Revenues under $1 billion (%) |
|---|---|---|---|
| Checks | 91 | 94 | 88 |
| ACH debits | 28 | 28 | 28 |
| Consumer credit/debit cards | 18 | 15 | 19 |
| Corporate/commercial purchasing cards | 14 | 14 | 14 |
| ACH credits | 7 | 6 | 6 |
| Wire transfers | 6 | 4 | 5 |

**Exhibit 4.1:** Prevalence of Attempted Fraud in 2008 (Percent of Organizations Subject to Attempted or Actual Payments Fraud)

Source: 2009 AFP Payments Fraud and Control Survey, *Report of Survey Results*, p. 6. Association for Financial Professionals, Bethesda, Maryland, www.afponline.org.

| | All Respondents (%) | Revenues over $1 billion (%) | Revenues under $1 billion (%) |
|---|---|---|---|
| No loss | 63 | 67 | 60 |
| Loss less than $25,000 | 23 | 20 | 31 |
| Loss between $25,000 and $49,000 | 5 | 5 | 2 |
| Loss between $50,000 and $99,999 | 2 | 1 | 1 |
| Loss between $100,000 and $249,999 | 4 | 3 | 4 |
| Loss greater than $250,000 | 3 | 4 | 2 |
| Median financial loss* | $15,200 | $15,900 | $10,000 |

**Exhibit 4.2:** Financial Loss Resulting from Payments Fraud in 2008 (Percentage Distribution of Organizations Subject to Attempted or Actual Payments Fraud)

*Of organizations that sustained financial losses resulting from payments fraud in 2008.

Source: *2009 AFP Payments Fraud and Control Survey, Report of Survey Results*, p. 7. Association for Financial Professionals, Bethesda, Maryland, www.afponline.org.

| Payment Methods | All Respondents (%) | Revenues over $1 billion (%) | Revenues under $1 billion (%) |
|---|---|---|---|
| Checks | 60 | 62 | 55 |
| Consumer credit/debit cards | 20 | 15 | 27 |
| Corporate/commercial cards | 10 | 9 | 13 |
| ACH debits | 5 | 7 | 6 |
| ACH credits | 3 | 6 | N/A |
| Wire transfers | 1 | 1 | N/A |

**Exhibit 4.3:** Payment Method Most Responsible for Financial Loss Resulting from Fraud (Percentage Distribution of Organizations Subject to Financial Losses Resulting from Payments Fraud in 2008)

Source: *2009 AFP Payments Fraud and Control Survey, Report of Survey Results*, p. 9. Association for Financial Professionals, Bethesda, Maryland, www.afponline.org.

## Creating Forged Checks

The Merriam-Webster dictionary defines forgery as "the crime of falsely and fraudulently making or altering a document (as a check)." Check forgery schemes are perpetrated by employees who lack check-signing authority. There are numerous ways to forge or alter a check, but according to the AFP, of all organizations hit by check fraud in 2006 (the most recent years for which data are available), altering the payee's name was the most common method of check fraud committed. Exhibit 4.4 shows that 61 percent of all organizations victimized by check fraud were hit by checks with fraudulently altered payees.

Counterfeiting checks with the victim organization's magnetic ink character recognition (MICR) line data but using another organization's name was second on the list; 57 percent of check fraud victims reported this method.

| Payment Methods | All Organizations (%) | Revenues over $1 billion (%) | Revenues under $1 billion (%) |
|---|---|---|---|
| Payee name alteration on checks issued | 61 | 65 | 42 |
| Counterfeit checks with the firm's MICR line data and another firm's name | 57 | 58 | 50 |
| Loss, theft, or counterfeiting of employee paychecks | 41 | 41 | 40 |
| Fraudulent checks caught by positive pay, then presented as ACH debits | 24 | 22 | 23 |

**Exhibit 4.4:** Prevalence of Check Fraud by Type (Percentage of Organizations that Reported Check Fraud Activity in 2006)

Source: *2009 AFP Payments Fraud and Control Survey, Report of Survey Results*, p. 13. Association for Financial Professionals, Bethesda, Maryland, www.afponline.org.

The frequency of theft or counterfeiting of employee paychecks is also extremely troublesome to banks and other organizations: 27 percent of organizations fell victim to these crimes in 2008.[15] Although statistics are unavailable for comparing the frequency of paycheck-related frauds perpetrated between insiders versus outsiders, it stands to reason that payroll checks are more readily accessible to bank employees than to outside fraudsters.

### Theft and Forgery of Blank Checks

Unfortunately for financial institutions (and for all other organizations as well), there are numerous other, albeit less thoroughly quantified varieties of check fraud that must be defended against.

One such method involves an employee stealing blank checks and making them out to him- or herself or to cash. Or the employee makes the stolen check out to a phony vendor or an accomplice and forges the signature of a person in the organization authorized to sign legitimate company checks.

This fraud is surprisingly easy to pull off in many banks. That is because many bank branch employees do not adequately scrutinize the details of presented checks. In fact, according to one experienced former bank fraud investigator, employees are *encouraged* to spend minimal time reviewing signatures because they are not considered "experts," and it is more important for them to keep the flow of transactions moving.

It is remarkable, in fact, how many conspicuously forged checks make their way into the payments system without getting flagged for possible forgery. The replication in Exhibit 4.5 of an actual forged check that was processed and paid is just one example.

Employees most likely to commit this fraud include those with access to blank check stock or with an internal accomplice who has such access. In a financial services firm, these employees typically include AP staff, other payments processing employees, bookkeepers, and office managers.

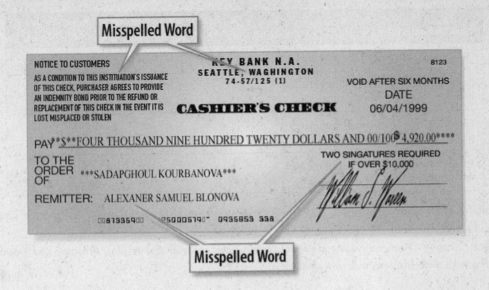

**Exhibit 4.5:** Replication of Forged Check

Source: International Accounts Payable Professionals, Orlando, FL, www.iappnet.org.

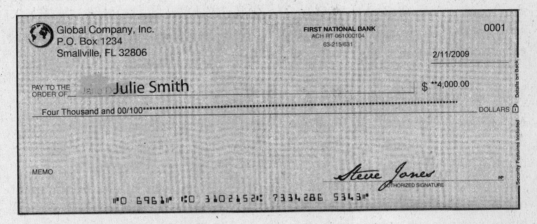

**Exhibit 4.6:** Replication of Altered Payee

Source: International Accounts Payable Professionals.

### Check Interception and Forgery of Endorsement

Some check fraud perpetrators prefer to steal checks that have already been made out to a legitimate payee and are signed and prepared for mailing or delivery. They intercept the check either before or after it is sealed in an envelope. After stealing the check, they change the payee by erasing or "whiting out" the existing payee's name and replacing it with their own name, either by hand or with a computer.

This fraud often is easy for a bank teller to catch, because these alterations, like the one in the image in Exhibit 4.6, often are very conspicuous.

Alternatively, the fraudster may set up a bank account with a "DBA" (doing business as) designation, such as "John Doe DBA ABC Company." The fraudster intercepts a corporate check, changes the payee to "ABC Company," and endorses it as "John Doe."

### Electronic Payee Alteration

Electronic payee alteration can occur in the AP department itself. Say a senior AP staffer who has authorized access to the secure computer system that stores all AP data and runs AP automation software decides to exploit this authorization. He simply accesses the system, changes the name of a legitimate vendor to a name that is similar enough not to be noticed, and uses a phony or old invoice number to initiate a payment. Of course, the fraudster also changes the payee's address to one that he controls.

After the fraud is executed, the vendor's name and address are changed back and disbursement records are fraudulently altered to conceal the transaction.

In many large financial institutions with tight internal controls over vendor files and other payments processes, covering up this ploy is difficult. Often it is easier and less risky simply to create a shell company or phony vendor, falsify the addition to the vendor master file, and generate phony invoices to be paid to that vendor.

### Check Altering by Inserting Numbers or Letters

According to the Office of the Comptroller of the Currency (OCC), there are two primary ways check fraudsters alter stolen checks by fraudulently inserting numerical or alphabetical characters before depositing or cashing them. The OCC illustrates these methods with two scenarios on which the next scenarios are based.

*Scenario 1: Numbers Games*   A fundraiser for what sounds like a reputable not-for-profit charity organization goes door to door soliciting donations. Most of her donors pay by check. In one instance, a superstitious good Samaritan whose lucky number happens to be 7 writes a check to the "charity" for "$77.77" to the far right in the box for the amount and the words "Seventy-seven and 77/100" to the far right of the text line.

The fraudster uses the blank spaces on both lines to alter the check by adding "9" before the numbers line and the words "Nine Hundred" before the text line. The $77.77 check is now a fraudulent check for $977.77, which the criminal cashes.

*Scenario 2: Alphabet Schemes*   Robinson Media Services Co. supplies Web site development services to small and medium-size companies. Its clients pay by check made out to "Robinson Media Services Co." or just "Robinson Media."

A mailroom worker at one of Robinson Media's client firms steals one of the latter's payment checks and uses a chemical solution to erase the word "Media." He then types in the name "Smith" and subsequently cashes the checks using false identification bearing the name Robinson Smith.[16]

### Hidden Check Fraud

Hidden check fraud is a scheme that requires some psychological cunning on the part of fraudsters. Here the criminals—usually a payments or other check-handling employee—submit a pile of prepared checks to an authorized signer for signature. Included among the pile is one check made out to the fraudster or to a phony vendor or accomplice. Attached to the fraudulent check is equally fraudulent documentation designed to camouflage the check among the rest of those in the pile.

Fraudsters are able to get the forged check approved because they know from experience that the signer is extremely busy and rarely looks at the details of the checks before hurriedly signing them.

Making an educated guess that this will result in the bogus check being signed along with all of the rest, fraudsters, in essence, have psyched out the signer by exploiting the individual's inattentiveness to the details of the checks, thereby securing a virtually automatic approval through the check-signing process.

Once the batch of signed checks is returned to the dishonest employee, he or she simply removes the fraudulent one from the pile and deposits or cashes it.

### Check Fraud by Intimidation

A senior executive instructs an AP manager to cut a check made out to cash or to "XYZ Corporation" for a significant six-figure amount.

The bank's rules say that any check request for more than $10,000 requires the written approval of two senior managers as well as full documentation of the payment (an invoice, purchase order, charitable gift documentation, etc.) and two authorized signatures.

The AP manager, concerned about being reprimanded for insubordination, musters the courage to meekly inform the executive that the rules require documentation prior to cutting the check. Unsurprisingly, the executive barks at the AP manager to mind her own business and just cut the check and have it on his desk within an hour.

Fearing the potential consequences of further protesting the violation of payments controls or of blowing the whistle by using the bank's confidential hotline, the employee reluctantly complies with her boss's demand.

This is not only a financial crime, it is a violation of workplace ethics in that it constitutes harassment and abuse of power that any financial institution with a minimal standard of integrity would not tolerate.

### ◄ Case Study #10

## Illegal Loans, Greed, and a Culture of Fear

*Although this case is not specifically a case of check fraud, it is believed that illegal check and funds transfers were part of this complex story of bank corruption and intimidation.*

Joseph Allbritton was a lightning rod for controversy stemming from illegal financial activities conducted on behalf of brutal dictators, including the late Chilean president, Augusto Pinochet, by the bank he controlled.

Allbritton was the largest shareholder of Riggs National Bank. He packed the bank's board with cronies and yes-men and reportedly ran Riggs with an iron fist, instilling fear in everyone who worked for him, from low-level employees to senior executives. Reported Allbritton is said to have berated a senior executive for sitting at his desk without his suit jacket on.

More disturbing was the discovery by a Riggs employee of a box of audio-tapes of some 150 board meetings. On one of the tapes, Allbritton is reported to have made "derisive" remarks about bank regulators who were pressing Riggs to correct its long history of money-laundering activities for which it had earlier paid a hefty penalty.

It is easy to see how a bank with such a negative tone at the top would be able to perpetrate fraud such as money-laundering and other illegal acts by literally scaring employees into complying with the corrupt and abusive boss's demands. Allbritton ultimately resigned when the bank was sold to a large financial institution.[17]

*How could this fraud have been prevented?* List as many controls as you can. Compare yours with those listed in Appendix B.

1. _____

2. _____

3. _____

## Remember

For obvious reasons, financial institutions are major targets of check fraudsters. Unfortunately, the techniques and technologies available to these crooks have become highly sophisticated and very inexpensive in recent years. This is one key explanation for the continued growth in check fraud attempts, despite the gradual shift away from checks to ACH for business-to-business transactions, as discussed in the next section.

### Automated Clearing House Fraud

When automated clearinghouse fraud is perpetrated, there is a good chance that your payroll account is the target. All employees have to do is provide your payroll accounts' American Bankers Association (ABA) routing number and bank account number to an organization that they owe money to, such as a utility company, phone company, cell phone service provider, or autofinance payments processor.

In one case, a man who was behind in his payments to his credit card company simply provided the collections agent with his employer's payroll account, which was debited successfully.

This particular fraudster executed the scam three times before getting caught. How was this possible? His employer lacked adequate internal controls over its payroll account: It failed to reconcile the account frequently enough to catch the fraudulent debits.

It is important to note, however, that according to the National Automated Clearing House Association (NACHA), which oversees the ACH system, corporate users of ACH services run a greater risk of being victimized by such frauds than do banks that process these transactions.

NACHA attributes this finding to the relatively small number of returned (i.e., fraudulent) ACH debits. Even when debits are returned, says NACHA, the bank may be able to charge the debit back to the fraudster's account if sufficient funds are available.[18]

The good news is that, according to the AFP, only about 20 percent of payment-originating organizations using ACH are victimized annually. This is in large part attributable to the ACH debit blocks and filters mentioned earlier.

### Payroll Fraud

Some business consultants and risk management experts consider payroll a sub-category of AP. Others—especially anti-fraud professionals—break it out separately because it has its own unique set of fraud risks that should not be confused with those associated with AP fraud.

Either way, payroll frauds committed by your organization's own employees can go undetected for many months and can result in substantial losses.

There is some good news, though, with regard to payroll fraud. According to the ACFE, the incidence of payroll fraud appears to be declining. In its latest research, the association determined that payroll fraud accounted for only 9.3 percent of all reported cases of internal fraud in 2008, down from 13.2 percent two years earlier. Unfortunately, the *cost* of individual cases of payroll fraud has remained steady at around $50,000 over the past several years.[19]

The most common form of payroll fraud involves the creation of ghost employees.

***How the scheme works.*** As you probably know or can guess, ghost employees are employees in name only. They are added to the payroll by insiders who have access to your systems that maintain payroll records and disburse payroll checks.

In some internally perpetrated ghost employee cases, the fraudsters are either too lazy or not quite smart enough to open new bank accounts for the ghost. This, of course, makes it easy for payroll managers, internal auditors, or others familiar with the mechanics of ghost employee schemes to flag cases of fraud simply by screening for direct deposit account numbers being used by two different employees.

Savvier fraudsters set up a separate bank account for the ghost or create a fictitious employee with a name similar to that of an actual employee, assuming that anyone reviewing payroll records will not notice the false entry.

In many of these schemes, the ghost may be a completely fictitious person with a bogus or stolen Social Security number, a deceased individual with a legitimate SSN, or a recently departed employee who was "mistakenly" left on the payroll and is continuing to receive paychecks and may or may not be splitting the proceeds with the internal employee who has the necessary access to your payroll system to stave off his or her removal.[20]

Another potentially costly form of payroll fraud by insiders involves the manipulation of your organization's computer-based payroll system. Most financial institutions are at potential risk of being victimized by these schemes even if they use an outside third-party payroll service.[21]

This, again, is a fraud that can be committed only by individuals with access to payroll operations. These fraudsters alter the computerized data applicable to their pay rate or salary details and simply give themselves a pay raise.

Alternatively, employees who lack access to payroll systems still can defraud the organization by creating phony time cards for hourly employees, punching the cards in and out and forging their supervisor's approval signature before submitting the cards to the payroll department, bookkeeper, or whoever is responsible for the payroll system.[22]

## ▶ Theft of Confidential Information

Although the term "embezzlement" generally refers to the theft of money, in today's information-based economy, confidential business information is becoming almost as attractive a target of internal thieves as cash. Hence the inclusion of information-related crimes in this chapter.

To conduct their day-to-day business, financial institutions have no choice other than to store vast amounts of sensitive and confidential data about their customers. Data includes credit card numbers, personal identification (PIN) numbers, Social Security numbers, dates of birth, credit scores, and more. It is no surprise that tens of thousands of banks have been victimized by employees out to steal this information in order to sell it on the vast and lucrative Internet black market or to abuse it by committing identity frauds, such as: fraudulent online purchases with bank customer credit card data; opening new bank accounts in victims' names; applying for home mortgages and other loans by posing as the legitimate customer whose personal identifying information (PII) they have stolen; or perpetrating any number of other identity-related frauds using stolen bank customer data.

The statistics are truly mind-numbing: Latest data from the Verizon Business RISK Team show that the majority of breaches of corporate information security originated from external sources; only 20 percent of these crimes were perpetrated by internal criminals. However, whereas the number of insider-perpetrated breaches was relatively small, the average number of records lost to insider attacks was approximately *three times greater* than those lost from externally perpetrated breaches.[23]

The top targets were financial services, retail, and food and beverage organizations. The 90 data breaches investigated by the Verizon Business RISK Team in 2008 resulted in a total of 285 million stolen records. According to the research, *93 percent of those records were lost by financial services companies.*

### Additional Findings

- The majority of internal perpetrators tend to be either information technology (IT) administrators or end users.[24]
- As shown in Exhibit 4.7, banks with between 1,000 and 10,000 employees experienced the largest number of breaches (27 percent), while small banks—those with between 11 and 100 employees—experienced essentially the same number of attacks (26 percent).[25]
- Ninety-six percent of all stolen data are related to credit or debit cards.[26]

According to latest data, many successful breaches result from employee error. Yet the majority are due to other weaknesses in the organization's information security defenses. In addition, many information thefts occur when employees lacking authority to access secure networks or databases that store customer or other sensitive information use social engineering tactics to persuade an authorized manager to allow "one-time" access to the information for a "special purpose." The term "social engineering" in the context of confidential, secure computer information, is the practice of persuading or "conning" a targeted individual who has access to such information to either provide the information or access to it to the perpetrator.

As you will learn in Chapter 5, many of these social engineering schemes are perpetrated by outsiders through scam e-mails targeting bank customers in an effort to obtain their account information. They know the bank's systems and its culture, and they may have earned the trust of someone who will provide them with access to secure data under false pretenses.

Once obtained, these data can be used to perpetrate a host of identity-related crimes, such as credit card fraud, unauthorized Internet purchases, check counterfeiting, consumer account takeover, and so on as discussed above.

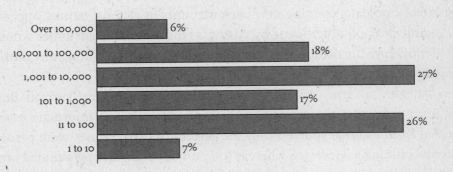

**Exhibit 4.7:** Number of Employees by Percent of Breaches

Source: Verizon Business RISK Team, *2009 Data Breach Investigations Report.* www.verizonbusiness.com/products/security/risk/.

## FACTS ABOUT FACTA

Closely related to social engineering in terms of objectives is the ongoing explosion of data breaches and the related boom in identity fraud. In response, Congress passed legislation requiring all financial institutions to implement programs to detect the red flags of identity theft and fraud.

As of November 1, 2009, all financial institutions were required to monitor their ongoing compliance with the Fair and Accurate Credit Transactions Act (FACTA). This federal law requires financial institutions and nonbank creditors to formulate and implement a "Red Flags Rule Compliance Program."

*Aim.* To equip financial institution employees with the knowledge to help detect, prevent, and mitigate identity theft that can occur as a result of the identity-related abuse of customer checking, savings, and credit card accounts as well as installment loans, mortgages, margin accounts, utility accounts, and cell phone accounts.

In short, the Red Flags Rule is designed to force financial organizations to implement anti–identity theft programs that alert organizations to the potential illegal use of personally identifiable information (PII) of employees, customers, medical patients, and so on, such as SSNs, license numbers, and medical information.

*Helpful.* After many months of confusion on the part of banks and their lawyers, the Federal Trade Commission (FTC) launched a Web site to help organizations come into compliance with the Red Flags Rule.

The FTC site provides articles and guides for helping create identity theft prevention programs, a key requirement of the rules. The most useful offering is a how-to guide called *Fighting Fraud with the Red Flags Rule.*

To obtain the guide and additional useful compliance information, visit www.ftc.gov/redflagsrule.

## ▶ Insider Abuse of Computer Systems

According to the U.S. Secret Service and the authoritative information security center Computer Emergency Response Team (CERT) at Carnegie Mellon University:

> Insiders pose a substantial threat by virtue of their knowledge of and access to their employers' systems and/or databases, and their ability to bypass existing physical and electronic security measures through legitimate means.[27]

This category of electronic white-collar crimes is very similar to insider theft of confidential information and social engineering, except that in addition to stealing data, the employee uses the organization's computer systems to:

- Steal money from customer deposit accounts—often by unauthorized electronic transfer to a personal account.

- Manipulate computerized processes, such as automated payroll systems to give themselves a pay increase.
- Alter vendor data in order to perpetrate billing schemes.
- Add, delete, disclose, or alter sensitive documents, such as proprietary loan application processes, intellectual property, financial documents, marketing materials, customer data, vendor account information, employee performance review details, and so on.
- Add ghost employees to the payroll.

In all instances—theft of information and the crimes just listed—the offenses usually are committed through one of these tactics:

- Exploiting poor controls. Many financial institutions lack the proper access controls to prevent unauthorized employees from breaking into databases storing sensitive information. In a surprisingly frequent number of cases, a simple mistake is the cause, such as forgetting to shut down a departing employee's access to the organization's secure systems.
- Hacking. Employees with exceptional computer skills electronically break into your organization's computer systems.
- Social engineering. Criminals persuade IT staff that they need or have special permission to access secure areas of the organization's computer system.

## ▶ Red Flags of Employee-Level Embezzlement

Keeping in mind the important soft indicators of employee-level fraud listed in Chapter 3, here are hard indicators of embezzlement and information-related thefts:

### Red Flags of Embezzlement

- Unusually high amount of bagged cash or coin tags. (May indicate skimming by tellers.)
- Currency wrapped in plastic when it normally is not. (Skimming.)
- Unusual frequency of teller cash transfers. (May indicate concealment of embezzled cash.)
- Excessive billing errors—where a customer receives a "Past Due" notice when the account is current. (Could indicate lapping/accounts receivable fraud.)
- Excessive write-offs of accounts receivable. (Lapping/accounts receivable fraud.)
- Customers complain about being past due on payments when they are not. (Lapping/accounts receivable fraud.)
- A records "error" showing a depleted CD account. (May indicate a branch employee has stolen CD deposit money and is running a lapping scheme with new incoming CD deposits.)
- Customers complain about unusual declines in account balances. (Skimming.)

- Fee reversals promised by a customer service employee do not show up or get posted to customer's account. (Skimming.)
- Dormant customer account suddenly shows signs of activity. (Customer account looting.)

### Red Flags of Billing Fraud

- Invoices have consecutive numbers despite being weeks or months apart.
- Vendor address matches an employee's address.
- Invoices are missing one or more key details, such as date, address, or quantities ordered.
- Invoices appear unprofessionally prepared.
- A vendor address does not match the address on the vendor master file.
- A vendor's pricing does not match "regular" prices.
- A new vendor suddenly is given contracts, replacing an existing competitor that has had your organization as a customer for a long time.
- A vendor's address is in a residential area or is a PO box or is not registered with the state department of corporations or secretary of state. (Could indicate a shell company.)
- Purchase orders lack key details, such as clear descriptions of items being ordered, payment terms, or dates.
- Sudden jumps in a vendor's pricing. (May indicate a kickback scheme.)
- Unusually low prices. (May also indicate a kickback or bribery scheme.)
- Invoices do not match purchase order details.
- Invoices are unfolded. (May indicate an employee is inserting invoices printed from a PC into a pile of legitimate invoices.)

### Red Flags of Vendor Master File Fraud

- An inactive vendor's file is suddenly reactivated.
- New vendors show up on the vendor master file with names similar to those of existing vendors.
- Vendor addresses in the vendor master file match addresses of employees.
- Key vendor information such as employer identification number (EIN), full address, or contact name are missing from the vendor master file.
- A vendor's Social Security number matches that of an employee.

### Red Flags of Collusion and Kickbacks with Vendors

- The same vendor is awarded numerous contracts on consecutive projects.
- Product or service prices jump unexpectedly.
- A longtime vendor is suddenly replaced by a new one.

- Inferior-quality product is delivered, but the invoice prices are for a higher-quality alternative.
- A pattern of growing frequency of "purchases" from a particular vendor.
- Purchases are recorded in amounts greater than what is normally purchased or are for products or services the organization does not use.
- Contracts are awarded without competitive bidding.
- Unusual price jumps or reductions.

### Red Flags of T&E Fraud

- Business trips are booked but not taken.
- Receipts for business meals, transportation, and service are falsified.
- Photocopies instead of originals are submitted for expenses such as boarding passes. This can be a sign of submitting expense reimbursement claims a second time.
- Sudden, unusually frequent business trips are recorded. Some could be personal/family trips.
- Lack of receipts or documentation for business expenses.
- Excessive amounts spent for "business" meals and entertainment.
- Claims for reimbursement for travel expenses outside of employee's ordinary travel routine or pattern.

### Red Flags of P-Card Fraud

- Unusual purchases made with a P-card, such as gift cards from retail outlets, online purchases of items of questionable business applicability, or items such as office equipment or supplies that are readily available at the cardholder's office.
- An unusual number of purchases for amounts just below the organization's minimum for requiring management approval.
- Photocopied receipts instead of originals are submitted with expense reports.
- Split payments. (Indicate an attempt to circumvent purchase limit rules.)
- Sudden, unusual patterns in a particular employee's monthly P-card purchases.
- Noticeably forged receipts.
- Charges for "business meals" from restaurants that are in the employee's neighborhood or that are made on weekends.
- Frequent returns of merchandise such as apparel—a potential sign of "wardrobing," where a retail customer purchases a clothing item, wears it once, and returns it for a refund. (This is naturally a fraud perpetrated against retailers, but it is conduct that, if detected through the paper trail on *your bank's P-card records*, can have a negative impact on your bank's reputation.)

## Red Flags of Check Fraud

- An unusual number of voided checks show up in bank reconciliations or audits. (May indicate that an employee is stealing cash payments and submitting phony invoices to cover up the theft.)

- Blank checks are missing.

- Canceled checks show signs of erasure or other alteration.

- Signatures are missing or appear forged.

- Ink comes off of the check when you crease it. (May indicate the check is a color photocopy of the original.)

- Nonpayroll checks are made out to employees.

- Vendors or other payees complain about not receiving payments, which might indicate checks have been stolen and altered.

- Canceled checks have fraudulent endorsements or dual endorsements.

- Customers complain about payments not being credited. (May indicate interception and forged endorsement of legitimate checks, or the existence of a lapping scheme in progress.)

- Unauthorized withdrawals are made from the organization's checking accounts. (May indicate simple embezzlement by an employee with access to your accounts or may be a sign of electronic fraud by an outside criminal who either has hacked into your bank's system to steal customer account numbers and PIN numbers, or has purchased this information illegally on the cyber-underground market.)

- Unauthorized debits from the organization's payroll account(s). (May be a red flag that a dishonest employee has used your payroll account's routing number and account number to fraudulently pay off personal debts.)

- Misspellings or other errors on your bank's cashier's checks. (May be a sign of counterfeiting of such checks.) See Exhibit 4.5.

## Red Flags of Payroll Fraud

- Former employees are still receiving paychecks.

- Two employees have the same address (one is likely a "ghost").

- An employee declines direct deposit of paychecks.

- Unusual patterns of hours worked.

- Sudden unauthorized debits from payroll accounts. (May indicate a hacking attack that has resulted in loss of payroll account information by a cyber-thief who uses it to counterfeit your institution's payroll checks.)

- Commission payments are unusually high. (May indicate that employees compensated in part by commission have generated false sales to fraudulently earn higher commissions.)

- Duplicate Social Security numbers. (May indicate existence of ghost employees.)
- "Employees" with no tax withholdings or insurance deductions or other normal deductions.

### Red Flags of Theft of Confidential Information

- An unauthorized employee requests special one-time access to secure computer systems.
- An employee uses a USB thumb drive for no apparent reason. (May indicate unauthorized transfer of confidential data from the employee's PC or that of a coworker.)
- The IT department detects attempts by unauthorized employees to access secure networks or databases.
- A particular IT employee shows a pattern of increasingly frequent access to secure databases. (May indicate collusion between an IT employee and an unauthorized coworker.)
- Vendors, customers, or others whose confidential identifying data are stored in your bank's systems complain about unauthorized use of their credit card or debit card information or other fraudulent transactions facilitated by identity theft.
- Your organization is billed for goods and/or services it never ordered. (Could indicate phony vendors have stolen key information about legitimate vendors to pose as them in order to perpetrate billing fraud.)
- A competing financial services institution appears to possess sensitive marketing, financial, customer, or other information about your company.

    This may be a sign that an employee who recently left your organization went to work with the competitor because he or she accepted a payment to share confidential data from your company.

    Or it may also indicate the existence of a "mole": an employee placed by a competitor inside your organization who has built trust and thereby gained authorization to access sensitive information such as customer bank account information or credit card data. This increasingly common threat is referred to as industrial espionage and almost always involves the theft of sensitive and proprietary information, especially from banks.

### Red Flags of Abuse of Secure Computer Systems

- Reports by the IT department of unauthorized attempts at access to funds via secure computer systems.
- Unusually frequent accessing of secure systems with a particular password. (May indicate knowledge and unauthorized use of a coworker's password.)
- Unauthorized access of secure systems by employees who no longer work at the bank.
- Missing organization-owned laptops.

# ■ Embezzlement Prevention Checklists

### Dormant Account Fraud

- Code all accounts that have had no activity for at least 12 months or whose owners can no longer be contacted.
- If activity suddenly attempts to post to one of these accounts, have at least two supervisory-level staff members review the activity for legitimacy.[28]

### Looting Customer Accounts

- Monitor activity on all employee accounts. (As discussed, dishonest employees sometimes simply transfer customer funds to their own accounts with the bank.)
- Immediately investigate all customer complaints about unusual or unauthorized account activity.
- Investigate unusually frequent withdrawals or transfers to or from a particular customer's account. Monitor activity in all dormant accounts to flag sudden activity.

### Teller Skimming

- Conduct surprise *manual* cash counts at least monthly. Include vault teller cash, such as loose bills; samples of strapped $20s, $10s, $5s, and $1s; open sample Fed-wrapped packages and fan bills to screen for counterfeits.
- Ensure that cash counts are scheduled for times when the teller has balanced to the general ledger.[29]
- Ensure that cash counts are conducted on all branch cash supplies on at least a quarterly basis. (Include all returned checks, food stamps, and other teller-assigned cash equivalents.)
- Reconcile all cash counts to teller records.
- Increase the frequency of branch audits.

# ■ Accounts Payable Fraud Prevention Checklist

Ensuring that an accounts payable staff member who is responsible for invoice approval does not also approve cash disbursements is essential to reducing the chances of a dishonest AP employee getting away with a phony invoice or a shell company scheme.[30]

Similarly, separating the main duties comprising the AP process from the key responsibility of reconciling bank accounts is equally critical for preventing many internal AP frauds.

Rotating AP employees from one position to another every six months or so also can prevent staff from getting too cozy with specific vendors who might try to offer kickbacks or bribes to secure business illegally.

In addition to these general segregation-of-duties and delegation-of-authority controls, be sure that these and other controls over *specific* AP-related processes are in place. And, importantly, delegate continuous monitoring of the effectiveness of *all* AP anti-fraud controls to a responsible manager who should be held accountable for the sound implementation and effective functioning of these measures.

Here is a list of specific internal AP fraud prevention measures. The applicable types of AP fraud appear in parentheses.

- Require approval of all purchase requests over a specified amount. (billing fraud, shell company schemes, kickback schemes, vendor master file fraud, check fraud)

- Establish and maintain tight controls over your vendor master file. (VMF fraud, billing/shell company fraud, kickbacks, check fraud) This includes establishing efficient vendor coding standards and monitoring for unusual departures from them. Select a sample of vendor master records and trace information to your vendor coding form to verify proper authorization of all additions and deletions of vendors or changes to existing vendor data.

- Prohibit people who are authorized to approve purchases from making changes to the VMF. (VMF fraud, billing schemes, check fraud, shell company schemes)

- Enforce consistent adherence to competitive bidding policies for all purchases over a certain amount. Monitor the bidding process carefully to screen for potential bribery or kickback schemes being perpetrated to avoid the bidding process. (billing schemes, kickback schemes, shell company fraud, bribery)

- Prohibit purchasing/procurement employees from accepting vendor gifts valued at more than the bank's policy limit. (bribery, kickbacks)

- Enforce monitoring for duplicate invoices. (billing/shell company schemes, VMF schemes, kickbacks, check fraud) To save time and money, consider implementing one of the many effective technological programs for conducting this function.

- Manually review all unmatched open purchase orders, receiving reports, and invoices. (billing/shell company schemes, VMF fraud, kickbacks, inventory schemes)

- Immediately document all purchasing databases and shipping documents with details of goods received. (billing/shell company schemes, inventory fraud, book cooking)

- Send all shipping documents and signed receipts for goods to AP within one business day. (billing schemes, inventory fraud)

- Never pay for partial shipments. (billing/shell company schemes)

- Require a W-9 with EIN/TIN (Employer/Taxpayer Identification Number) matching for all new vendors. (VMF, shell company/billing schemes)

- Conduct a periodic vendor master file cleanup to flag duplicate vendors. (shell company/billing schemes)

- Investigate multiple vendors with the same name but different operating addresses. This could be an indicator of an employee fraudulently altering the legitimate address of a vendor in order to have checks sent to the address he or she controls. (billing/shell company schemes, VMF fraud)

- Review any invoices that have been paid without a purchase order reference. (billing/shell company schemes, check fraud)

- Conduct detailed reviews of purchasing/procurement records to detect unusual pricing for certain vendors *before* payment is made. (kickback/bribery schemes, billing schemes, shell companies)

- Immediately investigate any changes in vendors who have been working with your organization for a long time. A dishonest employee may be attempting to replace them with new vendors who are willing to pay kickbacks in exchange for being awarded the organization's business. (kickbacks, bribery)

- Verify that a new vendor's address is in the same area code.

- Pull invoices, purchase orders, receiving documentation, and packing slips to check for anomalies.

- Trace sample documentation back to the original contract to ensure that everything matches.

- Call the phone number provided by the vendor to see if a business employee answers.

- Use Google maps to determine if the address is a residential address.

- Conduct a vendor audit if you suspect a billing, shell company, straw vendor, or kickback scheme. Include the right to conduct such an audit at your discretion in *all* contracts with outside suppliers.

- Use data analysis software, such as ACL (from ACL Services Inc., www.acl .com) or IDEA (from Audimation Services Inc., www.audimation.com), to streamline the review of documents for anomalies that could be indicators of vendor fraud. Other automated approaches include continuous transaction monitoring offered by Oversight Systems (www.oversightsystems.com) and audit recovery software such as that provided by APEX Analytix (www.apexanalytix.com), among others.

    If an automated forensic document examination identifies sufficient evidence of an at-risk vendor, use a vendor profile form to see whether it will be returned with the requested information (see Exhibit 4.8).

- Validate the vendor master file against the employee master annually to determine whether there are employees posing as vendors.[31]

### T&E Fraud Prevention Checklist

- Require traveling employees to submit original plane ticket stubs and boarding passes together with their credit card statements. Do not accept photocopies.

- Implement a T&E code of conduct with such rules as:
    - Personal expenditures are strictly prohibited.

Business Name/Taxpayer Name (Exact Legal Name): _____

Federal ID Number/Social Security Number: _____

Parent Company (if applicable): _____

❏ Domestic   ❏ Foreign

**Business Type:**           **Officers:**

❏ Corporation              Principal/Owner: _____

❏ Partnership              Chief Executive/President: _____

❏ Sole Proprietorship      CFO/Controller: _____

❏ Individual

**Contact Name for Negotiations:** _____   **Telephone:** _____

                                                     **E-mail:** _____

**Contact Name for Billing Inquiries:** _____   **Telephone:** _____

_____                                           **E-mail:** _____

**Primary Remittance Address:**              **Physical Business Address:**

Address 1: _____          Address 1: _____

Address 2: _____          Address 2: _____

City: _____ State: _____ Zip: _____   City: _____ State: _____

                                             Zip: _____

Telephone Number: _____   Fax Number: _____

Company Web Site (if applicable): _____

**Please attach at least three of the following:**

Proof of Existence:   ◯ Corporate Charter          ◯ Federal Tax Return

                      ◯ Recent Audited Annual Report   ◯ Vendor Contract/Agreement

                      ◯ City/County Business License   ◯ Product Catalog

                      ◯ Sales Tax Certificate          ◯ 1099

                      ◯ IRS Document/Notice            ◯ W-9

**Description of Business (or commodity code, i.e. SIC, NAICS, etc.):** _____

**Please check techniques you are currently using with your customers:**

❏ Evaluated Receipts Settlement (ERS)

❏ Electronic Data Interchange (EDI)

❏ Electronic Funds Transfer (EFT)

❏ Diskette EDI

❏ Online Pricing Catalog

**How would you like to receive payments?**   ☐ ACH   ☐ Wire   ☐ Check   ☐ Other

_____

**Estimated Sales Revenue from HealthSouth:** _____

I hereby certify, under the penalty of perjury, that to the best of my knowledge, the information
presented here is true and correct.

**Respondent's Name:** _____   **Respondent's Signature:** _____

**Exhibit 4.8:** Vendor Profile Form

- Only authorized personnel may approve expense reports. Delegating this authority to another employee is strictly prohibited.

- All T&E-related purchases must be properly documented in accordance with organization policy.

- Only authorized and allowable expenses may be submitted for reimbursement. Check with your department manager if you have any questions about the eligibility or the validity of a purchase.

- All dollar-value purchase limits must be adhered to. Splitting of transactions to avoid authorized limits is strictly prohibited.

- Prohibit up-front management authorizations of T&E expenditures.

- Prohibit cash advances.

- Require employees filing expense reports and reimbursement claims to include full descriptions of the business purpose of each expense, original receipt or other documentation, time and date, location, and exact amount.

- Examine the legitimacy of rounded dollar numbers lacking supporting documentation, or potentially counterfeit documentation, as well as a series of equal amounts claimed for a specific item or service.

- Scrutinize all currency conversions on expense reimbursement claims for overseas travel. (Employees traveling abroad may claim for amounts based on earlier exchange rates that give them a windfall.)

- Cross-reference receipts to the expense report and send the report directly to the processing group.

- Establish and enforce a minimum dollar level for requiring receipts for travel outlays.

- Regularly train appropriate managers in how to review T&E reimbursement documentation and pinpoint red flags of fudging.

## ■ P-Card Fraud Prevention Checklist

Keeping in mind that much of P-card fraud is perpetrated by outsiders who illegally obtain card numbers, expiration dates, and other data needed to create counterfeit cards, consult with your organization's IT department about securing these critical data.

However, as discussed, dishonest insiders with access to these data may steal the information and sell it to outsiders, who then either resell it or use it to produce counterfeit cards and make fraudulent purchases on them.

Ensure that your internal information security measures are as rigorous as possible. For even very large financial institutions, it may pay to retain an outside information security consultant to evaluate your organization's overall defenses against cyber-attack and to remedy any major weaknesses, at least, identified in your defenses.

To minimize abuse by P-card holders:

- Conduct random audits of P-card statements. Audit at least 10 percent of statements on a regular basis and ideally as many as 30 percent. *Screen for:*
  - Appropriateness (business-related) of purchase.
  - Personal purchases.
  - Preferred vendor spend.
- Conduct targeted audits on specific cardholders and/or object account spend. *Screen for:*
  - Preferred vendor spend on office supplies.
  - Charitable contributions.
  - Inappropriate use for retail or restaurant purchases.
  - Anomalies flagged by credit card online reporting service (if available).
- Block vendors who are paid via P-card from submitting invoices as well.
- Establish a detailed policy spelling out exactly what is permitted, and especially what is *not*, with regard to use of company P-cards. (The policy should include limits on amounts of individual purchases as well as all requirements for documenting transactions or submitting expense report.)
- Ensure that 100 percent of P-card statements have supporting documentation and authorized approval as required.
- Train all employees with newly issued P-cards in the details of your organization's P-card policy, including disciplinary and punitive policies for committing fraud.
- Require *original* itemized receipts for all P-card transactions. These should be merchant-produced receipts that include:
  - Quantities.
  - Price per unit.
  - Description of goods or services purchased.
  - Total charge amount.
  - Date of purchase.
  - Merchant's name and address.
- Instruct employees to ask merchants for a detailed receipt if one is not provided. Many merchants also will reprint a receipt that has been lost.
- Establish and distribute lists of permitted and prohibited P-card transactions and/or types of vendors.
- Require cardholders to turn in their reimbursement claims and accompanying receipts promptly after making purchases totaling a specified amount.
- Ensure that all receipts are accounted for when the billing cycle ends.
- Require cardholders to review and sign monthly statements if those statements are sent to them rather than to your organization. This is not to detect employee

abuse but rather to identify purchases they did not make and for which there is no supporting receipt or other documentation. Such transactions may indicate that the card was "swiped" by a retail employee using a "wedge" (a small hand-held card-swiping device) to record the data from the magnetic stripe, storing it in the wedge's memory device. Identity theft rings traffic in these data, which ultimately are used to create counterfeit cards or for making fraudulent purchases.

- Require the manager in charge of approving and signing employee P-card reimbursement claims or expense reports to carefully review all documentation prior to signing in order to verify:
    - Appropriateness of transactions.
    - Correct cost center and account.
    - Complete supporting documentation.
    - Cardholder signature.
- Require managers to review any transactions over a predetermined minimum amount.[32]

### Check Fraud Prevention Checklist

- Secure all checks used by finance staff and enforce dual control of check stock.
- Keep keys to the check storage off premises.
- Ensure that all checks used by AP are consecutively numbered.
- Enforce dollar-amount thresholds for check-signing authority (see Delegation of Authority above), as well as details as to when dual signatures are required.
- Do not permit any checks to be signed without required supporting documentation (i.e., requisition form, invoice, purchase order, statement).
- Enforce full monthly reconciliation of all AP checking accounts by a manager who does not have access to checks, signature plates, or AP software.
- Store unprinted check stock in a locked filing cabinet *under dual control*: Two locks are on the cabinet and two different managers each hold one of the keys. Store check signature plates the same way to prevent collusion with outsiders.
- Enforce check limits. These serve as a stop-loss control over cash disbursements.
- Use positive pay, payee positive pay, reverse positive pay, or a combination of the three.
- Conduct prompt bank reconciliations to ensure that any recent check fraud schemes are detected quickly and stopped.
- Ensure that all payables are mailed without delay, which helps prevent interception of checks by dishonest insiders.

### Payroll Fraud Prevention Checklist

- Conduct background checks on all new hires, including, at a minimum, contacting references, checking credit reports, and looking into criminal backgrounds.

Conduct further checking on candidates for jobs involving financial operations or access to sensitive information by verifying educational credentials, awards, military experience, and other information.

- Never permit hiring by a single person.

- Conduct monthly (or continuous) reviews of payroll records to screen for unusual employee addresses, such as PO boxes, dual employee addresses, or dual Social Security numbers (may indicate existence of ghosts).

- Segregate payroll duties by ensuring that the person who prepares payroll is not the person sending out paychecks.

- Conduct a periodic manual payroll distribution, instead of automated direct deposit, in order to determine whether any checks are left over, which might be intended for ghost employees.

### Confidential Information Theft Prevention Checklist

- Clearly define and enforce data classifications. It is quite easy to determine which types of electronic data should be made available publicly and which should not and which types should be accessible only to specific managers, supervisors, and line employees.

- Avoid being too open with sensitive information. Some financial institutions put on their Web sites sensitive information that should not be there. This is especially true for financial institutions, which are prime targets of information thieves, hackers, and phishers.

  Determine which specific types of data are "top secret," which are sensitive and must be made accessible under strictly enforced access policies and guidelines, and which are suitable for public consumption.

- Use software programs that analyze anomalies in normal patterns of sensitive information usage.

- Hire professional IT security staff or outside consultants to configure these systems and train appropriate staff.

- Implement policies specifying how employees can use the organization's e-mail system and what is prohibited. Also, enforce access controls as discussed.

- Ensure strict management enforcement through automated monitoring of employee usage. This requires special software and skilled staff.[33]

Just as there is no silver bullet for fully protecting customer data, there is no one-size-fits-all set of information security measures for financial institutions. Because each organization is structured in its own unique way and varies in size, complexity, and level of vulnerability to insider information theft, it is essential that management start the process of information security enhancement by conducting an information risk assessment. This is similar to the fraud risk assessment discussed in Chapter 7 but obviously focuses on the vulnerabilities that the bank may be exposed to with regard to sensitive data.

Moreover, financial institutions that lack the in-house information security expertise to tackle the problem should retain a qualified outside information security specialist. The Information Security Systems Association (www.issa.org) is a good place to start in finding such an expert.

### Abuse of Computer Systems Prevention Checklist

- Enforce strict system access controls. Ensure that employees who are promoted or moved to different areas of the bank have their system access shut down.

- Eliminate access of all departing employees.

- Enforce maximum-security password practices and implement sanctions for employees who violate these rules.

- Implement system security protocols requiring senior-level authorization for all requests for "one-time" or "special project" access that exceeds an employee's authorized access.

- If possible, log all data access (read, modify, and delete) for individual data items in *all* of the organization's databases. At a minimum, log all computer accounts, Internet Protocol (IP) addresses, actions taken, and times that actions were performed.

  This logging information often proves invaluable in detecting insider attacks. It is important to back up these logs so they can be recovered, along with the application data.

  A procedure for periodic review of all logs to screen for unusual activities or unauthorized access attempts is also recommended.

- Implement a layered security approach that allows remote access to e-mail and noncritical data but, whenever possible, restricts access to sensitive data and information systems to employees physically located inside the workplace. (In one reported case, an employee changed the passwords to his previous employer's master account remotely from his residence two weeks after his resignation.)

- For remote access to critical data, processes, and information systems, minimize risk with closer logging and frequent auditing of remote transactions. Frequently monitor logs of login accounts, date/times connected and disconnected, and IP addresses.

- Monitor failed remote logins, including the reason the login failed. If authorization for remote access to critical data is kept to a minimum, it should be possible to assign responsibility for reviewing these logs on a daily basis.

---

### Remember

Financial institutions are among the most frequent targets of insiders seeking unauthorized access to secure computer systems and databases. Their objectives are to steal money or to alter, add, delete, or disclose proprietary information, intellectual property, or other confidential information. Risk reduction is difficult and challenging but absolutely critical.

## ► Review Points

- Financial institutions are vulnerable to a wide range of internal frauds. These range from accounts payable fraud to check theft and tampering, theft of cash, looting of customer accounts, payroll fraud, and so on. Minimizing risk of these crimes requires implementation of carefully designed controls and deterrents.

- Financial institutions are especially vulnerable to attempts at theft of confidential information and abuse of secure data. Identity thieves, embezzlers, and confidential information traffickers are among the greatest insider threats in these areas.

- The first step toward preventing employee-level fraud is understanding and detecting the numerous red flags of such schemes.

- With a solid understanding of red flags, an organization can conduct detailed risk assessments to gather evidence of suspected frauds and put into place effective controls to minimize its vulnerability to most employee-level frauds.

- A virtually limitless variety of anti-fraud controls can be implemented to minimize the organization's fraud risk. Determine which controls to put into place by conducting a fraud risk assessment that pinpoints signs of specific fraud vulnerabilities.

## ► Chapter Quiz

True or False:

1. Fee reversal fraud occurs when a bank customer service representative credits a fee challenged by a customer to his own account.
   - ❏ True   ❏ False

2. When ACH fraud occurs, the bank account likeliest to be targeted is your payroll account.
   - ❏ True   ❏ False

3. The top targets of confidential information thieves are retail companies, financial services institutions, and food and beverage companies.
   - ❏ True   ❏ False

4. Soft indicators of potential employee fraud point to specific types of illegal activity.
   - ❏ True   ❏ False

5. The most common way that employee fraud is brought to management's attention is by tips.
   - ❏ True   ❏ False

6. Unfolded invoices may be a red flag of billing fraud.
   - ❏ True   ❏ False

Circle the correct answer to the following questions:

**7.** In bid-rigging schemes, bid pooling occurs in which of the following phases of the bidding process?

    **a.** Presolicitation

    **b.** Solicitation

    **c.** Submission

    **d.** Postsubmission

**8.** All of the following are examples of potential T&E fraud EXCEPT:

    **a.** Submitting handwritten receipts

    **b.** Making multiple expense claim submissions

    **c.** Claiming reimbursement for parking a personal car at the airport during a business trip

    **d.** Claiming expenses just below the minimum amount that requires documentation

**9.** The most common form of payments fraud is:

    **a.** ACH fraud

    **b.** Check fraud

    **c.** Consumer credit card fraud

    **d.** Wire transfer fraud

**10.** The most common form of payroll fraud is:

    **a.** Stealing blank payroll checks

    **b.** Counterfeiting payroll checks

    **c.** Adding "ghost" employees to the payroll

    **d.** Time-card fraud

Fill in the blank:

**11.** The term commonly used to describe cash theft by a teller is _____.

**12.** Traveler's checks, cashier's checks, and money orders are known as _____.

**13.** Employees in the accounts payable department who are able to fraudulently alter existing vendors' addresses, add phony vendors, or delete legitimate ones do so by tampering with the bank's _____.

**14.** _____ is a form of bid rigging designed to evade the competitive bidding process.

**15.** Customer complaints about unauthorized use of their credit cards may be a sign of _____.

*For the answers, please turn to Appendix A.*

# CHAPTER FIVE

# Internal Fraud: Management Level

In Chapter 2 you learned about the psychological elements of the Fraud Triangle and diamond, in the commission of top management frauds in financial services companies.

Now we go beyond the human element of senior management fraud to explore the specific types of financial crime most commonly committed at the top levels of financial institutions.

It is important to note that while the variety of these crimes is almost as great as at lower levels, there is an inverse ratio between the frequency of management frauds and the losses caused by individual criminal acts. Specifically, although management-level frauds are committed far less frequently than employee-level frauds, the losses resulting from management frauds are substantially greater than those of crimes committed by lower-level employees.

The main reason for this is fairly obvious: Management typically has greater authority than most lower-level employees to execute large-dollar transactions without the scrutiny or approval of others.

Less obvious are the realities that senior managers typically have more education than their subordinates, which often enables them to execute more complex frauds; they also tend to have a higher personal standard of living, which "requires" them to steal more in order to maintain their lavish lifestyles.

## Remember

Many types of fraud committed at the employee level also occur at the top management levels. The only difference is that, due to their greater authority, broader executive privileges, and costlier lifestyles, senior managers who commit crimes such as embezzlement, travel and entertainment (T&E) fraud, and billing schemes that are common at lower levels (as detailed in Chapter 3) cause substantially greater losses than their criminal counterparts in subordinate positions.

The next descriptions of the most commonly committed unlawful management-level transactions that generally *do not* occur at the employee level will give you a firm foundation of knowledge about such activity that could occur at your bank.

## ► Looting and Embezzlement

As discussed in Chapter 3, the variety of ways that bank employees can steal the organization's funds is seemingly limitless. The same applies to their bosses, although, as mentioned, the amounts lost to fraud usually are much greater. Common tactics used by dishonest bank executives to commit embezzlement include:

- Management-level check fraud
- Skimming from the vault
- Looting customer accounts
- Diverting incoming funds to personal account(s)

### ■ Management-Level Check Fraud

As you learned in Chapter 3, most check fraud is perpetrated by outsiders through counterfeiting, forged endorsements, new account fraud, and other identity-fraud schemes.

However, like employees at lower levels with access to the bank's blank checks or with authority to generate cashier's checks, senior managers can exploit their positions by stealing company checks and forging them or using forged checks to divert customer funds to their own accounts. These frauds are most often committed by managers with authority to sign outgoing checks.

As pointed out by Association of Certified Fraud Examiners (ACFE) chairman Joe Wells:

> In most situations, check signers are owners, officers, or otherwise high-ranking employees, and thus have or can obtain access to all the blank checks they need. Even if company policy prohibits check signers from handling blank checks, normally the perpetrator can use her influence to overcome this impediment.[1]

After all, Wells asks, what employee is willing to protest a boss's request for a blank check? A useful term for this type of crime is "fraud by intimidation." As you might imagine, this works well in most environments but especially during recessions, when employees are being laid off and bosses know that none of their subordinates will want to risk their jobs by invoking internal controls that prohibit managers from handling blank checks.

Thus, at senior levels of the bank, many check-related crimes involve what is commonly referred to as override of internal controls over check handling. In addition to requesting blank checks, such crimes may involve managers ordering subordinates to record check requests as being made to phony payees, such as bogus charities or political organizations, signing the checks, and depositing them in their own accounts or one belonging to a relative or a shell company. Or managers simply may establish an account in the name of the bogus payee to avoid having the payee name differ from that of the account holder.

## ■ Skimming from the Vault

Managers with access to the vault and responsibility for reconciliations enjoy a license to steal if, like Joe Green, they are inclined to do so.

### ◄ Case Study #11:

### The Vault Was His Personal Piggy Bank

Joseph Monroe Green Jr. was sentenced to 21 months in prison followed by three years of supervised release for embezzling bank funds. Green was also ordered to pay restitution of $151,774, the amount still owed after he had made a partial payment.

According to his guilty plea, Green was manager of the Chevy Chase Bank branch located at 1734 York Road, Lutherville, Maryland, when the bank's reconciliation department discovered discrepancies between amounts of money he had withdrawn from the vault and amounts he had turned over to the Dunbar armored car company. In interviews with bank officials and the Federal Bureau of Investigation (FBI), Green admitted that he altered the vault settlement receipts and Dunbar bank deposit tickets from the bank during 2005 to conceal his thefts. Green removed cash from the bank's minivault by hiding it in his pants or work apron. From December 9, 2004, to September 22, 2005, Green embezzled money on 56 occasions, stealing a total of $162,974.

*How could this fraud have been prevented?* List as many controls as you can. Compare yours with those listed in Appendix B.

1. _____

2. _____

3. _____

## ■ Looting Customer Accounts

If managers have the necessary authority, they simply can help themselves to customer funds in various ways, such as tapping a customer's personal credit line and depositing the proceeds into their own, as Tara Whitelock admitted to doing.

### ◀ Case Study #12:

## The Banker's Hand Was in the Cookie Jar for Five Years

According to a felony indictment filed in U.S. District Court, Tara Whitelock was employed as a loan officer at the Far West Bank in Provo between December 2000 and April 2005. During that time, Whitelock was accused of using a bank customer's credit line to direct funds to other bank accounts on which she was a signatory. The charges also stated that Whitelock falsified entries in Far West Bank's ledger to show payments were made to the line of credit. In all, Whitelock was accused of stealing $101,395. She ultimately pleaded guilty and received a one-year prison sentence. At her sentencing hearing she wept, playing the "soccer mom" card by telling the court that she had never done anything wrong before and never would again.

*How could this fraud have been prevented?* List as many controls as you can. Compare yours with those listed in Appendix B.

1. _____

2. _____

3. _____

### ■ Diverting Incoming Funds to Personal Account(s)

Managers with authority to move bank funds and oversee accounting activity often are able to abuse their positions of authority to divert customer deposits from third parties to their own accounts, as the bank manager in the next case study admitted to doing.

### ◀ Case Study #13:

## Trusted Trust Officer Abuses Trust for Five Full Years

Daryl Turner was sentenced to concurrent sentences of 41 months of incarceration and 3 years of supervised release, and ordered to pay $1,134,077 in restitution to U.S. Bank and $294,130 in restitution to the Internal Revenue Service, for committing bank embezzlement and income tax evasion. Turner previously pleaded guilty to the charges.

According to the indictment, during the years 2001 through 2006, Turner was employed as a manager of the Private Client Service Department of U.S. Bank (formerly Firstar). He had authorization to issue expense disbursements of up to $5,000 at his sole discretion and of up to $100,000 with further authorization.

*The scheme.* According to court documents, Turner's department regularly received payments from various mutual funds for deposit into Private Client customer accounts. Turner deposited several of these checks in a general sweep account of the bank. He then generated U.S. Bank checks payable to his wife or another individual whose accounts he had access to instead of directing the funds into the U.S. Bank accounts for the intended customers. To conceal the fraud, he generated fraudulent cash disbursement forms describing the illegal transactions as "interest repayments." Turner admitted that he used the stolen money for personal expenses.

*Insult to injury.* In addition, for the 2001 through 2006 income tax years, Turner failed to report the embezzled funds on his federal income tax returns. Turner evaded a total of $294,130 in individual federal income taxes.

*How could this fraud have been prevented?* List as many controls as you can. Compare yours with those listed in Appendix B.

1. _____

2. _____

3. _____

## ▶ Illegal Financial Transactions/Corruption

Illegal financial transactions/corruption are wide-ranging frauds, from the linked financing, daisy chain schemes and reciprocal loans that were widespread during the savings and loan (S&L) crisis of the 1980s (refer to Chapter 3 for details), to an array of similar high-level fraudulent transactions that sometimes are difficult to detect but often result in major losses to the financial institution. Some examples follow.

### ■ Kickback Schemes

Bank executives in a position to approve loans on favorable terms can do so for the benefit of friends, relatives, or outside business associates in exchange for illegal cash payments from the borrowers.

### ■ Approval of Loans to Oneself

Executives with the authority to abuse their positions by approving loans to themselves engage in what generally is referred to as self-dealing. Self-dealing also can include insider trading in securities, which is a crime under the Securities Exchange Act.

In the context of bank lending, self-dealing can result in shareholder lawsuits alleging fraud. However, in most instances of approving loans to oneself, the act represents both a violation of the bank's code of ethics and a breach of fiduciary duty.

The latter is defined by the online legal encyclopedia *The Legal Practitioner* as:

> wrongful conduct by a fiduciary. A fiduciary is a person who has duties of good faith, trust, special confidence, and candor toward another person. Examples

of fiduciary relationships include attorneys and their clients, doctors and their patients, investment bankers and their clients, trustees and trust beneficiaries, and corporate directors and stockholders. Fiduciaries have expert knowledge and skill, and they are paid to apply that knowledge and skill for the benefit of another party. Under the law, a fiduciary relationship imposes certain duties on fiduciaries because a fiduciary is in a special position of control over an important aspect of another person's life.

According to *The Legal Practitioner*:

> One important duty of a fiduciary is to act in the best interests of the benefited party. When a fiduciary engages in self-dealing, she breaches this duty by acting in her own interests instead of the interests of the represented party. For example, self-dealing occurs when a trustee uses money from the trust account to make a loan to a business in which he has a substantial personal interest. A fiduciary may make such a transaction with the prior permission of the trust beneficiary, but if the trustee does not obtain permission, the beneficiary can void the transaction and sue the fiduciary for any monetary losses that result.[2]

This definition of self-dealing is similar to that of conflict of interest, which, as described later in this chapter, involves conducting transactions for the benefit of a third party in which the perpetrator has a direct financial interest. Conflict of interest is one of the four types of fraud comprising the ACFE's definition of corruption (together with bribery, illegal gratuities, and economic extortion).

Significantly, corruption makes up a full 33 percent of all fraud against financial services institutions.[3]

---

### Remember

Bank executives with the poor judgment to authorize a loan to themselves run the risk of being terminated and charged through civil proceedings with breach of fiduciary duty, which can result in significant financial penalties.

---

## ■ Bribery

Although regulatory oversight of illegal business payments became more rigorous beginning in the years following the enactment of the Sarbanes-Oxley Act, senior bank executives still sometimes can abuse their authority to fraudulently manage the competitive bidding process, award lucrative contracts to preferred vendors, and execute similar acts in exchange for bribes. In one instance, a Connecticut bank vice president conspired with an outside attorney to accept bribes from parties seeking to purchase distressed loans that the executive's bank was selling.

◄ **Case Study #14:**

## The Banker's Bidding Bust

Kevin J. O'Keefe, who was a vice president at Fleet Bank (and Bank of America after it acquired Fleet Bank) in Hartford, Connecticut, pleaded guilty to conspiracy to commit financial institution bribery and to bank fraud in connection with a scheme he cooked up with attorney Paul Aparo, who also pleaded guilty, and a Connecticut real estate developer, identified by the Justice Department only as "Individual B."

*The scheme.* According to documents filed with the court and statements made during the case proceedings, Aparo, O'Keefe, and Individual B corrupted the bidding process on distressed loans that Fleet Bank was selling by colluding to set up shell companies through which to submit bids on the loans and with which to receive and distribute proceeds from the scheme.

The key to the scheme was that O'Keefe had access to confidential information belonging to Fleet Bank and provided that information to Aparo and Individual B so they could use it to submit winning bids on distressed loans. O'Keefe also intentionally provided outdated information to rival bidders in order to cause those bidders to submit artificially low bids.

O'Keefe also excluded bidders who he, Aparo, and Individual B believed would submit competitive bids for a distressed loan on which they wanted to bid.

Aparo admitted that Individual B paid him and O'Keefe $100,000 on one loan that Individual B obtained through the corrupt assistance of Aparo and O'Keefe. Individual B also agreed to pay a shell company, referred to in court documents as "LA," 15 percent of the profits on a second distressed loan on which Individual B, together with Aparo and O'Keefe's "corrupt assistance," had submitted a winning bid. The 15 percent that Individual B paid to LA through *his own* shell company amounted to more than $1.4 million, which Aparo and O'Keefe split evenly.[4]

*How could this fraud have been prevented?* List as many controls as you can. Compare yours with those listed in Appendix B.

1. _____

2. _____

3. _____

## ■ Violation of Overseas Antibribery Laws

The Foreign Corrupt Practices Act (FCPA) was passed by Congress in 1977 in the wake of the Watergate scandal. But it slipped into relative obscurity until 2002, when the Sarbanes-Oxley Act was passed and FCPA regained prominence as an additional legal tool for keeping company executives within the statutory and regulatory bounds of ethical conduct. Thus, in recent years, the Department of Justice and the Securities and Exchange Commission (SEC) began cracking down on U.S. companies that were paying frequent and substantial bribes to overseas authorities in order to obtain business.

The FCPA prohibits offering or giving bribes or other corrupt payments to foreign officials for the purpose of obtaining or retaining business. The FCPA also requires companies to keep accurate books and records and to maintain internal accounting controls for preventing and detecting FCPA violations.

To compete for overseas business without running afoul of the FCPA, U.S. companies must be extremely vigilant about how they prepare contract bids, communicate with local authorities, and negotiate deals.

◀ **Case Study #15:**

## The Greatest Corruption Story of All Time

The most stunning evidence of the bizarre lengths to which companies go to secure business in a tough global economy is the case of the German engineering and electronics conglomerate Siemens AG. Although not a financial services company, Siemens got its banks into trouble indirectly because federal prosecutors charged that the company's FCPA violations provided legal authorization for the company's overseas bank accounts to be forfeited.[5]

*Background.* In late 2008, the company settled charges in the United States of having violated the FCPA by paying more than $805 million in direct bribes to foreign officials to obtain large telecommunications and other infrastructure contracts around the world.

*Example.* According to federal court documents, a subsidiary of Siemens paid over $1.7 million in kickbacks to Iraqi government authorities to secure 42 contracts related to the widely publicized Iraqi Oil for Food program.

The illegal payments were concealed by falsifying the company's books and records.

Further bribes and kickbacks were paid in such countries as Argentina, Nigeria, Iran, Tunisia, Vietnam, and Bangladesh.

Although Siemens is headquartered in Germany, it became the subject of an FBI and SEC investigation in 2006 because it is listed on the New York Stock Exchange.

Once the SEC began digging into allegations of dubious payments made by the company to secure lucrative contracts, the company's top executives began resigning en masse.

Under the settlement deal with the United States, Siemens was ordered to pay penalties of $1.6 billion of which half was split between the U.S. Department of Justice and the SEC, with most of the balance going to the German government.[6]

*How could this fraud have been prevented?* List as many controls as you can. Compare yours with those listed in Appendix B.

1. _____

2. _____

3. _____

## Remember

The U.S. federal government has substantially increased its monitoring and enforcement activities with respect to the Foreign Corrupt Practices Act. While the temptation to offer bribes to overseas officials to obtain government or business contracts may be hard to resist, the danger of discovery and subsequent penalties indicate that the risk is usually too high.

Penalties for violation of the FCPA include fines up to $2 million per violation for companies and $100,000 and/or up to five years imprisonment for individuals. U.S. organizations also are prohibited from reimbursing their employees for fines they are forced to pay resulting from FCPA violations.

These frauds can occur in both lending and operational functions. In operations, procurement is the area where most high-level conflict-of-interest cases occur. Senior executives with the power to sidestep the bank's required competitive bidding procedures, for example, may award business to a vendor in which they have an ownership interest.

A variation on this fraud would be awarding contracts to vendors owned by friends or relatives in exchange for a kickback.

Executives with the authority to approve loans obviously have the opportunity to "adjust" lending standards or falsify the application of a commercial borrower in which they have a direct financial interest.

Conflicts of interest in the lending process were especially egregious during the S&L debacle. As former federal banking regulator and author, William K. Black, wrote:

> The S&L debacle proved that human nature had not changed; conflicts of interest still caused damage. [Lincoln Savings Bank CEO], [Charles] Keating's actions demonstrate that . . . maximizing conflicts of interest made it easier for him to suborn auditors and attorneys. He engineered [Arthur] Andersen's and [Arthur] Young's involvement in nonaudit work while they were the auditors. Keating placed the accountants in an advocacy role requiring them to attack [bank] examiners in order to help Keating retain control of Lincoln Savings.[7]

Today, while less widespread, such loan schemes still can be perpetrated if proper controls are not in place. Referring back to the Fraud Triangle, senior lending officers may authorize fraudulent loans to family, friends, or business associates if they are under personal financial pressure and need the proceeds of the loan or the kickback from the loan recipients who might otherwise not qualify for a loan. If managers are senior enough and proper segregation of duties is absent, they will be able to conceal the scheme by falsifying the recording of these illegal transactions.

## ▪ Other Forms of Management-Level Loan Fraud and Misconduct

Conflicts of interest are by no means the only motivators for executives to commit loan fraud. As discussed in Chapter 3, the opportunities for employees to commit loan fraud are numerous, to say the least. While many of these frauds do not require the direct involvement or approval of senior management, it is clear that the financial crisis of 2007–2008 was at least *partially* caused by tacit executive approval of the loosening of lending standards that enabled lower-level loan officers to process loans that were unequivocally fraudulent.

Many informed observers suggest that this syndrome was driven by a kind of tsunami of executive greed that engulfed Wall Street executive suites, leading top decision makers to sanction the frenzied creation and aggressive selling of exotic subprime loan-backed securities that ultimately imploded. Although most of the actions of top banking and Wall Street executives in connection with the crisis cannot technically be described as fraudulent, the difference between legal and illegal in this context is imprecise and almost certainly will be defined and refined by a long string of legal actions brought by investors, shareholders, regulators, and others in coming years.

Writes Frank Partnoy, a former Morgan Stanley derivatives trader and now a professor of securities law:

> Without derivatives, the complex risks that destroyed Bear Stearns, Lehman Brothers, and Merrill Lynch and decimated dozens of banks and insurance companies, including AIG, could not have been hidden from view. Without derivatives, a handful of financial wizards could not have gunned down major mutual funds and pension funds and then pulled the trigger on their own institutions. Derivatives were the key: they enabled Wall Street to continue its destructive run until it was too late.[8]

### Remember

The determination as to whether many of the actions of top banking and Wall Street executives in connection with the subprime crisis were legal or not is unclear and will be determined only after many years of arduous legal debate and adjudication.

### ▶ Fraudulent Financial Reporting

According to the ACFE, fraudulent financial reporting ranks third on the list of most frequently committed frauds against financial institutions, behind only corruption and theft of cash.[9]

Fraudulent financial reporting—commonly referred to as cooking the books—has a voluminous record in the annals of American business. The financial services industry has not been exempt from these crimes.

However, these frauds did earn renewed notoriety after the Enron debacle, which, as is well known, was a book-cooking scandal of epic proportions. Since Enron, literally hundreds of organizations have been caught falsifying their financial records and statements.

Similar to such frauds in nonfinancial industries, the most common motives driving dishonest financial services executives to falsify financial records and statements are to boost share price, increase executive bonuses, conceal illegal financial transactions, and secure financing.

How is fraudulent financial reporting perpetrated at financial institutions? Given the exceptionally complex nature of financial institution accounting rules and procedures, it is not surprising that, according to one important study, 88 different methods of financial statement fraud were used to commit 64 examined financial institution frauds.[10] The study found that the most frequently misstated areas are investment value, loans receivable, loan loss reserves, accounts receivable, cash reserves, and revenue gains or losses. The top methods of committing these frauds at financial institutions are:

- Making inaccurate accounting estimates
- Inaccurate or misleading disclosure
- Misclassification of financial information
- Lack of detailed transaction records
- Unsupported accounting entries
- Fictitious documentation
- Premature (revenue) recognition[11]

Details of some of the most frequently committed financial statement frauds, often collectively referred to as earnings management, are provided next.

## ■ Recording False Revenues or Earnings

This tactic for misrepresenting financial performance involves recording nonexistent revenue or misrepresenting the period in which the revenue was received.

You learned in Chapter 3 about recording fictitious loans and other records manipulation schemes. The purpose there was to steal money—without getting caught. In the context of fraudulent financial reporting, organizations falsify their financial records to make investors, Wall Street analysts, and the general public think that they are in better financial shape than they actually are. Financial institutions can do this by adding fictitious loans to the bank's portfolio and then inflating its interest income figures for a particular reporting period. Similarly, this type of fraud can be perpetrated along the lines of the real case involving Freddie Mac, the government-sponsored enterprise (GSE) that bought billions of dollars of mortgages leading up to the crisis of 2007–2008.

On January 22, 2003, Freddie Mac announced that it would revise its reported earnings for 2001 and 2002. On November 21, 2003, the company disclosed the results of its restatement for 2000, 2001, and 2002. The restatement revealed that Freddie Mac had misreported its net income in each of those years by 30.5, 23.8, and 42.9 percent, respectively. The picture the company had presented to investors of an enterprise with steadily growing and predictable GAAP earnings was false; in fact, according to court documents in a lawsuit brought against Freddie Mac by the SEC:

> Freddie Mac's restated net income reflects significantly greater volatility than previously reported, and the company anticipates that its net income for periods following the restatement will continue to reflect greater volatility than previously

reported from quarter to quarter. . . . The company's combined net income for 2000 and 2001 was approximately $6.6 billion, but income that should have been reported in 2000 was shifted to 2001 to show smooth and steady growth. Had the company reported income properly for those years, as in the restatement, it would have shown an earnings decrease of over $500 million between 2000 and 2001.[12]

## ■ Fraudulent Revenue Recognition

Fraudulent revenue recognition is a category of accounting fraud with an objective similar to that of recording false earnings, as Freddie Mac did to make the organization's financial performance appear rosier than it was. These accounting frauds can involve recording revenue—typically loan interest income and interest from investments and related revenue—from a future reporting period in the current period or understating amounts set aside for loan losses.

In one of the few authoritative research studies on financial institution financial statement fraud, it was discovered that accounts receivable frauds commonly involved simple overstatement of amounts owed to the institution.

Investment frauds involve reporting values on an institution's financial statements that exceed the investment's "realizable value" (the value of an asset that can be realized by a company upon the sale of the asset). For example, according to the research, in some cases, "banks and S&Ls held investments at higher book values per share even when they had knowledge that the companies they had invested in were insolvent."[13]

Loans receivable fraud, by contrast, occurs when the institution maintains on its books loans that it knows to be uncollectible. For example, in one three-year period, now-defunct American Pioneer Bank intentionally maintained on its books (and continued to accrue interest on) a $25 million loan to a Texas developer who was both delinquent in loan payments and insolvent.

However, typical frauds involving loan loss reserves, according to experts, entail failing to maintain allowances sufficient to cover the estimated probable loss.

## ■ Manipulating Liabilities

Also referred to as concealing liabilities or underreporting expenses, manipulating liability schemes are perpetrated in a number of ways. For example, by simply neglecting to record expenses and burying vendor invoices, management can make it appear as if expenses for a particular reporting period are lower than they actually are, thereby making earnings appear *greater* than they are.

A related ploy involves classifying expenses as capital expenditures. This bookkeeping trick essentially results in converting liabilities into assets, which is what happened on a grand scale when WorldCom improperly reported $3.8 billion in expenses as capital expenditures.

## ■ Overstating Assets

Overstating assets is the flip side of neglecting to recognize or record expenses. Examples include failure to mark investments to market when the securities markets decline, overstating the amount of cash, or recording the value of an outstanding loan as being greater than its estimated market value. This was a major point of debate in the period 2007 to 2009 with regard to the value of "toxic assets"—such as non-performing mortgages and securities backed by such loans and other loans that were approaching foreclosure.

### ◀ Case Study #16:

## The Case of the $2.7 Million "Segregated Cash"

The accounting personnel at each branch of CapitalBanc, the holding company of New York City-based Capital National Bank (CNB), maintained a "vault general ledger proof sheet" that reconciled the amount of cash on hand at the branch to the balance of the branch's general ledger cash account. During the surprise cash count at the 177th Street branch, the bank's outside auditor, Arthur Andersen, discovered a $2.7 million reconciling item listed on the branch's proof sheet.

When the staff auditors asked to count the $2.7 million of cash represented by the reconciling item, they were told that Carlos Cordova, the chief executive officer (CEO), had segregated those funds in a locked cabinet within the bank's main vault. According to bank staff, three keys were required to unlock the cabinet. Cordova, who was out of the country at the time, maintained custody of one of those keys.

In response to this information, a staff auditor called one of the Andersen engagement partners to share the "segregation" story with him. The Andersen partner told the staff auditor that the cash could be counted when the CEO returned, despite the unusual circumstance of having a substantial portion of a bank's cash inaccessible for long periods of time.

Nonetheless, on the date of the CEO's return, the Andersen partners arrived at the branch. The locked cabinet in the main vault was opened in the presence of the staff auditors. The auditors then proceeded to count the $2.7 million that had not been counted on December 29, 1987. All of the cash was present.

After counting the cash in the locked cabinet, the staff auditors asked Cordova why those funds were kept segregated. The CEO replied that a customer had previously cashed a large certificate of deposit and insisted on having the funds available on demand at all times. According to the CEO, the customer intended to use the funds to buy foreign currencies when market conditions became favorable. The volatility of the foreign currency market dictated that the customer have access to the funds on a daily basis.

*Problem.* When the staff auditors were asked to confirm that there was an offsetting liability to the given customer in CNB's accounting records equal to the amount of the segregated funds, the staff auditors obtained the documentation for this liability directly from CNB personnel. However, the auditors did not confirm this information with the customer or independently verify it in any other way. The staff auditors also did not even obtain documentation confirming that the customer in question had cashed a certificate of deposit.

*(Continued)*

◀ **Case Study #16 (*Continued*)**

Finally, the staff auditors had no evidence to corroborate Cordova's assertion regarding the customer's planned use of the funds.

Shortly thereafter, the Office of the Comptroller of the Currency declared CapitalBanc insolvent and placed it under the control of the Federal Deposit Insurance Corporation (FDIC). The following year, Banco Popular de Puerto Rico purchased the assets of CNB from the FDIC.

Eventually Carlos Cordova pleaded guilty to three counts of bank fraud and conspiracy to commit bank fraud.[14]

***How could this fraud have been prevented?*** List as many controls as you can. Compare yours with those listed in Appendix B.

1. _____

2. _____

3. _____

## ▶ Deceiving Borrowers, Investors, and Regulators

Deception by bank executives of regulators and their own investors about illegal activity or about the institution's true financial condition in order to conceal poor performance, poor management, or questionable transactions is not new to the world of finance. In fact, it was a widespread practice during the meltdown of the financial markets in 2007. In addition, this period saw heated debate about alleged deception by the rating agencies, Standard & Poor's, Moody's, and Fitch, of major institutional investors, which depended on the agencies' valuations of subprime-backed securities in making investment decisions. Thus, not only deceptive borrowers and unscrupulous mortgage brokers and appraisers contributed to the meltdown. The maelstrom of lies and deception that drove the entire U.S. financial system in the mid- to late 2000s accelerated to the point of no return, and the crisis that ensued proved unavoidable.

As already noted, there were ample instances of bank deception in the years leading up to the Great Depression. That information came out with considerable drama and fanfare through the work of the Pecora Commission.

However, the executive deceptions that came under the legal and regulatory microscope following the financial market meltdown of 2007 to 2009 represent some of history's most brazen cases of concealment of irresponsible lending practices, fraudulent underwriting, shady financial transactions, and false statements to investors, federal regulators, and investigators.

Indeed, according to several learned analysts, the lion's share of direct blame for the meltdown lies with top executives of major banks, investment firms, and rating agencies. They charge the bank bosses with perpetuating a boom in reckless mortgage lending and the investment bankers with essentially tricking institutional investors into buying the exotic derivative securities backed by the millions and millions of toxic mortgages sold off by the mortgage lenders. The bank bosses and investment bankers were, according to these observers, aided and abetted by the rating agencies, which lowered their rating standards on high-risk mortgage-backed securities that should never have received investment-grade ratings but did so because the rating agencies are paid by investment banks, which issue those bonds. The agencies reportedly feared losing business if they gave poor ratings to the securities. As William Black wrote:

> Fraud is the principal credit risk of nonprime mortgage lending. It is impossible to detect fraud without reviewing a sample of the loan files. Paper loan files are bulky, so they are photographed and the images are stored on computer tapes. Unfortunately, "most investors" (the large commercial and investment banks that purchased nonprime loans and pooled them to create financial derivatives) did not review the loan files before purchasing nonprime loans and did not even require the lender to provide loan tapes.
>
> The rating agencies never reviewed samples of loan files before giving AAA ratings to nonprime mortgage financial derivatives. The "AAA" rating is supposed to indicate that there is virtually no credit risk—the risk is equivalent to U.S. government bonds, which finance refers to as "risk-free." We know that the rating agencies attained their lucrative profits because they gave AAA ratings to nonprime financial derivatives exposed to staggering default risk. A graph of their profits in this era rises like a stairway to heaven. We also know that turning a blind eye to the mortgage fraud epidemic was the only way the rating agencies could hope to attain those profits. If they had reviewed even small samples of nonprime loans they would have had only two choices: (1) rating them as toxic waste, which would have made it impossible to sell the nonprime financial derivatives or (2) documenting that they were committing, and aiding and abetting, accounting control fraud.[15]

A statement made during the October 2008 House of Representatives hearings on the topic of the rating agencies' roles in the crisis presents an apt summary of how the financial and government communities view the actions and attitudes of the three rating agencies in the years leading up to the subprime crisis. During those hearings, Chris Myer, an S&P employee, testified that "the rating agencies continue to create an even bigger monster, the CDO [collateralized debt obligation] market. Let's hope we all are wealthy and retired by the time this house of cards falters."

Committee member Elijah Cummings summed up several hours of testimony by the three rating agency bosses by saying:

> It seems to me that . . . there was a climate [at the rating agencies] of mediocrity because when we go on, we realize that there were other people [besides Myer] saying the same thing your organization. Now although you may not think it reflected the culture, I think it reflected the culture and my constituents think it reflected the culture, and to you Mr. [Raymond] McDaniel [chairman of Moody's,] you know this is your watch. You made a nice statement about your organization being around since 1909.
>
> But I wondered whether the folks who started your organization in 1909 would be happy with what they see today. Because there is, without a doubt, . . . a loss of trust. And somebody has to recover that. You have to get that trust back. We can never get these markets back, get them back right unless the investors

feel comfortable about what is going on. And you're the gatekeepers. You're the guys. You're the ones that make all the money. You're there.[16]

With respect to bank executives, the examples of alleged deception are too numerous to describe here. Among the most noteworthy are:

- The SEC investigated Citigroup as to whether it misled investors by failing to disclose critical details about troubled mortgage assets it was holding as the financial markets began to collapse in 2007. The investigation came after some of the mortgage-related securities being held by Citigroup were downgraded by a rating agency. Shortly thereafter, Citigroup announced quarterly losses of around $10 billion on its subprime-mortgage holdings—an astounding amount that directly contributed to the resignation of then-CEO Charles Prince.

- The SEC conducted similar investigations into Bank of America, now-defunct Lehman Brothers, and Merrill Lynch (now a part of Bank of America).

- The SEC filed civil fraud charges against Angelo Mozilo, cofounder and former CEO of Countrywide Financial Corp. In the highest-profile government legal action against a chief executive related to the financial crisis, the SEC charged Mozilo with insider trading and *alleged failure to disclose material information to shareholders*, according to people familiar with the matter.

Mozilo sold $130 million of Countrywide stock in the first half of 2007 under an executive sales plan, according to government filings.

Insider trading (buying and selling stocks on the strength of information available only to company or investment firm insiders, *not* to the investing public), as Mozilo is accused of doing, has been against the law since enactment of the Securities Exchange Act of 1934. The act prohibits "short-swing profits [from any purchases and sales within any six-month period] made by corporate directors, officers, or stockholders owning more than 10% of a firm's shares."

The rule was implemented to prevent insiders, who have greater access to material company information, from taking advantage of information to make short-term profits. For example, if an officer buys 100 shares at $5 in January and sells these same shares in February for $6, he would have made a profit of $100. Because the shares were bought and sold within a six-month period, however, under the short-swing profit rule, the officer would have to return the $100 to the company.[17]

The 1934 act also makes it illegal "to use or employ, in connection with the purchase or sale of any security registered on a national securities exchange or any security not so registered, any manipulative or deceptive device or contrivance in contravention of such rules and regulations as the [SEC] may prescribe."[18] However, criminalization of insider trading was much more clearly codified in the Insider Trading Sanctions Act (ITSA) of 1984, which gave the SEC the ability to request courts to impose monetary penalties on violators of the insider trading laws. Further toughening came with the Insider Trading and Securities Fraud Act of 1988, which, in short, makes it clear that a penalty can be imposed against "tippers" of material nonpublic information and authorized the SEC to pay up to 10 percent of fines to informers as bounty in certain cases.[19]

Unfortunately, history tells us that statutory and regulatory deterrents to insider trading have not stopped dishonest financial institution managers from making illegal securities trades based on privileged information.

In fact, many of the criminal charges against Michael Milken, the famed inventor of "junk bonds," was in collusion with investment tycoon, Ivan Boesky, involved incidents of insider trading, mainly in connection with the numerous junk bond–financed takeover deals that Milken and his team engineered. (Thanks to successful plea bargaining, Milken never was actually *convicted* of illegal insider trading, although the evidence against him overwhelmingly pointed to repeated incidents of such activity.)

More recently, many of the high-profile corporate fraud cases, such as Enron, WorldCom, Deutsche Bank, and others, have consisted in part of insider trading violations.

## ▶ Red Flags of Management-Level Internal Fraud

Now that you know the most common forms of management-level fraud, the next step toward being able to take action against fraud is understanding the telltale indicators of these crimes.

Being able to identify red flags is the first step toward apprehending a senior-level fraudster and taking the appropriate disciplinary or legal action. It is important to remember that not all red flags are definite signs of fraud. Conducting a proper fraud risk assessment, as you will learn in Chapter 7, prevents your auditors and investigators from pursuing red flags that are actually mere errors or an abuse of authority and *not* fraud.

In the next pages, you will find lists of the common red flags for each of the major types of management fraud discussed in this chapter. However, it is also essential to be on the lookout for certain *behavioral* red flags of management-level frauds (also referred to in Chapter 3 as soft indicators). Some examples include:

- Managers have lied to internal or external auditors or others in response to audit-related questions.

- Management places excessive emphasis on meeting financial performance or budget goals.

- Management frequently argues with or intimidates auditors—especially in defense of "aggressive" accounting practices that misrepresent the organization's financial condition.[20]

You may wish to make photocopies of the next few pages, which provide specific hard indicators (explained in Chapter 3) of the types of management-level fraud you have learned about in this chapter. Keeping them handy may prove useful in your day-to-day activities.

As discussed, many of the frauds described in Chapters 3 and 4 in the area of employee fraud also occur at the management level. The major difference is in the amounts of money lost. The next pages address the red flags of frauds that occur primarily at the management level.

### Red Flags of Management-Level Check Fraud

- Evidence of manual alterations to bank statements.

- Unusual number of voided checks. (May indicate a senior manager is making false entries in disbursements journal and is intercepting and destroying returned fraudulent checks.)

- Bank reconciliation issues. (May indicate an executive is making fraudulent checks and neglecting to record them or instructing subordinates not to record them.)

- Missing blank checks.

- Sudden increase in checks to a particular vendor. (May indicate a manager is making blank checks out to self but having them recorded as payable to a known vendor in the expectation that the unusual pattern will not be noticed.)

- Supporting documentation for specific checks is missing key details. (May indicate a manager intimidating a subordinate into creating false documentation on a fraudulent check made out to the manager.)

### Red Flags of Looting or Embezzlement

- Signs of altered documentation on funds transfers.

- Complaints by customers of unusually low balances or unauthorized withdrawals/transfers.

- Unusual details of funds transfers (such as interest repayment in Case Study #13).

- Unusually high volume of funds transfers from particular customer accounts.

- Missing checks or unsupported check requests by senior managers.

- Evidence of check forgery or alteration.

- Bank statements are not being sent to the customer.

- "Miscellaneous" debits from a customer account.

### Red Flags of Illegal Loan Transactions, Kickback Schemes, and Self-Dealing

- Manager personally delivers disbursement of loan proceeds. (May indicate an illegal loan approval in exchange for a kickback.)

- Ratio of deposits to outstanding loan amounts is unusually high compared to industry levels. (May indicate linked financing schemes.)

- Large-dollar deposits are offered as consideration for favorable treatment on loan requests, but deposits are not pledged as collateral for the loans. (May indicate a linked financing scheme.)

- Loans with excessive number of renewals and increasing balances. (May indicate a manager authorized a loan to a borrower who is unable to make payments in exchange for a kickback or is simply perpetuating an ongoing kickback scheme.)

- Missing loan documentation.

- Loans are not grouped or identified by loan officer; therefore, loan officer activity cannot be monitored effectively. (May indicate kiting of payments from one account to another on fictitious loans.)

- The same vendor is awarded numerous contracts on consecutive projects.

- Indicators of intimidation of subordinates. (May indicate senior manager is forcing override of controls to fraudulently alter key records.)

- Outspoken disdain for bank regulators. (May indicate a lack of regard for lending or operational rules or standards.)

### Red Flags of Operational Fraud

- A longtime vendor is suddenly replaced by a new one.

- Inferior-quality product is delivered, but the invoice prices are for a higher-quality alternative.

- A pattern of growing frequency of "purchases" from a particular vendor.

- Purchases are recorded in amounts greater than what is normally purchased, or of products or services the organization does not use.

- Contracts are awarded without competitive bidding.

- Unusual price jumps or reductions.

### Red Flags of Bribery (Nongovernmental)

- Longtime valued vendors are suddenly replaced.

- Contract change orders lack sufficient justification.

- Delivery of shoddy quality merchandise or substandard service.

- Unusual offshore accounts are set up (usually slush funds for funneling bribes to overseas "agents").

- Prices for regularly purchased goods or services suddenly increase.

- Circumvention of bidding rules and procedures (including shortening of bidding submission time, imposing unusual and unconventional "qualifying" conditions for prospective bidders to meet, allowing individual bidders to submit bids *after* the submission deadline).

### Red Flags of Illegal Overseas Bribery

- Evidence of offshore slush funds.

- Unusually strong financial performance of an overseas affiliate.

### Red Flags of Conflicts of Interest

- Signs that entities owned by a manager or friend or family member are receiving loans that have been approved without compliance with appropriate approval process.

- Special terms or concessions on loans to family members, friends, or organizations in which the executive has a direct financial interest.

- Signs that entities owned by a manager or friend or family member are receiving contracts without going through the proper bidding process.

- Evidence of unusually high volumes of business with a particular vendor, especially a new one.

- Disclosure statements by top managers are missing key details.

- One or more vendors begin to obtain an unusual number of consecutive contracts from your organization.

### Red Flags of Fraudulent Financial Reporting/Management Override (Includes Red Flags of Deceiving Borrowers, Investors, and Regulators)

- Unusual/subjectively calculated drops in expenses/liabilities. (Misclassification of expenses.)

- Unusual names of new customers. (Fictitious loans.)

- Sudden increases in revenues compared to previous reporting periods and to industry trend. (Fictitious loans, mistimed revenue recognition, or overstatement of investment income.)

- Unusual decline or lack of change in accounts payable for a specific accounting period during which sales significantly increased. (Revenue recognition or misrepresentation of liabilities.)

- Unusually low costs recorded for routine processes or projects. (Understatement of expenses.)

- Unusually high accounts receivable.

- Unusually strong earnings growth compared to industry norms, especially during economic downturns. (Revenue recognition or misrepresentation of asset or liability values, deceiving investors, borrowers, and regulators.)

- Sudden increase in loan default rates. (Fraudulent loan approval, deceiving investors, borrowers, and regulators about level of high-risk loans underwritten.)

- Frequent changes in outside auditors.

- Unusually high profits/margins compared to the industry norm. (Fictitious loans, fraudulent loans.)
- Unusually high cash reserves during periods of economic downturn or tight credit markets.
- Odd patterns in asset values. (May indicate false representation of loan or investment value.)

### Red Flags of Insider Trading

- Securities trades that have a price significantly different (at least 10 percent above or below) from the stock's prevailing price.[21]
- Anomalies show up in computer monitoring records of stock exchange self-regulatory organizations, such as the Financial Industry Regulatory Authority.[22]

Aside from receiving a tip from another insider, it is virtually impossible to detect potential illegal insider trading without the use of sophisticated computer systems. Several software vendors offer such products designed specifically for financial services institutions. An Internet search will produce several offerings.

## Remember

Being able to detect management-level fraud at your organization depends on your ability to recognize the numerous red flags of the many types of fraud. These red flags can be complicated and unclear, especially as they apply to potential senior management misconduct. Thus, reviewing them from time to time will help you to focus on the *evidence* of potential fraud. Doing so is important because investigating executives often results in extreme scrutiny of the investigator and potential resistance.

## ▶ Management-Level Fraud Prevention Checklists

Every financial services company has its own unique internal structure and management policies. Some are more effective than others in reducing the risk of management-level fraud. The best anti-fraud controls are those designed to reduce the risk of a specific type of fraud threatening the organization.

Designing effective anti-fraud controls depends directly on accurate assessment of those risks. How, after all, can management or the board be expected to design and implement effective controls if it is unclear about which frauds are most threatening? It can't. This is why a fraud risk assessment (FRA) is essential to any anti-fraud program. This is an essential exercise designed to determine the specific types of fraud to which your organization is most vulnerable within the context of its existing anti-fraud controls. This enables management to design, customize, and implement the *best* controls to minimize fraud risk throughout the organization.

According to the ACFE, the Institute of Internal Auditors, and the American Institute of Certified Public Accountants, an organization's internal audit team must play a direct role in this all-important process:

> Internal auditors should consider the organization's assessment of fraud risk when developing their annual audit plan and review management's fraud management capabilities periodically. They should interview and communicate regularly with those conducting the organization's risk assessments, as well as others in key positions throughout the organization, to help them ensure that all fraud risks have been considered appropriately. When performing engagements, internal auditors should spend adequate time and attention to evaluating the design and operation of internal controls related to fraud risk management. They should exercise professional skepticism when reviewing activities and be on guard for the signs of fraud. Potential frauds uncovered during an engagement should be treated in accordance with a well-designed response plan consistent with professional and legal standards. Internal auditing should also take an active role in support of the organization's ethical culture.[23]

Chapter 7 will introduce you to the methodology for conducting an FRA that pinpoints the specific fraud scenarios and schemes most likely to threaten the organization. You will learn how the FRA provides the foundation that auditors can use to adjust their audit plans to include procedures that specifically target these fraud risks.

Before turning to the topic of the FRA, however, carefully review the next checklists covering *basic* but essential fraud prevention measures for the categories of fraud discussed in the earlier parts of this chapter.

### Check Fraud Prevention Checklist

- Reconcile all bank accounts immediately to prevent falsification of statements.
- Do not allow check signatories to prepare checks.
- Do not allow employees who approve invoices to prepare checks (or sign them).
- Harden physical security of check stock. Store unprinted check stock in a locked filing cabinet *under dual control*: Two locks are on the cabinet and two different people each hold one of the keys. In addition, enforce check limits. The system's limitation of the maximum amount of any check can serve as an overall stop-loss control over cash disbursement.
- Consider using high-tech check printing with security features.
- Conduct background checks on all managers who handle checks.
- Enforce segregation of duties (SoD) for bank reconciliations. (No signatories should be permitted to do reconciliations.)
- Set up positive pay and/or payee positive pay and/or reverse positive pay.
- Secure all checks used by accounts payable staff and enforce dual control of check stock.

- Keep keys to the check storage off premises.

- Ensure that all checks used by accounts payable are consecutively numbered.

- Enforce levels of check-signing authority (see the discussion of delegation of authority [DoA] in Chapter 3), including when dual signatures are required.

- Prohibit signing of any checks lacking supporting documentation (i.e., requisition form, invoice, purchase order, statement).

### Looting or Embezzlement

- Reduce opportunities for management-level check fraud by following preventive measures discussed earlier.

- Implement proper DoA for customer funds transfers over a specific amount.

- Implement and monitor compliance with SoD governing handling of all incoming payments to the bank *or* to customers.

- Conduct surprise cash counts on a monthly or quarterly basis to monitor for cash skimming.

### Overseas Bribery Prevention Checklist

- Adopt a zero-tolerance policy toward bribing overseas officials. Top management must lay down the law and communicate the company's seriousness about keeping its overseas dealings clean and fully compliant with both FCPA and local business regulations.

- Assess and, if necessary, reinforce the stringency of your FCPA compliance policies and procedures. Although it is all but impossible to secure foreign business without retaining a local agent to assist in navigating the bureaucratic and cultural challenges to winning the business, you must be exceedingly cautious about how you select, manage, and compensate these individuals.

    You can never do too much due diligence on prospective local business agents or partners. Basic background checks are essentially worthless. Thorough scrutiny of prospective consultants' previous business record, along with rigorous reference checking and other research, is required if your company is serious about a zero-tolerance position on FCPA compliance.

- Station an experienced, bilingual compliance officer in the country your bank is seeking to do business in. This officer's task is to monitor your bank's dealings with its local consultant and with local government, regulatory, and business entities. Your local consultant should be fully aware of your compliance officer's duty to monitor FCPA compliance meticulously. A mutually respectful and constructive working relationship should exist between the individuals.

- Be prepared to disclose promptly and thoroughly any unintentional violation of FCPA rules. The Catch-22 regarding FCPA and doing business in many countries is that no matter how serious your organization is about the zero-tolerance standard, the path to successful business dealings is littered with legal traps. However, attorneys and business consultants who specialize in guiding U.S. companies through the legal minefield of FCPA often can facilitate the launch of a successful overseas presence *without* running afoul of the FCPA. If you receive a hotline call or other tip about a potential violation of antibribery rules, do not dismiss it as the cost of doing business overseas. Management must take all such tips seriously. Immediately initiate investigations, take swift remedial action, and promptly disclose all details of such incidents to the proper Department of Justice and SEC regulatory offices.[24]

### Bribery and Kickback Prevention

- Rotate staff members who are authorized to approve vendors—every quarter, if possible.
- Segregate the duties for approving vendors and awarding contracts or approving invoices.
- Implement a crystal-clear policy about the illegalities of accepting and paying bribes/kickbacks.

    The aim is to provide a deterrent to managers who are on the fence about committing these crimes.

### Conflict-of-Interest Prevention

- Implement and enforce strict policies defining and prohibiting this activity.
- Enforce a policy requiring all managers to complete an annual disclosure statement detailing their personal financial interests in other organizations. Compare disclosed names and addresses with vendor lists to screen for potential conflicts.
- Advertise your whistleblower hotline to outside vendors, customers, strategic partners, and so on.
- Investigate any sudden increase in amounts paid for regularly purchased items or services.
- Investigate sudden changes from established vendors to new ones.
- Investigate all loans with apparent or suspected preferential terms.

### Fraudulent Financial Reporting Prevention

- Strengthen the wording in your code of conduct regarding compliance with the laws and regulations governing financial reporting. Emphasize to all employees the critical importance of accuracy in all of the organization's financial reports and filings. Encourage anyone who detects actual or suspected fraudulent financial reporting to use the organization's confidential hotline or other reporting channel immediately.
- Establish a competent and independent audit committee (refer also to Chapter 4). If we look back at some of the big accounting scandals, one common characteristic

of the victimized organizations was a climate of privileged cronyism among board members that served the purposes of self-congratulation by a clique of influential people, with a bare minimum of time or genuine effort given to matters of corporate governance.

- Continuously monitor transactions and business relationships among managers, vendors, purchasing staff, and others involved in financial transactions. Transactions often can be monitored to screen for anomalous patterns that could be indicative of individually perpetrated or collusive frauds.

- Harden physical control/security of assets, records, and computer systems housing financial applications.

- Reduce pressure, opportunity, and rationalization. The key for board-level committees as well as honest senior managers is to create a workplace culture in which the Fraud Triangle or fraud diamond will have no bearing on the activities of managers in a position to influence the organization's financial records.

    Some steps to take include:

    - Reduce *pressure* to cook the books.

        - Avoid setting unrealistic financial performance goals for management.

        - Adjust (downgrade) goals when the economy or market conditions worsen.

        - Be sure that compensation levels are competitive, and avoid excessive performance-based compensation plans.

        - Review and if necessary eliminate bureaucratic or other procedural obstacles to performance.

    - Reduce *opportunity* to commit fraudulent financial reporting.

        - Consistently maintain detailed and accurate accounting records—to eliminate lapses or errors in accounting practices that dishonest managers can exploit.

        - Fortify and sustain physical security of assets, including blank check stock, cash, and salable goods.

        - Enforce proper SoD for all finance-related management duties. Have an independent reviewer assess the integrity of the SoD procedures to prevent management collusion.

        - Conduct thorough background checks on *all* managers.

        - Eliminate any exception clauses in accounting procedures.

        - Enlist and insist on audit committee oversight of financial reporting functions and controls.

        - Consider retaining an external financial reporting controls expert, such as a forensic accountant, Sarbanes-Oxley consultant, or certified fraud examiner, to assist in developing, implementing, and enforcing controls of financial reporting.

- Reduce *rationalization* of fraudulent financial reporting.
    - Establish and maintain the right tone at the top and promote a culture of doing the right thing. Not only does this establish an example of integrity for all employees to adhere to, it greatly reduces the temptation of executives to cook the books, thereby eliminating the need for rationalization for doing so.
    - Enforce a policy that attaining financial goals is *never* as important as maintaining integrity and adhering to high ethical standards.

### Remember

Financial statement frauds are among the least frequently committed frauds in most organizations. However, they are by far the costliest. Implementing effective internal controls for this type of fraud is usually challenging.

### Borrower, Investor, and Regulator Deception Prevention

- Have a well-designed and clearly worded section in the code of conduct— drafted by a senior compliance or legal executive and reviewed and approved by the CEO and the board—emphasizing the importance of adhering to all laws and regulations governing the dissemination of information to the public.

- Establish a policy of imposing consequences for violation of the rules on accuracy of disseminated information.

- Have an active and independent governance committee in place that includes, among its general duties, the responsibility to scrutinize executive conduct and communications with a close eye on accuracy and honesty.

- Establish a senior executive–level corporate compliance position, and ensure direct access for the chief compliance officer to the board. The compliance officer's responsibilities should encompass monitoring of the organization's adherence to all applicable regulatory and legal standards, *including* those contained in the Sarbanes-Oxley Act defining internal controls over financial reporting.

- Consider assigning to a board-level committee the job of monitoring senior executives' internal communications (primarily e-mail). Although this step can be controversial, a company with a culture of integrity and honesty should have no reservations about having its top managers' communications monitored. Too many criminal cases have emerged based on the incriminating and often deceptive internal e-mail communications between executives seeking to bend the rules. This step is especially applicable in the prevention of illegal insider trading (see next list).

### Insider-Trading Prevention

- Implement procedures that limit employee discretion—by providing personnel with clear and specific guidance on buying and selling of the bank's stock.

  According to the SEC:

  > Whenever a trader is given non-public information concerning an investment banking engagement, the trader's continued ability to transact in the relevant securities should be evaluated by compliance personnel or legal counsel with appropriate training and knowledge.[25]

- Maintain watch lists and restricted lists and the reviews of proprietary and employee trading in securities on those lists.

- Formally structure and enforce procedures rather than relegating them to "a loose mixture of internal memoranda, excerpts from employee manuals, and certifications."[26]

- Document all actions taken pursuant to the firm's procedures in order to facilitate subsequent reviews and compliance efforts.

- Implement clear procedures for the restriction or review of proprietary trading when the firm is in possession of material, nonpublic information.

- Establish a central executive-level compliance function for administering procedures, including monitoring significant interdepartmental communications of nonpublic information, the placement and removal of securities from watch or restricted lists, and trade surveillance.

- Train all employees in the rules and restrictions governing insider trading and nonpublic financial information.[27]

- Include in the organization's code of ethics and/or conduct standards of business conduct governing the fiduciary obligations of financial advisors and their supervised staff as well as provisions requiring advisory personnel to comply with all federal securities laws.

- Require advisors' "access persons" to report, and the advisor to review, personal securities holdings and transactions on a periodic basis. ("Access person" is a term contained in SEC regulation referring to employees of financial organizations who have access to nonpublic information that is pertinent to compliance with rules prohibiting illegal insider trading.)

- Ensure that a compliance official of the organization informs all access persons of their status and maintains an up-to-date list of all access persons.

- Require preclearance of personal investments by access persons in initial public and private placements.[28]

### ▶ Review Points

- Although management-level frauds are committed far less frequently than employee-level frauds, the losses resulting from management frauds are substantially greater than those of crimes committed by lower-level employees.

- ACFE chairman Joe Wells explains executive-level check fraud this way:

  > In most situations, check signers are owners, officers, or otherwise high-ranking employees, and thus have or can obtain access to all the blank checks they need. Even if company policy prohibits check signers from handling blank checks, normally the perpetrator can use her influence to overcome this impediment.[29]

- Conflict of interest is one of the four types of fraud comprising the ACFE's definition of corruption, together with bribery, illegal gratuities, and economic extortion.

- Although the temptation to offer bribes to overseas officials to obtain government or business contracts sometimes may be tough to resist, the risk of discovery and subsequent penalties indicate that the risk is usually extremely high.

- The sanctioning by Wall Street bosses of rampant derivatives development and marketing cannot technically be defined as fraudulent. However, the courts will be occupied for many years with cases whose outcome may produce new definitions of legal and illegal conduct in the C suites of major financial institutions.

- The most common motives driving dishonest financial services executives to falsify financial records and statements are to boost share price, increase executive bonuses, conceal illegal financial transactions, and secure financing.

- The three rating agencies—Moody's, Standard & Poor's, and Fitch—have been criticized by financial thought leaders and politicians for acting without objectivity in rating certain mortgage-backed securities.

- Buying and selling stocks on the strength of information available only to company or investment firm insiders and *not* to the investing public has been against the law since enactment of the Securities Exchange Act of 1934.

- Rules governing the trading conduct of employees with access to nonpublic financial information are numerous and extremely detailed. However, adherence to all laws and regulations applicable to insider trading is of critical importance to your financial institution.

## ▶ Chapter Quiz

True or False:

1. Overlooking certain qualifications for a loan for a company in which the loan officer has a direct financial interest is *not* a conflict of interest.

   ❑ True    ❑ False

2. One of the main motives for top management to falsify financial reporting is to get bigger bonuses.

   ❑ True    ❑ False

3. Fraudulent revenue recognition is sometimes referred to as earnings manipulation.

   ❑ True    ❑ False

Circle the correct answer to the following questions:

4. All of the following are forms of looting or embezzlement EXCEPT:

    a. Skimming from the vault

    b. Transferring funds from a customer's account to one's own

    c. Tax evasion

    d. Stealing and forging company checks

5. "Corruption" is a term applying to which of the following:

    1. Conflict of interest

    2. Bribery

    3. Extortion

    4. Breach of fiduciary duty

      a. 1, 2, 3

      b. 2, 3, 4

      c. 1, 3, 4

      d. 1, 2, 3, 4

6. The Foreign Corrupt Practices Act (FCPA) makes it illegal to:

    a. Accept gifts from foreign business executives.

    b. Purchase goods or services on discounted prices from foreign vendors.

    c. Pay bribes to foreign government officials.

    d. Pay bribes to foreign joint venture partners.

7. The top methods of committing frauds at financial institutions include:

    1. Making inaccurate accounting estimates.

    2. Inaccurate or misleading disclosure.

    3. Misclassification of financial information.

    4. Lack of detailed transaction records.

      a. 1, 2, 3

      b. 1, 3, 4

      c. 1, 2, 4

      d. 1, 2, 3, 4

8. The following are preventive measures against check fraud EXCEPT:

    a. Prohibiting check signatories from preparing checks.

    b. Prohibiting employees who approve invoices from preparing checks (or signing them).

    c. Hardening physical security of check stock.

    d. Not using positive pay.

9. Which of the following are important measures to prevent insider trading?

    1. Train all employees in the rules and restrictions on use of nonpublic information.

    2. Require access persons to report personal securities holdings and transactions on a periodic basis.

3. Require postclearance of personal investments by access persons.

4. Restrict or review proprietary trading when the firm is in possession of material, nonpublic information.

    a. 1, 2, 3

    b. 1, 3, 4

    c. 1, 2, 4

    d. 1, 2, 3, 4

Fill in the blank:

10. One crime that Michael Milken was not convicted of was _____.

11. One key red flag of possible looting of customer accounts is _____ from customers.

12. Approving loans to oneself is an example of _____.

*For the answers, please turn to Appendix A.*

# CHAPTER SIX

# External Fraud against Financial Services Companies

As discussed in Chapter 2, financial institutions are especially desirable targets of external fraudsters. Although, as mentioned, it is difficult to profile external white-collar criminals, it is probably safe to say that if nothing else, most external fraudsters share the storied reasoning of Willie Sutton, who explained that the reason he robbed banks was because "That's where the money is."

Unlike bank robberies, however, most of which involve an element of actual or threatened violence, frauds against financial institutions involve stealthy, nonviolent acts of deception, manipulation, and concealment.

Violent or not, external fraud results in serious losses for financial institutions. This chapter addresses the numerous and ever-evolving varieties of fraud attempted against financial institutions by outsiders—based in the United States *and* abroad.

## ▶ Externally Perpetrated Loan Fraud (Nonmortgage)

As you progress through this chapter, it will become abundantly clear that externally perpetrated mortgage fraud is vastly more serious than other forms of loan fraud initiated by outsiders. Yet the next *non*mortgage frauds by outsiders are potentially very costly to many financial services firms and therefore cannot be overlooked.

## ■ Commercial Construction Loan Fraud

According to Blake Coppotelli, former head of a construction fraud unit in the Manhattan District Attorney's Office and subsequently with Kroll's Consulting Group, "Having investigated hundreds (of construction projects) all over the world, I have not come across one that was totally clean."[1]

This is the assessment of a highly experienced and prominent construction fraud expert. Coppotelli further states that 10 percent of total worldwide expenditures on construction is lost to fraud and corruption. The crimes targeting construction projects are countless. However, several occur with exceptional frequency. Clifton Gunderson, a major international accounting and consulting firm with extensive experience in the construction industry, published a report on fraud in the industry. In it, the firm describes the common construction fraud schemes that lenders should be alert to at all times, including tools theft, materials waste, product substitution, duplicate payments, employee ghosting, vehicle maintenance schemes, and bid rigging or collusion.[2]

### Tools Theft

Tools theft typically is perpetrated by a solo fraudster, who removes hand tools or small machines from the job site and then reports them as lost. The fraudster then sells the stolen tools and keeps the proceeds. Although this scheme is not limited to small tools, it is more difficult to carry off larger equipment without detection, and the it-was-lost story is less convincing.

Why, you might ask, should bankers care about the theft of tools on a construction project their bank is financing? The answer is that if committed on a large scale, this crime can result in significant financial losses, potentially resulting in cost overruns that directly impact the financing conditions of the project.

### Materials Waste

In materials waste schemes, the fraudster orders more materials than necessary for the job under an existing purchase order. The excess material is reported as scrap or waste and then is sold by the fraudster.

If an auditor conducts a reconciliation of materials ordered versus materials estimated and/or authorized, the excess may be detected. Further investigation would then be required to determine whether there was a justification for the excess material being ordered. As with theft of tools, excess ordering can produce cost overruns that a bank would want to be aware of.

### Product Substitution

In the product substitution scheme, one grade of materials is specified, submitted, and approved, but a lower grade of materials is delivered to the construction site. However, billing is prepared using the original high-grade of materials.

### ◄ Case Study #17

## New Yankee Stadium Construction Shows Red Flags of Concrete Crime

State racketeering and fraud charges were filed against about a dozen officers and employees of Testwell Laboratories, a company hired to tewst the strength of the concrete at some of the biggest construction projects in the New York City area.

The charges accuse the company's president and several senior officials of failing to conduct some required tests and falsifying others over a period of about five years.

Concrete testing like that done by Testwell is a basic safety measure at construction sites, and investigators found irregularities in tests conducted at the new Yankee Stadium and the Freedom Tower, among other locations. But officials said they did not believe any falsified tests created hazards because most of the concrete poured in New York is of a high quality. Nonetheless, the city's Department of Buildings began retesting concrete at some construction sites that the firm had monitored.

The investigation began after monitors hired by the Yankees and by the Port Authority uncovered irregularities in the concrete testing at Yankee Stadium and at ground zero, as did the Authority's own own engineers.

*How could this fraud have been prevented?* List as many controls as you can. Compare yours with those listed in Appendix B.

1. _____

2. _____

3. _____

## Duplicate Payments

In this scheme, duplicate payments are issued to a legitimate vendor for a legitimate invoice related to the project. One check is delivered to the vendor and the fraudster cashes the other check but shows the check on the general ledger as being voided or canceled. Alternatively, both checks can show up in the general ledger (GL) if the person issuing the checks also has responsibility for reconciling the GL and the bank statements.

## Employee Ghosting

You learned about the employee ghosting scheme in Chapter 3, when it is perpetrated by an insider. In construction fraud, the scheme can be either field based or office based. A field-based fraud involves someone creating hours for an employee who was not there at the time recorded.

In one example, an insulation subcontractor commissioned by a general contractor issued several notices reminding employees to punch in only their own time cards and *not* those of another employee. The problem became so severe that the subcontractor ultimately had to revamp its entire clocking-in system.

In an office-based fraud, additional hours typically are added to bills by adding a fictitious employee. The fraudster has payroll checks directed to an address where he or she can pick up and cash the check later.

## Vehicle Maintenance Schemes

In vehicle maintenance schemes, a fraudster agrees to send construction company-owned or leased vehicles to a service provider for what is described as legitimate, ordinary maintenance. However, either the pricing for the actual services rendered is greater than the market price or the services documented are not actually rendered. In either case, the service provider gives a kickback to the company employee.

### Bid Rigging or Collusion

Refer back to Chapter 4 for details of how bid rigging and collusion frauds are perpetrated. As noted, construction is a sector that is especially vulnerable to these schemes—in which a contracting company's bid-management employee colludes with dishonest contractors to fix bids or otherwise abuse the bidding process in exchange for kickbacks or bribes.

## ■ Asset-Based or Working Capital Loan Fraud

Asset-based commercial loans typically are made by committing the borrower's receivables, inventory, or other assets as collateral.

According to the prominent banking industry consortium BITS, commercial loan fraud is committed most often by companies experiencing financial difficulties. Typically, the borrowing organization is cash-strapped and is having trouble paying vendors, making payroll, or covering payroll taxes.

If the company has a working capital line of credit with funds availability based on a minimum percentage of qualified receivables and inventory, the owner or senior executive may attempt to increase the company's borrowing power by falsely overstating the values on the certifications submitted to the bank.

One variation on this fraud occurs when business borrowers create false invoices to document bogus receivables or otherwise cook the books to appear financially sound to a lending institution.[3] They also may accelerate revenue recognition on contracts or double-count contracts.

In addition, borrowers may use lines of credit for unapproved purposes. For example, a business borrower may use the line for personal or other purposes but generate a phony invoice for the purchase of a piece of equipment to mislead a loan officer into thinking that the loan proceeds were used for that purchase.[4]

Alternatively, if the lending institution's loan officer or manager is in collusion with a prospective borrower with assets worth less than the amount of credit sought, the necessary due diligence required to verify the true value of the pledged assets can be circumvented with the payment of kickbacks by the borrower.

Since these loans typically would not meet the institution's lending standards, there is a good chance that the fraud will lead to eventual default, leaving the lender with an unsecured loan balance.

## ■ Floor Plan and Dealer Loan Fraud

A related fraud involves pledging high-value in-stock merchandise, such as automobiles, boats, or furniture, as collateral for a loan. This sometimes is called floor plan lending. In a legitimate transaction, the loan is repaid as the merchandise is sold.

In a loan fraud, the merchant sells an asset but fails to use the proceeds to repay the loan. Instead, a kickback is paid to the loan officer or manager who ensures that the appropriate due diligence procedures to verify the value of the merchandise are ignored and that any documentation falsification required to conceal the loan is taken care of. As with asset-based lending, a fraudulent floor plan loan ultimately will become nonperforming and the bank will be left holding the bag.[5]

In related schemes, the owner of a dealership makes misleading statements to the financial institution by:

- Falsely claiming that the dealership owns specific vehicles.
- Falsifying vehicle identification number information/unit.
- Failing to pay off trade-ins.
- Double-financing a single sale and pocketing the proceeds of the fraudulent second deal.[6]

## ■ Asset Shifting

In the asset-shifting fraud, a business owner or executive shifts assets to entities where loan guarantees are nonexistent.

For example, a commercial customer who owns several companies shifts bank collateral out of guaranteed entities and moves it to other corporations where guarantees were not obtained. In essence, the owner or executive is using the same collateral for two different loans, without the banks' knowledge.

## ▶ Externally Perpetrated Mortgage Fraud Schemes

In Chapter 3, you were introduced to the role of bank insiders in perpetrating mortgage fraud. Unfortunately, in many if not most instances of mortgage fraud, the line between internal and external initiation is blurry. This is one reason why, in the aftermath of the so-called subprime meltdown of 2007–2008, there was an explosion in legal action by borrowers, brokers, lenders, and others in attempts to place the blame for the massive loan losses on someone who might be forced by the judicial system to provide restitution for alleged lending improprieties.

It will be years before the courts determine who was responsible for which civil or criminal elements of the subprime crisis. But for now, suffice it to say that mortgage fraud in the 1990s to the early 2000s was perpetrated by financial institution insiders *as well as* outsiders. The next pages discuss how externally perpetrated mortgage fraud has occurred most frequently in recent years.

Not all external mortgage fraud qualifies as subprime lending. However, according to Richard Bitner, a subprime lender during the hottest years of subprime financing, "About three-quarters of all subprime loan applications sent by mortgage brokers to lenders for approval and funding were in one form or another misleading, incorrect or outright fraudulent in the heyday of subprime lending."[7]

According to Bitner, common subprime mortgage deception occurred mainly by:

- Indicating that the borrower will occupy a property when he or she is actually buying it as an investment.

- Falsifying a borrower's employment history by having a friend or relative who owns a business say the person works there.

- Hiding a critical piece of information or not disclosing something about the loan and hoping the lender will not find out.

Within each of these categories is a long list of specific document falsification ploys aimed at deceiving the bank. Several of them are red flags that fraud is being perpetrated.

Bitner further explains that as investment banks bought more and more mortgages from lenders in the 1990s in order to securitize and sell them, they boosted demand for subprime loans. This in turn caused lenders to drastically relax the standards for approving mortgages, thereby further fueling more broker fraud in order to generate more income from selling the loans.

Says Bitner, "While subprime lending fraud did not alone cause the financial system to 'fall off a cliff' in 2008, it substantially accelerated its inexorable slide to the precipice."[8]

This assessment underscores the unanswered question of who is to blame for what in the subprime mess. However, as he and many other industry experts suggest, while greedy or overly competitive bankers looking to boost profits from securities backed by risky mortgages may have catalyzed the mad dash to a crisis, they could not have succeeded without the aggressive and widespread activities—often blatantly illegal—of outside brokers, appraisers, builders, and sales reps.

### Remember

The boom in subprime mortgage lending accounted for a substantial portion of total mortgage lending in the 1990s and early 2000s. A solid majority of subprime mortgage applications contained at least some element of deception, misrepresentation, or outright fraud.

### ■ Mortgage Fraud Modus Operandi

External mortgage fraud occurs in two primary ways: fraud for profit and fraud for property. The former encompasses schemes designed mainly to defraud borrowers or lenders through the real estate system, while the latter involves borrowers and/or brokers and other dishonest outsiders falsifying mortgage applications so that a loan that normally would not be approved due to its failure to meet bank lending standards *is* approved.

It is important to note that in the subprime mortgage crisis, many loans approved by banks were not technically fraudulent, even though they were approved for borrowers with poor credit histories and therefore were excessively risky. As Richard Bitner points out, in the late 1990s and early 2000s, banks did not care much about a particular borrower's lack of creditworthiness because once the loan was approved, it was quickly sold off to a larger financial institution, which bundled it with other subprime loans to be collateralized into mortgage-backed securities for sale on the open securities markets.

This practice was not fraudulent—as long as the brokers who were submitting mortgage applications on behalf of subprime borrowers did not include false or misleading information on those applications. In many instances, however, they did exactly that in order to ensure that a loan would be approved. This in spite of the fact that, by the mid-1990s, most lenders had so drastically liberalized their mortgage lending standards that it was unnecessary for most applications to be fudged in order to gain approval, or loan underwriters simply overlooked intentional falsification of applications.

Some of these externally perpetrated frauds may sound similar to the straw buyer schemes discussed in Chapter 3 in which an unscrupulous bank employee initiates or colludes with brokers or other outsiders to get an unqualified borrower approved for a mortgage. During the subprime mortgage boom, independent brokers often were the main perpetrators of these deceptive tactics. However, to a large extent, the bank lending environment *encouraged* broker malfeasance because, as explained, in the 1990s and early 2000s, large banks had a voracious appetite for new loans that they could sell off at a profit.

You will learn more about the various schemes and ploys used in the subprime mortgage fraud game in upcoming sections.

## ■ Fraud-for-Profit Schemes

Fraud-for-profit schemes are not unique to the subprime crisis, although as implied, they did play a key role in bringing on the crisis. They also were extremely common during the savings and loan crisis of the 1980s. Moreover, even after the worst of the mortgage meltdown had passed, fraud-for-profit schemes were still being perpetrated by unscrupulous entities. The major types of fraud-for-profit schemes are discussed next.

### Builder Bailout Schemes

Builder bailout schemes can involve straw buyers or legitimate buyers who are led to believe that they are getting a great deal in buying a new home with no money down. The builder, typically desperate to sell the property, agrees on a "bargain" sale price of, for example, $100,000 when in fact the home is worth only $80,000. The builder offers buyers a $20,000 loan as the down payment and instructs the buyers to tell the bank that they have paid $20,000 to the builder and are seeking an $80,000 loan to conclude the purchase. The lender approves the loan and sends the $80,000 check to the builder. The builder then "forgives" the original $20,000 down payment loan and skips town. The lender is on the hook for a loan for 100 percent of the home value, and the buyers may or may not be able to make the payments on the $80,000 mortgage.

### Chunking

The chunking scam comes in several forms and fashions. In most, the victim is a gullible investor who is recruited by a fraudster to purchase a residential property, site unseen, with no money down and with no risk because, according to the perpetrator, the property is either currently or soon to be occupied by a tenant whose payments will be made to the investor and will be more than adequate to cover the mortgage payments.

In some cases, there is no actual property, or it is a rundown home for which the fraudster has obtained a falsely inflated appraisal to submit along with the victim's mortgage application. In other cases, there is no tenant or never will be one. In yet other instances, the perpetrator agrees to lease back the house or condo with monthly payments adequate to cover the mortgage payments, but he or she never actually makes a single lease payment.

In all of these cases, the trusting investor is left with a mortgage on a property that is overvalued and for which there is no income to cover the mortgage payments. Usually the mortgage goes into default and the fraudsters are long gone with the loan proceeds, leaving the investor with a blemished credit report for defaulting on the mortgage, and the bank on the hook for the property that it must foreclose on.[9]

In a somewhat different form of chunking, the fraudster poses as a mortgage broker, or is in collusion with one, and recruits the unwitting investor, promising to take care of everything from obtaining the appraisal, to submitting the mortgage application, to finding a tenant. Unbeknownst to the victim, the perpetrator submits the mortgage application to multiple banks. Ultimately, multiple closings occur on the same property, with the individual banks having no clue that they are sharing the collateral—that is, the property—with other lenders. The fraudster, who has acted as the investor's power of attorney, collects loan proceeds from all of the duped banks, pays off the legitimate seller, and pockets the often-substantial excess. The investor is left holding multiple mortgages on which he or she has neither the means nor the desire to make payments.[10]

In each category of fraud, buyers, sellers, mortgage brokers, real estate agents, appraisers, and other industry professionals can use numerous schemes, misstatements, and misrepresentations for financial gain from property sellers and legitimate lenders.

### Equity Skimming

In equity skimming frauds, an individual or group buys one or more single-family homes with mortgages in amounts equal to 80 to 90 percent of the property value, with the rest of the purchase amount invested by the buyer(s) as equity.

The properties are then rented, but the owner/perpetrators fail to make the mortgage payments. They collect rent until they have recouped their equity investment and continue to collect until the mortgage is foreclosed. Any rental payments they receive in excess of the equity "investment" are proverbial gravy—until the bank forecloses. The lending bank is left holding the bag.

### Committing Identity Theft to Obtain or Transact Mortgages

To obtain a mortgage by committing identity theft, a fraudster files a bogus deed to make it appear that he or she has acquired the property legitimately. In reality, the perpetrator is stealing the actual title or deed to the property of a legitimate owner. Then he or she obtains a loan on the property and takes the money and defaults on the loan, leaving the legitimate owners with the outstanding debt.[11]

### Overstating Appraisal Values to "Flip" a Particular Property Multiple Times

One example of overstating appraisal values to sell property is property flipping. A home is purchased using an initial mortgage. The property then is fraudulently appraised by an unscrupulous appraiser at a much higher value. The home is then quickly resold for maximum profit. Often this is a one-time event. But sometimes the same process is initiated again and again by a group of co-conspirators who buy and flip the same property to each other at progressively higher prices, applying for bigger and bigger mortgages each time.

Other appraisal fraud schemes involve inflating the value of a property to obtain a second mortgage or to pad the commissions of real estate brokers or agents.[12]

### Recruiting Straw Buyers to Secure Mortgage Loans

As you learned in Chapter 3, straw buyer schemes sometimes can be perpetrated with the collusive involvement of a senior banking officer. However, more often these straw buyer schemes are the dirty work of outsiders.

*How the scheme works.* Straw buyers are loan applicants who are used by fraudsters to obtain home loans and have no intention of occupying the home being "purchased." Straw buyers are chosen—and compensated—for their good credit rating. They may be active participants in the scheme; they also may believe they are simply investors, not knowing the true nature of the scheme; or they may be led to believe they are helping people with poor credit obtain a mortgage, who, without the straw buyer's personal information, would not be able to qualify for a mortgage.

In many mortgage fraud instances, straw buyers are approached by "friends" or acquaintances and told of a creative way to make money. They are falsely assured by the perpetrator of the legitimacy of the proposed deal. Straw buyers may receive a flat fee to use their credit or a percentage of the sale proceeds.

In a common scheme, straw buyers misrepresent their intention to live in the home on the loan application. They enter into contracts specifying the purchase price, the terms of the sale, and other basic contractual elements.

The straw buyers then purchase the property by obtaining a mortgage through filing a generally legitimate application, except for the representation that they plan to live in the home.

If the straw buyers are just pawns in the scheme, thinking that the purchase is an investment, they may receive a fee from the perpetrator. Any other promises made, such as paying the mortgage or dividing profits from the property with the straw buyers, may not be fulfilled, especially if the straw buyers' cooperation was fraudulently obtained.

If the straw buyers are colluding in the scheme, the loan proceeds may be split with them.[13]

### Remember

Fraud-for-profit mortgage schemes typically are perpetrated by dishonest outsiders, such as brokers, investors, or buyers, who have no intention of living in the property. Instead, their schemes are designed to defraud banks or unwitting buyers in order to make a quick, illegal profit.

### ■ Fraud-for-Property Schemes

Fraud-for-property schemes are committed by prospective borrowers (often with the illegal actions of brokers, appraisers and other parties) who may or may not intend to repay the mortgages. They misrepresent themselves and their financial qualifications to secure the mortgage. The most common frauds are committed by individuals who overstate their income, assets, collateral values, or other essential loan qualification factors.

*How the scheme works.* Potential buyers submit a loan application containing fraudulent income, credit, asset, employment, or appraisal documents to obtain a mortgage for which they are not qualified.

During the peak of the subprime mortgage boom, these buyers were "assisted" by dishonest mortgage brokers who encouraged them to falsify their applications, assuring them that there was nothing inappropriate about doing so because no one would be checking the details. The rapid proliferation of these liar's loans (designated by lending institutions as stated income loans) is what caused millions of borrowers to take out loans that offered low payments at the beginning of the loan term and then "reset" at market rates. This resetting often doubled the borrowers' monthly payments, causing them to default.

In these schemes, again, banks are typically the victims. However, as mentioned, lenders typically sell off these loans to other financial institutions, which package them into securities for sale in the financial markets.

### Remember

Mortgage fraud has become an immensely costly drain on the U.S. economy in recent years. This is partly due to loopholes in regulatory systems that enable dishonest mortgage brokers, appraisers, and lenders to perpetrate lending schemes that victimize mortgage banks, unwitting borrowers, or both. The debate over mortgage fraud shifted into high gear as the so-called subprime mortgage business collapsed in the 2007–2008 period. However, it is important to remember that mortgage fraud did not begin with the subprime crisis. It has been around since the early decades of American history.

## ■ Nonloan External Fraud

External fraud against banks and other financial institutions is by no means limited to lending operations. As with internal fraud, many of a bank's basic business functions are potential targets of dishonest outsiders looking for control weaknesses that can provide opportunities to steal financial or information assets.

### Social Engineering and Pretexting

Social engineering is technically not a type of fraud. Rather it is a psychological tactic aimed at obtaining information needed to commit fraud.

The basic method involves getting trusting people to divulge information that they should not be divulging to someone who, in most cases, plans to use that information to commit an identity-related fraud. Not surprisingly, given the large volumes of customer financial information stored on their systems, financial services companies have been among the prime targets of social engineering schemes.

According to the Business Software Alliance (BSA), a nonprofit industry association, social engineering is

> [A] scam that preys upon our acceptance of authority and willingness to cooperate with others. The Social Engineer's objective is to extract sensitive information such as your social security number, bank account information, or login name and password to a Website.
>     Social Engineering scams are most commonly perpetrated over the telephone or via e-mail.[14]

Although financial institutions are top targets of social engineering attacks, consumers are also highly vulnerable.

For example, one recent consumer scheme involved criminals calling people and stating there was a warrant out for their arrest because they failed to show up for jury duty. The callers then asked for the person's Social Security number to "verify their identity."

The BSA further notes that "social engineering revolves around getting an employee or customer to do something that they're not supposed to do, or 'bending the rules' just once to allow someone access to a document or account."

As discussed in Chapter 3, clever insiders can use social engineering to persuade information technology (IT) staff to allow them access to secure networks and databases that store confidential information. Outsiders have a variety of approaches, including in-person or telephone deception and the much more dangerous and costly online attacks called phishing (described on page 135).

Social engineering is especially troublesome in financial institution call centers. Unless call center employees are trained in the scams that dishonest customers or criminals posing as customers try to pull off, your organization's risk of being a victim of account takeover, fraudulent transactions, and other crimes is extremely high.

For example, a bank call center employee receives a call from someone claiming to be a customer. She is able to pass the verification process because she has stolen the legitimate customer's mail containing his bank statement with the account number, name and address, as well as the last four digits of his Social Security number, which appear on a stolen investment account statement.

The fraudster then asks the call center representative to help with a funds transfer to an account at a different bank or asks to change his address.

---

◄ **Case Study #18**

### How to Use Social Engineering to Defraud Just about Any Organization

*Summary of an actual ploy by a technology whiz . . .*

I enter the bank dressed in Dickies coveralls, a baseball cap, work boots, and sunglasses. I approach the young lady at the front desk.

"Hello," I say. "John Doe with XYZ Pest Control, here to do your pest inspection." I flash her a smile followed by the credentials. She says, "*Uhm . . . okay . . . let me check with the branch manager*" and picks up the phone. If all goes according to plan, the fake e-mail I sent out last week notifying branch manager of our inspection will allow me access.

It does.

The manager greets me and brings me into the wsecure area behind the teller line. She says she received an e-mail from the bank's facilities supervisor saying that we would be by on Monday. I nod and explain this visit is not for spraying, but just to see if there's a problem to begin with.

The bag I'm carrying contains only a flashlight, a paper mask, a pair of work gloves, a tiny wireless access point disguised as a pager, two key loggers, and lots of space to store whatever I might find of interest or value.

The manager wanders off, leaving me to my "work."

As soon as she disappears I move into a room where documents are stored. I look around the area for anything "of interest." A stack of checks for deposit catches my eye, so I grab them and shove them into my clipboard. Each check has a name and account number on it.

I walk back to the manager's office and ask her if she could please grant me entry into "this back room, whatever's in there." She explains that this room houses their computer equipment. I nod and say that rodents are known to bed up in warm areas, and in my experience, computer rooms generate heat.

As she unlocks the door, she asks only that I notify her when I am finished so that she may lock it again.

I enter the computer room and immediately notice several tower servers on the floor beneath the rack. I could plug any number of items into the switch at this point—a rogue access point, key loggers, etc.

I find a company phone directory and take it. Near one of the terminals, I see a pink sticky note. "Bingo," I say aloud. Written on the note are login credentials to the core processor. This information should allow me to query the bank's core processing software for account numbers, names, and Social Security numbers, once I have determined its IP [Internet Protocol] address. I note the credentials in my clipboard.

I let the manager know I'm finished. Per my request, she signs my fake work order. I date it and sign my initials as well. I thank her for her time and cooperation and leave the building.

Inside my car, I inspect the items I have collected:

- 27 customer account names and numbers
- Copies of 13 loan applications complete with Social Security numbers, names, birthdays, and driver's license numbers
- One phone directory with (what appears to be) extensions for everyone in the bank
- One login to the core processor

This should be enough to start some new bogus eBay accounts.[15]

*How could this fraud have been prevented?* List as many controls as you can. Compare yours with those listed in Appendix B.

1. _____

2. _____

3. _____

### Phishing

If you have not received a phony e-mail appearing to be from your bank or another financial institution, asking you to update or resubmit your account information, including your Social Security number and other personal identifying information (PII), you are probably the only person on the planet who has not (see Exhibit 6.1).

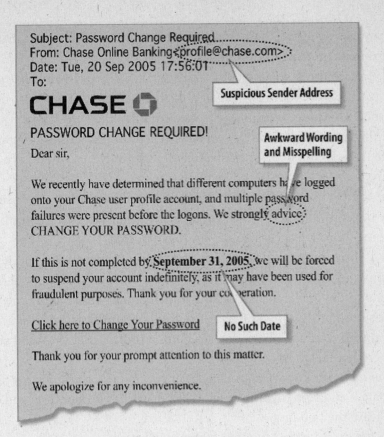

**Exhibit 6.1:** Sample Phishing E-mail

In these phishing schemes, Internet, or cyber, criminals disseminate hundreds of thousands of so-called "spoof," or fraudulent e-mails urging recipients to click on a link that takes them to a Web site purporting to be that of their bank, their credit card company, or another trusted entity.

This is simply an Internet-based version of conventional social engineering.

Although most Americans have by now learned that these e-mails are scams, a large enough percentage of victims still fall for the ploy and provide the perpetrators with PII requested by the bogus e-mails that typically indicate the need to update credit card information, online banking usernames and passwords, date of birth, and other PII.

According to the Anti-Phishing Working Group (AFWG), a prominent association dedicated to fighting phishing, attacks against financial institutions represent approximately one-half of all such attacks reported. The good news is that this figure represents a decline from earlier years when over 90 percent of all phishing attacks targeted financial institutions.

The AFWG's definition of phishing is:

> A criminal mechanism employing both *social engineering* and *technical subterfuge* to steal consumers' personal identity data and financial account credentials.
>
> Social engineering schemes use spoofed e-mails purporting to be from legitimate businesses and agencies to lead consumers to counterfeit Websites designed to trick recipients into divulging financial data such as usernames and passwords.[16]

The problem for financial services institutions is that they are targeted in two ways: (1) to illegally harvest secure customer credit card data or other PII as described here and (2) when the stolen data or PII is used to defraud the organization's customers themselves.

As you will learn later in this chapter, preventing phishing requires a two-pronged approach, focused on enhanced security for the data and on keeping customers informed about the potential fraudulent use of their credit cards and other PII if or when it is stolen.

### Information Security Breaches

Unlike phishing attacks, which, as discussed, are social engineering schemes aimed at getting unsuspecting Internet users to divulge their secret online banking activities, shopping, and PII, information security breaches target the secure networks of financial institutions, national retail chains, and other organizations to steal very large volumes of customer data.

The biggest breach of corporate information security on record so far is the early-2008 attack on Heartland Payment Systems, one of the country's largest processors of credit card transactions. The crime, which affected customers of over 600 financial institutions, resulted in the loss of more than 100 million card numbers and related data.

To illustrate the magnitude of the Heartland breach, Tom Mahoney, founder of the online credit card resources Web site Merchant911.com, said:

> We'll never know the exact numbers of records affected by the breach. The whole Heartland mess is shrouded in corporate secrecy, but here's what we do know. BankInfoSecurity.com [reported] that over 600 institutions had card accounts breached. It's important to note that these are only *reported and confirmed* numbers. There could be hundreds, if not thousands, more. Remember that Heartland processes payments for 175,000 merchants at the rate of over 100 million transactions per month and this breach was on-going for 6 months.[17]

Kimberly Kiefer Peretti, senior counsel in U.S. Department of Justice's Computer Crime Section, told *BankInfoSecurity.com* that the most popular tactics among cyber-criminals for perpetrating data breaches are:

- War-driving, where hackers penetrate the wireless networks of businesses or other organizations that store confidential personal information
- Internet-based attacks
- Malicious code
- Social engineering

The majority of external organized crime attacks originated in Eastern Europe. As for internal perpetrators, the overwhelming majority tend to be either IT administrators or end users.[18]

Banks of all sizes in every state are vulnerable to credit card information theft through information breaches against themselves and against retail companies and other organizations that store the critical data on cards they have issued.

The end result of these attacks is a host of identity-related frauds. Illegal purchases via the Internet or phone in so-called card-not-present frauds rank high on the list of crimes involving illegal use of legitimate credit and debit card data.

The threat is expected to worsen, and financial institutions are scrambling to devise methods of at least *reducing* the risk to which their card customers are exposed while at the same time seeking better ways of detecting suspicious activity.

### Online Banking Fraud against Customers

Although more often than not, data breaches are aimed at stealing credit card data, that is by no means their sole objective. Together with phishing attacks, data breaches also present a formidable threat to online banking customers and to the banks themselves.

As mentioned earlier, phishing is a form of online social engineering. If victims fall for the ploy, they type their online banking username and password, Social Security number, and any other "updated" information requested by the scammers. Having collected this vital data, the fraudsters are able to take total control of victims' online bank account. They usually simply empty out victims' checking or savings account by fraudulently transferring the funds to an account they control. In instances of what is commonly referred to as online account takeover, both the bank and the legitimate account owner lose money.

As Shirley Inscoe, former Wachovia Bank senior vice president and current director of Financial Services Solutions at bank fraud prevention software providers Memento, Inc., says:

> Once a fraudster has online access to a [customer's] accounts, they can open new accounts to direct deposits to, submit fraudulent ACH files, generate wire transfers and much more. Extremely large losses result when banks are unable to detect and prevent these activities, so this type of fraud will continue to appeal to fraudsters.[19]

The challenge for banks is that online fraudsters move more quickly than the security professionals who are constantly striving to thwart them. This is particularly problematic in the area of so-called Trojan horses, which are sophisticated software programs that plant themselves on the hard drives of online banking customers when they click on a link in a spam e-mail message. Once embedded in victims' computers, the programs record and transmit keystrokes when they type in their username and password to access online bank accounts.

Surprisingly, this method of illegally accessing online banking customers' accounts has been a threat to both U.S. and foreign banks for many years. It is a clear example of how difficult it is for even the most highly skilled computer and Internet security professionals to engineer technological protective measures for banks and their customers. As has been widely reported, one of the most effective anti-fraud measures in the area of illegal account takeover is communication: notifying customers of the threat they may subject themselves to if they click on a spam e-mail that contains a piece of malicious software such as a Trojan horse.

## ▶ New Forms of Identity Theft and Fraud

As you have probably noticed, the fraud-related attacks discussed earlier sound very much like identity theft. That is because when outside fraudsters initiate a social engineering, information theft, or phishing attack, they are going after confidential information that enables them to assume victims' identities in one way or another.

For example, in social engineering attacks, the fraudster may be after information about a company's office supply vendor to use to assume the legitimate office vendor's identity in order to send phony invoices or perpetrate a related fraud.

In phishing schemes, collecting customer usernames and passwords by tricking them into visiting a Web site that looks exactly like that of their bank and having them "update" their username and password enables fraudsters to use that information to pose as legitimate customers in order to loot their account, open fraudulent new accounts, submit fraudulent automated clearinghouse files, and so on.

The same idea applies to information security breaches. When outside attackers hack into a bank's databases to steal customer account information and PII, they are able to create a host of costly identity frauds: creating counterfeit credit cards and debit cards; applying for loans in the legitimate victim's name; and opening new bank accounts, online purchasing accounts, and so on.

An increasingly worrisome variety of this identity theft and fraud involves what Memento director of solution strategy Mike Mulholand refers to as "teams of pros working together to commit fraud." Mulholand says that such teams

> can generate larger, more damaging fraud losses. Their schemes tend to be more sophisticated and better-planned than the work of fraudsters working alone on quick-hit attacks. Their work can be harder to detect. And collusive fraud covers all fraud types—from new account fraud to employee fraud. A lot of times, it means cross-channel fraud, and most banks struggle to find it, much less shut it down completely.
>
> It appears that [these gang members] may be loosely related, and groups change in their makeup over time. Regardless of how they are connected, they need to control their fraud operations, and in the process may do suspicious things like change their address right after opening an account. They may reveal sketchy access patterns, like [accessing] multiple accounts . . . from the same IP address or phone, [o]pen[ing] multiple accounts with the same funding source or mak[ing] suspicious deposits or withdrawals. But they all want one thing—your customer's money.[20]

Mulholand further offers an especially sobering assessment:

> Collusive behavior accounts for nearly 50% of new account fraud. More sophisticated schemes like on-line account takeover are often performed by organized

fraudsters (from virtually anywhere in the world). New account fraud detection strategies need to be focused on protecting your bank from organized fraudsters. Only then can you protect your customer base from victimization and your bank from eroding profits.[21]

The relentless assault on financial institutions to steal the information needed to commit these identity frauds is one major reason that identity theft has become the fastest-growing crime in America.

It is also to a large degree responsible for Congress's enactment of the "Red Flags" Rules implementing Sections 114 and 315 of the Fair and Accurate Credit Transactions Act of 2003 (FACT Act).

Starting November 1, 2009, all financial institutions were required to have an Identity Theft Prevention Program in place to comply with the terms of the new FACT Act Identity Theft Red Flags regulations.

---

### IDENTITY THEFT VERSUS IDENTITY FRAUD

It is important to keep in mind the difference between identity *fraud* and identity *theft*. The latter is the crime of fraudulently obtaining a person's confidential identifying information through social engineering . . . or by stealing the information. Identity fraud, in contrast, is the act of abusing this stolen information to fraudulently transact personal business in the victim's name. Identity frauds occur when the perpetrator poses as the victim to apply for credit cards, open bank accounts, make fraudulent online purchases, or fraudulently apply for personal loans or mortgages.

---

If your financial institution is like most, it already has in place basic procedures for preventing identity theft in new credit card applications, address changes, address discrepancies, and the host of other financial account-related identity theft risks that are detailed in the new Red Flags Rules of FACTA. These rules are aimed at detecting, preventing, and mitigating the risk of identity theft in connection with so-called covered accounts, which essentially encompass most types of consumer checking, savings, credit card, debit card, and other accounts offered by most financial institutions. The Federal Trade Commission (FTC) together with the five financial industry regulatory agencies are responsible for enforcing the Red Flags Rules.

According to current FTC guidelines, your organization's Red Flags compliance program must be based on existing anti–identity theft policies and procedures as well as other vulnerabilities to identity theft that the organization has—or should have by now—identified through an enterprise-wide risk assessment. Such an assessment is designed to pinpoint specific weaknesses in the organization's business processes and procedures that could be exploited by identity thieves (see Chapter 7).

In one set of guidelines, issued by the Office of Thrift Supervision, as part of the regulatory agencies' enforcement measures, examiners will assess whether the financial institution has

> conducted a risk assessment to identify [all] accounts that pose a reasonably fore-seeable risk of identity theft, taking into consideration the methods used to open and access accounts, and the institution's previous experiences with identity theft.[22]

The Red Flags requirements have specific rules for credit and debit card issuers. Most important, issuers are required to have in place procedures for authenticating cardholders' requests for changes of address. Bank examiners will assess financial institutions' policies in this regard based on four tests:

1. Can the card issuer assess the validity of a change of address?
2. Do the institution's policies and procedures prohibit issuance of a card until it verifies the change of address?
3. Are electronic notices sent for verification clear and conspicuous?
4. Is sampling performed, if needed?

## ■ Credit Card, Debit Card, and Automated Teller Machine Fraud

Some bank anti-fraud experts are skeptical about how effective the Red Flags Rules will be in reducing the incidence of credit and debit card fraud. That is because while the rules aim to identify potential cases of card-related identity fraud, they do not address the enormous threat of having large volumes of credit card data stolen from bank networks and databases. As long as external cyber-thieves continue to succeed in breaching bank security systems and compromising credit and debit card information, the card-related identity fraud problem will continue to grow.

As alluded to earlier, the most common and obvious types of fraud related to these breaches are cases where a thief who has stolen someone's credit card data simply uses it to make fraudulent online purchases or to open cell phone accounts, PayPal accounts, and so on. These accounts will remain open and active until the victim notices from the monthly statements that the accounts are fraudulent and refuses to pay the bills.

More sophisticated credit card frauds involve the sale of large batches of stolen credit card records to third parties, often organized crime rings located in Eastern Europe or Asia. These buyers use the stolen data to manufacture counterfeit credit or debit cards and then either sell them on the Internet black market or use them to make hundreds or thousands of fraudulent purchases—often of expensive consumer electronic equipment, which can in turn be sold for a profit.

Other credit card fraud gangs operate domestically, trafficking in large volumes of stolen card data and generating enormous ill-gotten profits.

Among the increasingly common—and potentially costly—forms of credit card fraud is one called the "credit card bust-out." Criminals use stolen PII or create entirely fictitious identification documents to apply for credit cards. When the

◄ **Case Study #19**

## International Card Gang Went to Town to the Tune of $75 Million

Four members of a South Florida–based criminal gang that generated $75 million in credit card fraud losses were arrested by the U.S. Secret Service.

More than 200,000 credit card account numbers, two pickup trucks, about $10,000 in cash, and one handgun were also recovered in connection with the gang's activity, according to a Secret Service statement.

The gang was uncovered through an earlier investigation by the Secret Service's Miami and Nashville field offices that targeted an individual named Julio Lopez, who used the screen name "Blinky" to traffic in counterfeit credit cards and stolen IDs.

Lopez, based in Hialeah, Florida, and his girlfriend, Anett Villar, were arrested earlier, and an investigation into their activities led to the discovery of an organized fraud ring made up of Cuban nationals operating in South Florida.

The Secret Service reported that the gang sent "large amounts" of money using E-gold accounts to cyber-criminals in Eastern Europe in exchange for "tens of thousands" of stolen credit card numbers. (E-gold is an illegal form of online currency.) The numbers were then used to create counterfeit cards in several "plants" throughout Florida.

***How could this fraud have been prevented?*** List as many controls as you can. Compare yours with those listed in Appendix B.

1. _____

2. _____

3. _____

applications are approved and the cards are sent, the criminals immediately max out the credit lines by taking cash advances and making purchases of items, often for resale. Of course, they never have any intention of paying off the balances; the issuing bank is stuck with the loss.

◄ **Case Study #20**

## "Cardbusters"

U.S. Immigration and Customs Enforcement (ICE) agents arrested Akbar Wrind and Rafael Marte on charges of "knowingly, willfully, and with the intent to defraud and conspire, obtaining things of value aggregating over $1,000."

Wrind and Marte established lines of credit using false identification documents in the names of nonexistent persons. They used those fraudulent credit cards to obtain cash and merchandise with no intent of paying back the lenders.

According to ICE, Wrind and Marte leased properties in Union and West New York, New Jersey, as "drop addresses" for the fraudulent bills and cash payouts. They also allegedly established shell companies to fraudulently establish credit card processing terminals and initiate fraudulent transactions. The victimized banks included Bank of America, Citibank, JPMorgan Chase, Wachovia, and others.

In connection with the arrests, ICE stated:

This type of non-traditional money laundering crime is commonly referred to as a credit card "bust-out" scheme. Fraudulent credit cards are obtained for the sole purpose of removing all available credit and not repaying the lender. Commonly, criminals use false identification documents to create fictitious identities, or purchase credit portfolios from individuals leaving the country.

*How could this fraud have been prevented?* List as many controls as you can. Compare yours with those listed in Appendix B.

1. _____

2. _____

3. _____

Another critical threat to financial institutions is that of fraud related to purchasing cards (P-cards). As discussed in Chapter 3, banks are vulnerable in two ways:

1. As issuers of P-cards to corporate clients, banks are at risk of loss of P-card data in information security attacks. When cyber-thieves steal large volumes of card data, corporate P-card data often are among the digital booty.

2. Cardholders themselves too often find it difficult to resist the temptation to abuse their card privileges by making personal purchases and disguising them as business-related expenditures.

The fraudulent transactions committed by a user of these stolen data may not become evident until several months after the initial breach. That is because the stolen data may be bought and sold several times before a criminal finally uses the data to perpetrate illegal transactions. It may take up to an additional 30 days before cardholders receive their statements and discover that someone has hijacked their account.

Closely related to credit and debit card theft are frauds targeting automated teller machines (ATMs). Some retail bank anti-fraud experts believe that ATM fraud ranks as the top fraud problem of all for such organizations.

Whether it is or not, the indisputable reality is that ATM fraud is *huge* and growing continuously. In the old-fashioned but still widely deployed fraud attack on ATMs, crooks insert a card-reading mechanism into the ATM slot where customers insert their ATM/debit cards. These devices record data from the magnetic strip on the back of the card for use in counterfeiting the cards. Of course, the cards are of little use to the criminals unless they also have the customer's personal identification number (PIN) codes to go with them. To obtain those, fraudsters typically install a small camera behind where the customer stands and record the keystrokes victims make when entering their PIN codes on the ATM keypad. With that, the fraudsters have all they need to empty out victims' bank accounts.

New ATMs are equipped with card slots that require fraudsters to take extra mechanical steps to outfit the machines with card-reading devices. This improvement has deterred many potential crooks from attempting conventional ATM/debit card information theft.

Increasingly, however, this low-tech method of victimizing ATM users is being replaced by data breach attacks similar to those described earlier with regard to credit card data.

Sophisticated cyber-criminals have learned how to steal not only the debit card data but also the encrypted PIN data that goes along with the cards. To complete the crime, the fraudsters are now stealing the "keys" required to decrypt the PINs.

As described by one industry expert:

> While industry losses due to debit card fraud—including both signature and PIN based—increased 21 percent from $546 million in 2004 to $662 million in 2005, PIN debit card fraud at the point of sale almost trebled, increasing from $8 million in 2004 to $21 million in 2005 . . . .
>
> From the perspective of a financial institution, the relevant fraud metric is debit fraud losses as a percentage of total debit card purchase volume. In 2005, issuers experienced a net fraud rate of 4.71 basis points on signature debit card purchases and 0.61 basis points on PIN debit card purchases. (That is, for every $100 spent on a debit card, on average, financial institutions lose 4.71¢ on signature transactions and 0.61¢ on PIN transactions.) On a relative basis, therefore, the loss rate on signature debit transactions is 7.7 times higher than on PIN debit.
>
> While PIN debit card fraud at the point of sale remains relatively low, it is obviously increasing and . . . issuers are developing and applying new strategies to address the risks presented by the use of PIN debit, along with continuing efforts to combat signature debit card fraud.[23]

### Remember

For financial institutions, the problems of credit card fraud, debit card fraud, ATM fraud, and information theft are all interrelated. To understand how many modern credit card frauds are executed, you also must understand the mechanics of debit card fraud and card information theft.

## ■ Check Fraud

As discussed in Chapter 3, checks remain the primary method of business-to-business payments by far. According to the Association for Financial Professionals, automated clearing house (ACH) credit, ACH debit, corporate purchasing cards, and wire transfers all trail far behind.

Nonetheless, check fraudsters are hard at work attacking banks and other financial institutions in a continuous barrage of fraud attempts.

The list of frauds popular among internal bank employees that was discussed in Chapter 3 is rivaled by the numerous types of check-related crimes attempted by outsiders.

Not only must banks keep up with the continuously evolving types of check-related crime, they must scramble to devise ways to detect these frauds faster and of course persevere in the endless quest for effective deterrents and preventive measures. Today, the main types of externally perpetrated check fraud affecting financial institutions include:

- Creating forged checks
- Forged on-us checks
- Check altering by inserting numbers or letters
- Cashier's check counterfeiting
- ACH fraud
- Bank employee collusion with outsiders
- Deposit or payments fraud
- Vendor fraud

### Creating Forged Checks

The Merriam-Webster dictionary defines forgery as "the crime of falsely and fraudulently making or altering a document (as a check)."

Check forgery schemes are perpetrated by outsiders who steal checks from payees' mailboxes or other locations and fraudulently alter the payee, much as employees do with made-out checks prepared for mailing to legitimate payees.

All they have to do after changing the payee is to forge the endorsement and deposit the check. Some outsiders execute these alterations the low-tech way by whiting out the legitimate payee name and replacing it with their own.

### Forged On-Us Checks

On-us checks are checks that are cashed or deposited at the same bank or one of its branches on which it was drawn. Among the most common on-us check frauds are those that involve payroll checks. An outsider steals an employee's paycheck and creates a counterfeit using a computer and actual check stock. The counterfeit, if done skillfully, is nearly indistinguishable from a legitimate paycheck. The fraudster can then simply cash the check at a branch of the bank where the employer's payroll account is held.

However, it is just as easy to commit this fraud by stealing a regular business or consumer check and using the routing number and account information to make high-tech forgeries.

Often these crimes are committed by organized crime rings, with large numbers of counterfeits being generated and cashed by groups of criminals or by recruits who are given a stack of checks to cash one at a time at different branches in exchange for a percentage of the amount stolen.[24]

### Check Altering by Inserting Numbers or Letters

According to the Office of the Comptroller of the Currency (OCC), there are two primary ways check fraudsters alter stolen checks: by fraudulently inserting numerical or alphabetical characters before depositing or by cashing them. These methods are illustrated by the OCC with two hypothetical scenarios.

*Scenario 1: Numbers Games*   A dishonest door-to-door prepared-meal salesman sells a week's worth of frozen dinners for $69.99. The customer pays by check, writing "$69.99" to the far right in the box for the amount and the words: "Sixty-nine and 99/100" to the far right of the text line. The criminal uses the blank spaces on both lines to alter the check by adding "9" before the numbers line and the words "Nine Hundred" before the text line. The $69.99 check is now a fraudulent check for $969.99, which the criminal cashes.

*Scenario 2: Alphabet Ploys*   A company that provides computer service to several small clients is paid by checks made out to "Johnson Co." or "Johnson Company." A mailroom worker at one of Johnson Co.'s client firms steals a payment check and uses a chemical solution to erase the word "Co." or "Company."

He then types in the word "Cooper" and subsequently cashes the checks using false identification with the name Johnson Cooper.[25]

In these schemes, not only is the financial institution on which the checks are drawn a victim, so is the account holder whose checks have been altered and against whose account the bad check is debited.

---

### ◀ Case Study #21

#### Student Learns Tricks of the Check Fraud Trade

Heather Anne Morshead of Magalia, California, was sentenced to 15 months in prison for felony conspiracy and bank fraud offenses related to a scheme to create counterfeit checks.

According to the U.S. Attorney's office in Sacramento, Morshead, working with several codefendants, manufactured bogus checks using financial information stolen from the U.S. mail and during residential burglaries and vehicle break-ins. Morshead used computer software and authentic check stock to manufacture checks with the names of her co-conspirators and used bank account numbers obtained from stolen financial information.

Morshead, who was a student at Butte County Community College, also cashed checks that were stolen from the mail.

*How could this fraud have been prevented?* List as many controls as you can. Compare yours with those listed in Appendix B.

1. _____

2. _____

3. _____

### Cashier's Check Counterfeiting

A growing problem of check fraud is counterfeiting of bank cashier's checks. In 2004, the Federal Deposit Insurance Corporation (FDIC) issued 106 special alerts concerning counterfeit cashier's checks. That number almost doubled to 202 in 2005 and more than tripled to 342 in 2006. The number of special alerts for counterfeit cashier's checks issued through mid-August 2007 was 226.

This type of check fraud is more of a problem for unsuspecting consumers who are targeted by scammers. In the most common ploy, fraudsters buy from individuals items that are advertised in newspaper ads or on the Internet. To pay for the item, they send a genuine-looking but bogus cashier's check to the victim for more than the purchase amount. Claiming that the check is the only means of payment they have, they ask the victim to send a personal check back to them for the difference. Once the victim deposits the cashier's check, it is processed and eventually returned to the victim's bank as fraudulent. The victim's bank then debits the customer's account to cover the fraudulent cashier's check amount. The victim is out the amount of the cashier's check, the amount of the "reimbursement" *and* the merchandise if it has already been shipped.

Once cashier's checks are counterfeited and circulated, banks incur sizable administrative costs along with potential reputational damage as publicity about the crime is generated through the news. Refer to Exhibit 4.5 for a graphic illustration of a fraudulent cashier's check.

### ACH Fraud

As indicated in Chapter 3, ACH fraud perpetrated by insiders poses a comparatively low risk to most financial institutions. However, as the volume of ACH transactions grows, replacing checks, the risk to banks of being victimized by ACH-related fraud will increase.

According to Shirley Inscoe of Memento Inc.:

> ACH fraud will continue to be a growing threat, both from an origination and receiving bank perspective. With the advent of check conversion, fraud became an inherent part of the ACH network. Every time a fraudulent (counterfeit, forged or altered) check is converted to an ACH debit, it creates a fraudulent ACH transaction.[26]

In other words, when retail businesses accept checks from consumers and convert them to ACH transactions, any counterfeit or forged checks included in the processing automatically become fraudulent ACH transactions as well. An innocent consumer whose check was forged could be a victim. Consumers have 60 days to report the unauthorized debit to their bank, but the business that accepted the check has only two days.[27]

---

### ◀ Case Study #22

## Even Fraud Fighters Can Get Bitten by the Bad Guys

Nearly $2 million was stolen from the West Virginia Auditor's office via ACH fraud.

According to news reports, the Federal Bureau of Investigation and the U.S Attorney's Office began investigating the fraud scheme after more than $1 million was stolen via ACH fraud and transferred to banks out of the state. The fraud was perpetrated by an overseas individual who somehow acquired the federal employee identification numbers (EINs) of two companies that provide services to the state auditor's offices and wrote letters asking that checks for payment of amounts owed be remitted to new bank accounts, the details of which were contained in the letters.

West Virginia state auditor Glen Gainer said at the time that a total of three payments were collected from banks out of state and then transferred to offshore banks. He also said one of the payments was for around $900,000, but he was not sure of the exact amount of the other two transfers. In all, the amount was close to $1.99 million.

The names of the companies whose EINs were stolen were not officially released by the auditor's office. However, news reports indicated that one of the vendors was Sedgwick CMS, a company that served as third-party administrator for the West Virginia Insurance Commission and manages workers' compensation claims for the state.

Gainer, who by coincidence was chairman of the National White-Collar Crime Center (www.nw3c.org) at the time of the fraud, said that this type of fraud also occurred in Florida, Maine, Massachusetts, and North Carolina.

According to the National Association of State Auditors, Comptrollers and Treasurers, other states have been targeted by this scheme of using ACH payments to certain vendors. But not all states have lost money.

*How could this fraud have been prevented?* List as many controls as you can. Compare yours with those listed in Appendix B.

1. _____

2. _____

3. _____

### Bank Employee Collusion with Outsiders

Bank branch managers, tellers, or other employees with access to cash or bank checks are often in positions to collude with outside criminals. For example, organized crime groups are known to recruit individuals to apply for jobs as tellers or other positions in one or more bank branches. Once these insiders have been trained and have been employed long enough to gain the trust of their superiors, they begin to steal customer account information and other PII and transmit it to their handlers. They are paid a modest fee for this service and usually quit before any suspicion is raised about their illegal conduct.

Such collusion is by no means limited to organized crime rings. Law enforcement agency files are full of cases involving collusion between bank employees and friends or relatives on the outside in check fraud, identity theft/fraud, credit card scams, and the like.

### Deposit or Payments Fraud

The term "deposit fraud" refers to several of the varieties of financial crime already discussed in this chapter. However, new varieties of common deposit frauds are being cooked up by fraudsters all the time.

A study on deposit fraud conducted by KPMG concluded:

> While "traditional" forms of [deposit] fraud such as [check] kiting, forged signatures and counterfeit checks continue to constitute a threat, an entirely new level of fraud has recently surfaced and is rapidly escalating. Examples of this new, more menacing type of fraud include identity theft, personal computer-produced counterfeit checks, internal theft of information, ATM deposit available-balance policy manipulation, and kiting through ACH processing.[28]

Of all the fraud types mentioned here, check kiting is the one we have not yet addressed. In its simplest form, the term refers to the crime of depositing a legitimate check in an account at one bank, writing a bad check for much more than the initial deposit and depositing it into an account at a second bank, and then withdrawing the majority of the funds in cash from the second account before the bad check bounces. Sometimes these frauds can go on for months before being detected.

◀ **Case Study #23**

## Kite Soars to $1.3 Million in a Week before Crashing

John T. Quaid pleaded guilty in federal district court in Phoenix to having executed a check-kiting scheme that inflated his account balances with Bank of America and USAA Federal Savings Bank (FSB).

*The scheme.* Quaid owned and operated several small businesses, including Security Holdings, LLC, and Property Management & Advisors, LLC, in Scottsdale, Arizona. Quaid admitted to writing worthless checks and depositing them into his business accounts with the banks. Doing so artificially increased the balances in the accounts.

His fraud reflected a fairly straightforward check-kiting scheme: After depositing one bad check into one business account, Quaid then drew a second check on a second account with insufficient funds, and then deposited the second check into the first account to cover the first check.

According to court documents, over a period of about a week, Quaid deposited checks totaling $1,340,000, of which at least eight totaling $740,000 were worthless.

*The bust.* Officials at USAA FSB discovered the scheme after it had caused the two banks that Quaid used to perpetrate the scheme to lose approximately $487,015. After being apprehended, Quaid admitted that he perpetrated the scheme to obtain cash for his personal use and to fund his business interests.

As a result of subsequent civil litigation and negotiations among Quaid and the two banks, Quaid repaid all the banks' financial losses as well as their legal expenses.

### Vendor Fraud

In Chapter 3, you learned how insiders create phony vendors by setting up shell companies to generate bogus invoices or by manipulating the vendor master file (VMF) to add false vendors or change the addresses or other details of legitimate vendors in order to divert disbursements to their own accounts.

The latter type of fraud cannot be perpetrated by an outsider (unless he or she is colluding with an accounts payable [AP] or procurement employee with access to the VMF). However, external fraudsters *are* known for creating shell company vendors with all of the necessary corporate documentation, EINs, TINs (taxpayer identification numbers), Social Security numbers (SSNs), and the technical resources to generate legitimate-looking invoices.

Sometimes these criminals will generate invoices from phony companies with names very similar to legitimate suppliers. In other instances, they simply generate a generic invoice and send it to numerous target companies in the expectation that one or more lack the internal controls to flag the invoice as potentially fraudulent.

In cases where legitimate vendors are the perpetrators, the common ploys are to send the same invoice a second time in the hope that the financial institution's internal controls are not set up to flag duplicate invoices. They also may try to get away with delivering substandard goods or short deliveries.

Also, as discussed previously, keep an eye out for dishonest vendors who engage procurement personnel in bribery or kickback schemes.

---

### EXTERNAL FRAUD AGAINST FINANCIAL INSTITUTIONS: THE TECHNOLOGY WEAPON

**Technology in the wrong hands is a costly weapon.**

Zeldon Morris was the controlling partner in the computer consulting firm Lee & Morris. Morris, who took on Eunyong Lee as a partner in April 2008, had been retained as an independent contractor by Provo, Utah–based Open Solutions Inc. to repair and maintain the data processing systems of Family First Credit Union in Orem.

Morris, it turns out, proceeded to use his estimable technical skills to plunder over $1 million from the credit union over about 10 months ending in January 2009, when his crimes were reportedly discovered.

Morris, who initially was considered a flight risk because he had made frequent trips to Korea and was married to a woman of Korean descent who had family in that country, was released under undisclosed conditions.

*Details.* According to the indictment, Morris was given passwords by Open Solutions to access the credit union's computer system at its Orem office and via remote locations. From June 13, 2008, through mid-January 2009, he accessed the credit union system and executed several fraudulent electronic funds transfers, depositing more than $1 million into his personal accounts and into a business account of Lee & Morris.

An investigation by credit union officials reportedly found that Morris made the fraudulent transfers either by using bogus trace numbers—numbers that, according to banking officials, are "serial number[s] for ACH transaction[s], similar to a check number, that identifies the payment"—or, according to court documents, by "duplicating other legitimate trace numbers but using fictitious amounts, or by remotely accessing the bank's system through the 'E-teller' system and overriding it to accept deposits" to Morris's own accounts.

*Additional details.* The sources of the stolen funds were one or more internal general ledger accounts, in particular, according to legal filings, "the interest income general ledger account because it recently had a larger-than-expected drop."

According to the indictment, Morris transferred the stolen funds to his personal accounts at other financial institutions and to other businesses or individuals as well as to a Family First account in the name of his wife.

*(Continued)*

Among the red flags was the fact that several cashier's checks were purchased with the stolen funds, and the checks included the phrase "Re: Zeldon Thomas Morris" on the face of the checks. The endorsements on the checks were either to Morris or to an account that required his signature.

*The bust*. Court documents indicate that Family First would not have discovered the fraud scheme if Eunyong Lee had not blown the whistle after investigating odd details in the company's accounts in October.

Lee initially suspected Morris of embezzling funds from the company after he made suspicious withdrawals from the company and failed to pay Lee for his work.

When Lee reviewed Morris's accounts at the credit union, he found several very large deposits that appeared to be "real estate related." Morris, who told Lee of his financial difficulties, reportedly explained that the deposits were proceeds of mortgage refinancings. But in court documents, Lee said he found no recorded real estate transactions on Utah County online property records to support the refinancing and also discovered that Morris's original mortgage loans were still outstanding.

Lee informed credit union officials of the suspicious deposits to Morris's accounts in March 2009, resigned from the company, and asked Morris to buy out his interest.

Family First vice president Jason Craddock said Morris had taken no money from any of the credit union's 26,000 members and that the institution's losses were covered by the National Credit Union Association.[29]

## ▶ Red Flags of External Fraud

As explained earlier, the key to preventing fraud is being able to detect the key indicators of the many types of such crimes threatening your organization. Unfortunately, the list of red flags is extremely lengthy, thanks to the ingenuity of bank fraudsters. A list of the most common indicators of the frauds discussed in this chapter follows. Although it is not exhaustive, it does provide you with a firm foundation of red flags to work with.

### Red Flags of Commercial Loan Fraud

- Vehicle identification numbers provided for dealer financing contain wrong number and sequence of characters. (Dealer loan/line of credit fraud.)
- Number of vehicle sales is unusually high or low compared to local competitors and past years' history.
- Contracts are awarded without competitive bidding. (May indicate corruption by vendors and/or collusion with your purchasing department.)

- High turnover in the borrowing company's personnel. (May indicate that management is embezzling cash or other illegal conduct is taking place, causing employees to leave after short stints.)

- Unusually numerous change orders. Most major construction projects require changes to be made at some point during the construction process. However, high numbers of such changes may be an indicator of collusive bidding and should be investigated.

- Missing documentation. Commercial projects involve mountains of paperwork. Missing documents, such as professionally prepared budgets, lists of subcontractors, and major environmental regulatory filings, may be signs of a fraudulent loan application.

- Cash flow problems. (May indicate that contractor management is skimming cash.)

- Sudden increases in labor costs. (May indicate employee ghosting.)

- Unusually frequent delays in progress. (May indicate employees are accepting kickbacks from vehicle or equipment maintenance vendors for steering business their way but not performing services ordered.)

- Frequent replacement orders for tools, equipment, and materials. (May indicate diversion of materials, theft of tools and equipment, etc.)

### Red Flags of Externally Perpetrated Mortgage Fraud
General red flags:

- A mortgage broker insists that a buyer use a particular lender.

- The appraiser referred by a mortgage broker or lender has never been used by the broker or lender before.

- Appraisal fee is unusually high.

- Improper or random use of comparable property sales.

- Appraised value of the property is substantially higher than market levels.

- Borrower resides in a state other than that where the property is located but the property is denoted on the mortgage application as the borrower's intended primary residence.

- Unrecognized names are added to the purchase contract.

- Parties to the transaction are related.

- No real estate agent is involved.

- A third party signs on behalf of the borrower.

- Address discrepancies within the loan file.

- Verifications are completed on the same day they were ordered.

- Verifications of employment (VOEs) are completed on weekends or holidays, or show an employee's hire date was on a weekend.

- Builder is overanxious to sell. (May indicate builder bailout scheme.)

- Sales price and/or appraisal appear to be inflated.

- Internet advertisements for the propert(ies) with no money down. (Possible builder bailout scheme.)
- Inconsistent handwriting or type styles within a document.
- Excessive number of AUS (Automated Underwriting System) submissions.

Mortgage application red flags:

- Borrower's Social Security number includes one or more of these indicators:
  - Issue date is inconsistent with the borrower's age.
  - Three or more leading zeros.
  - Zeros in positions 4 and 5.
  - Numbers ending in four zeros.
  - A leading number of 73 through 79.
  - A leading number of 8 or 9.[30]
- Significant or contradictory changes from handwritten to typed application.
- Application is unsigned or undated or both.
- Borrower's age is inconsistent with stated employment or the number of years employed.
- Employer's address is a post office box.
- Loan purpose is cash-out refinance on a recently acquired property.
- Buyer currently resides in the property.
- Same telephone number for applicant and employer.
- "Buyer" shows surprise or shock when learning about payment amount. This may indicate that he or she is a straw buyer and/or the fraudster has falsely inflated income on the application.
- Pay stubs are handwritten.
- Pay stubs show round numbers for earnings.
- Documentation includes deletions, whiting out, or other alteration.
- Numbers on the documentation appear to be squeezed due to alteration.

Sales contract red flags:

- Non–arm's-length transaction: The seller is also the real estate broker, or a relative, employer, friend, or so on.
- Seller is not named on the property title.
- Purchaser is not the applicant.
- Purchaser(s) are deleted from or added to the sales contract.
- No real estate agent is involved.
- Sales price has changed numerous times.
- Seller is a real estate broker, employer, or relative of the borrower.

- Power of attorney is used.

- Indications of a second mortgage on the property exist, but none is disclosed on the contract.

- Earnest money deposit equals the entire down payment or is an odd amount.

- Multiple deposit checks have inconsistent dates (i.e., #303 dated 10/1, #299 dated 11/1).

- Name and/or address on earnest money deposit check differs from that of the buyer.

- Real estate commission is excessive.

- Contract is dated later than the date on the credit documents.

- Contract is boilerplate with limited fill-in-the-blank terms, not reflective of a genuine negotiation.

- Invalid SSN appears on the application, or the number is different from that on other documents.

- Recently issued SSN number.

- Liabilities shown on the credit report do not appear on the mortgage application.

- Length of established credit indicated on the contract is not consistent with the applicant's age.

- Credit patterns are inconsistent with income and lifestyle.

- Authorized user accounts all have superior payment histories.

- Significant differences appear between original and new or supplemental credit reports.

- Also known as (AKA) or doing business as (DBA) names appear on the contract.

- Employment history discrepancies.

Employment and income documentation red flags:

- Employer's address is a post office box, the property address, or applicant's current residence.

- The property's address is unusually far from the applicant's place of employment.

- Employer name is similar to a party to the transaction, such as the applicant's initials.

- Employment verification form contains whiting out, erasures, or other signs of alteration.

- Spelling errors appear on verification of employment document.

- Employer cannot be contacted.

- Year-to-date or past-year earnings are even dollar amounts.

- Withholding is incorrectly calculated.

- Abnormalities in paycheck numbering.

- W-2 form presented is not the employee's copy.

- Employer's identification number has a format other than 12-3456789.

- Income appears to be out of line with type of employment.

- Self-employed applicant does not make estimated tax payments.

- Applicant has a high income but tax return is not prepared by a professional paid preparer.

- Pay stubs are handwritten.

- Pay stubs show round numbers for earnings.

- Documentation includes deletions, whiting out, or other alteration.

- Numbers on the documentation appear to be squeezed due to alteration.

- Interest and dividend income do not substantiate assets.

- Applicant reports substantial income but has no cash in the bank.

- Stated income appears out of line with type of employment, applicant age, education, and/or lifestyle.

Asset documentation red flags:

- Applicant does not utilize traditional banking institutions.

- Account balances are greater than Federal Deposit Insurance Corporation or SIPC (Securities Investor Protection Corporation) insured limits.

- High-asset applicant's investments are not diversified.

- Excessive balance maintained in checking account.

- Dates of bank statements are unusual or out of sequence.

- Recently deposited funds have no plausible paper trail or explanation.

- Bank account ownership includes unknown parties.

- Two-month average balance is equal to current balance.

- Source of earnest money is not apparent.

- Earnest money is not reflected in account withdrawals.

- Bank statements do not reflect deposits consistent with income.

- Assets appear excessive for type of employment, applicant age, education, and/or lifestyle.

- Falsified pay stubs.

- Altered W-2 forms.

Appraisal fraud red flags:

- Appraisal is ordered by a party to the transaction. (May indicate an attempt to falsely inflate property value.)

- Appraiser is not certified.

- Owner is someone other than the seller indicated on the sales contract.

- Appraisal indicates that the transaction is a refinance but other documentation reflects a purchase.
- Purchase price is substantially higher than prevailing market values.
- Purchase price is substantially lower than prevailing market values.
- Comparable sales are not similar in style, size, and amenities.
- Old sales are used as comparable sales.
- Borrower already owns an excessive amount of real estate. (May indicate misrepresentation of intent to occupy the property.)
- For new construction, all comparable sales are located in the same development as the property being financed.
- Comparable properties are a significant distance from the subject or located across neighborhood boundaries (main arteries, waterways, etc.).
- Appraiser's map scale distorts the distance between comparable properties.
- "For Rent" sign appears in photographs of the property.
- Photos appear to be taken from an awkward or unusual angle.
- Address reflected in photos does not match property address.
- Appraisal is dated before the sales contract date.

Title-related red flags:

- Income tax, judgments, or similar liens are recorded.
- Delinquent property taxes.
- Notice of default or modification agreement recorded.
- Seller is not on the title.
- Seller has owned the property for a very short time.
- Buyer has a preexisting financial interest in the property.
- Date and amount of existing encumbrances do not add up.
- Buyer and seller have similar names. (Property flips often utilize family members as straw buyers.)[31]

These lists of commercial loan and home mortgage frauds are adapted from publications by BITS and the Federal Financial Institutions Examination Council (FFIEC). They are partial lists only, and the reader is encouraged to visit the Web sites of the respective sources for additional details.

### Red Flags of Phone or Face-to-Face Social Engineering

- Caller or visitor sounds nervous or hesitant when making a request for information.
- Perpetrator is unable to provide an adequate reason for needing the requested information.
- Caller's or visitor's voice sounds familiar. (Could be an ex-employee or manager seeking unauthorized information.)

- Individual's affiliation sounds unfamiliar or suspicious. ("Big Computer Services" or "LK Suppliers and Maintenance.")

### Red Flags of Phishing, External Theft of Confidential Customer Data, and Identity Theft/Fraud against Customers

- You receive unsolicited e-mail messages that ask, either directly or through a Web site, for your financial or other personal identifying information. This could include bank account information, Social Security number, username, passwords, or other confidential personal data.

- An unsolicited e-mail message leads you to a supposedly secure Web site that lacks the familiar "lock" icon at the bottom of your browser and "https" in front of the Web site address.

- An e-mail message leads you to a Web page with an unusually long header address (URL). Most legitimate sites have a relatively short Internet address that depicts the business name followed by ".com," or ".org." Spoofed sites often have exceedingly long strings of characters in the header, with the legitimate business name somewhere in the string or not at all. Refer to Exhibit 6.1 to see a graphic illustration of the telltale signs of a phishing e-mail.

Because phishing's ultimate objective is to facilitate identity theft and identity fraud in order to loot customer accounts, the 26 red flags of potential identity theft or fraud contained in the FACT Act's Red Flag Rules represent an excellent starting point for monitoring signs of potential phishing attacks. In addition, familiarize yourself with your organization's *own* list of red flags, as each organization has its own telltale signs of identity fraud that may not be on the official list.

### Red Flags of an Information Security Breach

- An organization's IT department reports a pattern of unauthorized attempts by outsiders to access a secure computer system.

- An organization's accounts payable department suddenly receives invoices from an existing or new vendor that seem suspicious. This may be a sign that the vendor's information was stolen from your AP files by an outside hacker and used to generate bogus invoices.

### Red Flags of Online Banking Fraud

- Complaints from customers about unauthorized debits/withdrawals.
- Evidence of multiple online accounts being accessed illegally.
- Unusual patterns in multiple online customer accounts.

### Red Flags of Credit and Debit Card Fraud

- Customers complain of unauthorized purchases.
- Sudden unusual patterns in multiple customer card accounts.

- Sudden surge in credit cards maxing out in short periods of time. (May indicate perpetration of bust-out schemes.)
- Unusual increase in numbers of chargebacks.
- Unusual increase in out-of-pattern purchasing by cardholders.

### Red Flags of Check Fraud or Tampering

- Blank checks are missing.
- Canceled checks show signs of erasure or other alteration.
- Authorized signatures are missing or appear forged.
- Vendors or other payees complain about not receiving payments (May indicate that checks have been stolen and altered.)
- Canceled checks have fraudulent endorsements or dual endorsements.
- Account reconciliation anomalies: Canceled checks do not match checks disbursed (or outstanding checks with numbers not appearing in bank statements or other payables records—a sign of stolen blank checks that have not yet been used.)

### Red Flags of ACH Fraud

- Requests from new vendors to allow ACH debits to receive payment of invoices. (Can be a sign that an actual vendor is trying to gain access to client accounts with ACH authorization in order to get a quick payoff before the fraud is discovered. Such a requests should trigger an immediate review of the vendor's background and credit history).
- Sudden high volume of payroll check fraud. (May indicate a fraudster has obtained your payroll account routing number and account number and is counterfeiting paychecks.)
- Sudden increase in customer complaints about unauthorized ACH debits.

### Red Flags of Vendor Fraud and Billing Schemes

- Vendor charges unusually high prices. Vendor may be inflating prices for substandard goods, hoping no one in your organization questions the discrepancies.
- Vendor charges unusually low prices. Vendors sometimes claim they are substituting a regular order with an alternative brand because it "is just as good or better for less money." In reality, while the price is lower, so is the quality; but for the vendor, the profit margin is greater.
- End users complain about defective or malfunctioning products. (Can be a sign that either of the last two scams has been perpetrated.)
- Delivery is for product of higher quality compared to "normal" orders. Here the vendor charges more and delivers high-quality product, and justifies it by claiming that the less-expensive alternative you ordered was out of stock.
- Vendor's name on an invoice does not show up on your vendor master file.
- Delivery address on the invoice differs from that of an approved vendor.

- A post office (PO) box is the only address of the vendor.

- Numbers on invoices sent to the victim organization by a particular vendor are sequential.

- Round dollar amounts are suddenly invoiced.

- Unusual volume of invoices from the same vendor (e.g., a vendor who usually submits 2 invoices per month suddenly submits 12 per month).

- Invoices do not match purchase orders and/or delivery documents.

- Billing for unusual change orders, overtime charges, or supplemental orders.

- Prices on invoices are plus or minus 3 percent of each other.

- Invoices are identical except prices have the same first four digits (e.g., $259.66 and $2,596.77).

- Vendor sends two identical invoices except the amount of one is exactly twice that of the other (e.g., $412.33 and $824.66).[32]

### Red Flags of Kickback Schemes

Note: Because kickback schemes are carried out in the same ways whether they are initiated by an employee or by an outsider, the red flags of an externally initiated kickback scheme often closely resemble those of such a fraud instigated by an insider.

- Same vendor is awarded numerous contracts on consecutive projects.

- Product or service prices jump unexpectedly.

- A longtime vendor is suddenly replaced by a new one.

- Inferior-quality product is delivered, but the invoice prices are for a higher-quality alternative.

- Pattern of growing frequency of purchases from a particularly vendor.

- Purchases are recorded in amounts greater than what is normally purchased, or of products or services the organization does not use.

- Contracts are awarded without competitive bidding.

- Unusual price jumps or discounts.

## ► External Fraud Prevention Checklists

### Externally Perpetrated Commercial Loan Fraud Prevention Checklist

- Recommend that borrowing organizations implement and enforce a code of ethics. The code should specify how the organization will conduct its external business dealings and how the organization expects its employees to conduct their business.

- Encourage borrowers to have their employees execute an annual compliance statement affirming that they have not violated these standards. Suppliers and subcontractors also should agree to abide by the code of ethics before conducting business.

- Encourage institutional customers to conduct fraud awareness/ethics training coupled with the organizational code of ethics. Fraud awareness and ethics training has been shown to be effective at reducing the average fraud loss to half of what it is in organizations without this training.[33]

- Improve whistleblower hotline operations. Review the performance of the organization's hotline service provider to determine if it is receiving a volume of complaints that at least matches, but preferably exceeds, that of competitors. Perform other hotline benchmarking activities, such as those outlined in Deloitte's very useful report, *2006 Corporate Governance and Compliance Hotline Benchmarking Report*, downloadable at www.tnwinc.com/downloads/2006benchmarkingReport.pdf.

- Urge borrowers to conduct regular internal fraud audits. An internal audit program demonstrates the borrower's commitment to its ethics program. Research suggests that organizations with an internal fraud audit program have a shorter average duration to their fraud schemes, with smaller average losses than those without an internal audit program.

- Suggest that borrowers conduct surprise audits—either on a project or on an internal operational basis. These audits are effective but often underutilized fraud deterrents. Research by the Association of Certified Fraud Examiners suggests that fraud detection is quicker and smaller average losses are incurred when surprise audits are conducted. For example, organizations that conduct surprise audits sustained a median loss of $70,000, while those that did not had a median loss of $207,000.[34]

- Require contractors to include a right-to-audit clause in all commercial/construction loan contracts. This allows a company to inspect the books and records of subcontractors for any reason for a defined period after the job ends.

- Ensure that contractors protect their receiving areas. They should routinely reconcile the quantity of materials estimated, ordered, and delivered by project. Ask for reports comparing pricing obtained for materials from one vendor across multiple projects or across multiple vendors.[35]

- Conduct random on-site audits. Periodically have the borrower instruct its internal auditors or an outside construction audit specialist to conduct an assessment of labor costs, materials, equipment usage, and job site security procedures.

- Reconcile material requisitions and deliveries with estimates and account for any significant differences. Attention should also be given to change orders—a common area of fraudulent activity.[36]

### Consumer Loan Fraud Prevention Checklist

- Manually review loan documents. Compile scores for accounts based on overdrafts, nonsufficient funds, and uncollected loans to anticipate downgrades based on deposit activity.

- Use routing, transit, and demand deposit account (DDA) information to search databases (lockbox/payment data functions). This information can be used to extract the magnetic ink character recognition (MICR) line on a check to screen for a common payment source and bad deals within broker portfolios.

- Monitor additional accounts when fraud is identified. If fraud is confirmed on a DDA account, but no fraud is found on other accounts (such as a line of credit), Regulation Z prohibits the bank from closing those secondary accounts. However, the accounts can be monitored to prevent *additional* fraud.

- Use fraud detection technology tools, such as Carreker-Antinori's ASI-16 or ASI-19, and Falcon to identify fraudulent transactions and/or compromised accounts.

- Confirm check orders from borrowers if they are made soon after an address and/or phone number change.[37]

## ■ Externally Perpetrated Mortgage Fraud Prevention Checklist

Although most mortgage frauds are committed by outsiders, many of the methods for committing these crimes can be carried out by either insiders *or* outsiders. That is because so much of mortgage fraud requires manipulation of documentation. It is almost always just as easy, for example, for a dishonest mortgage broker or borrower's attorney to doctor the asset or employment information on a mortgage application as it is for a mortgage loan officer to do so.

Given this often gray area between internal and external mortgage fraud, many of the preventive measures discussed in Chapter 3 apply to preventing external mortgage fraud as well.

However, some important preventive steps apply *only* to externally perpetrated mortgage fraud. BITS details these very clearly in its white paper, *Fraud Prevention Strategies for Consumer, Commercial and Mortgage Loan Departments*. The next list is a digest of the most critical measures.

- Periodically review your organization's closing instructions to ensure that the language includes latest external fraud schemes to beware of.

     Closing instructions should clearly define the role of closing agents and outline their responsibilities to the financial institution. The document should clearly establish liability on the closer's part when instructions are not followed or information is hidden from the financial institution.

     Specifically, closing instructions should require that:

  - The HUD-1 be signed by the bank's settlement agent and the agent sign a statement acknowledging that he or she will follow specific closing instructions provided by the financial institution.

  - All funds provided at closing pass through escrow to avoid funds changing hands outside of the closing.

  - The settlement agent notify the financial institution if:

    - Any mortgage, judgment, or lien has been satisfied within the last eight months (or another internally defined timeframe).

- Any privately held mortgage requires payoff.
- Any mortgage lien of judgment has been entered in the last eight months (or another internally defined timeframe).
- Any transfers of title have occurred within the last eight months (or another internally defined timeframe).
- There have been any significant changes to the sales price.

■ The settlement agent obtain the financial institution's written consent before closing if the settlement agent or anyone in his or her office is a party to the transaction; is a family member, relative, or close friend of one of the parties; or otherwise has a conflict of interest. (Relatives include a spouse, parent, child, brother, sister, aunt, uncle, niece, nephew, cousin, grandparent, fiancé or life partner as well as in-law and step relations.)

■ If the settlement agent has reason to believe there is a fraud or scheme related to the transaction, or if he or she is aware that any party to the transaction made a material misstatement in the loan documentation, the agent will immediately suspend the loan closing and contact the financial institution.

■ If the settlement agent knows or believes that any document has been tampered with or falsely generated; includes false dates, names, or addresses; or if a party's handwriting is inconsistent throughout the file, the agent will suspend closing and immediately contact the financial institution.

■ If the borrower or seller appears to be coerced or under undue influence, the bank's agent must suspend closing and immediately contact the financial institution.

■ If the borrower cannot produce an unexpired driver's license, passport, or other form of identification, the financial institution should be contacted for assistance in independently verifying the identity of the customer.

If the settlement agent cannot be assured that the true identity of the borrower is known, he or she should suspend the closing and contact the financial institution.

■ The borrower must affirm that no third party is paying him or her to provide credit or identification documentation to the transaction.

If the settlement agent has knowledge that there is, or will be, a silent second mortgage placed on the property, or that any funds the borrower is required to pay or deposit at closing are not from the borrower's own funds or a bona fide gift, the settlement agent will suspend the loan closing and immediately contact the financial institution.

■ The settlement agent accepts borrower funds only from the borrower's deposited accounts in the financial institutions verified and disclosed on Fannie Mae Form 1003, or Freddie Mac Form 65, or from the account and institution specified elsewhere in the closing instructions. If borrower funds come from a different and/or out-of-state institution, the settlement agent should suspend the closing and immediately contact the financial institution. (The settlement agent should, of course, also verify the source of funds.)

- For an owner-occupied property transaction in which the settlement agent learns at closing that the borrower owns and occupies a *different* residence that is not subject to sale, or that the borrower does not intend to occupy the property, the settlement agent must obtain the written consent of the financial institution to proceed with the closing. (This measure is to avoid funding a property flip transaction.)

- The mortgage broker and the property seller are not the same person or entity and are not owned or controlled by the same person. If they are, the settlement agent must inform the bank immediately and await instructions to proceed or suspend the closing.

- The financial institution must be informed immediately if the borrower had a former interest in the property, or if other parties to the transaction, such as the real estate agent, mortgage broker, appraiser, or settlement agent, had or has an interest in the property.

- If a business entity is acting as the seller, the settlement agent must confirm that the borrower does not control, and is not related to, the owner or the seller. (This is another possible red flag of a property flipping scheme.)

- For purchase transactions, the settlement agent must confirm that a property inspection has occurred. If no real estate commission is payable, the agent should provide the financial institution with an explanation.

- The financial institution must be contacted prior to closing if the real estate commission appears excessive for the market area.

- The financial institution must be contacted immediately if there are any unusual payouts, including payouts with missing, incomplete, or unclear descriptions, noted on the seller's column on the HUD-1 settlement statement.

- If the legal documents are incomplete or inconsistent with other information in the mortgage file, the settlement agent must contact the financial institution immediately.

### ■ Social Engineering Fraud Prevention Checklist

According to BITS, due to the high volume of calls coming in to bank call centers, loan servicing representatives play a key role in identifying suspicious activity.

By establishing policies and procedures relating to changing customer information, handling returned mail, and responding appropriately to unusual customer phone requests, the organization's loan servicing department is well situated to uncover incidents of attempted fraud by dishonest customers or fraudsters posing as customers using the social engineering ploys discussed in this chapter.

Call center reps should be trained to:

- Review returned payment books and returned mail. A pattern of returned items can indicate broker fraud.

- Obtain signatures from all parties for address changes.

- Send verification letters to old and new addresses for address changes.

- Use outside vendors or bureaus to validate address changes. A number of vendors offer software programs that monitor address change information and determine if the new ZIP code matches the salary demographics of a particular area.

- Validate Social Security numbers or tax identification numbers when a request is made to change the tax identification on an account. Validate the number either by contacting the Social Security Administration directly or through a third-party service provider.

- Compare signatures on checks over a certain dollar amount using technology such as Carreker-Antinori's ASI-16 or a comparable product.

## Phishing and Online Banking Fraud Prevention Checklist

Unfortunately, there is no stopping the countless cyber-criminals trying to trick your financial institution's customers into giving up their bank account information, PIN numbers, and other data to be used to commit identity theft and fraud.

The critical preventive measure is customer *communication*. Financial services institutions should:

- Repeatedly inform customers about potential phishing e-mails that appear to be legitimate urgent requests to "update" their account information by clicking on a link in the e-mail. Fortunately, most financial institutions have taken this step and continue to alert customers to new forms of phishing attacks as they emerge. This is the most effective preemptive measure against phishing attacks and the most effective way to protect customers from potentially ruinous identity-related frauds associated with phishing.

- Maintain compliance with the FFIEC's "strong-factor" online banking security guidance contained in its "Authentication in an Internet Banking Environment," available at www.ffiec.gov.

  This standard involves a technology-based approach for enhancing security by requiring customers to provide more personal information than just their username and password to access their online accounts.

  As discussed earlier, it is recommended that strong-factor (or multiple-factor) authentication be used to provide better online banking security for your customers. Some of the technologies used in strong-factor authentication include:

  - Shared secrets, including passwords and PINs
  - Tokens, such as USB tokens and smart cards
  - Biometrics, such as fingerprint or retina scans
  - One-time password cards
  - Out-of-band authentication, including fax, phone, and short message service (SMS) confirmation
  - Geolocation verification[38]

Geolocation technology monitors Internet banking users by determining where they are or, conversely, where they are not. Geolocation software inspects and analyzes the small bits of time required for Internet communications to move through the network. These electronic travel times are converted into cyberspace distances. After these cyberspace distances have been determined for a user, they are compared with cyberspace distances for known locations. If the comparison is considered reasonable, the user's location can be authenticated. If the distance is considered *un*reasonable or for some reason is not calculable, the user will not be authenticated.[39]

### Information Breach Prevention Checklist

- Avoid placing secure login boxes on insecure pages. Nearly one-half of all financial institutions violate this critical security measure.

  A hacker could reroute data entered in the boxes or create a spoof copy of the page to harvest information. In a wireless situation, it is possible to conduct this man-in-the-middle attack without changing the bank URL for the user, so even a security-conscious customer could fall victim.

  Use the standard secure socket layer (SSL) protocol on pages that ask for sensitive information. (SSL-protected pages begin with https rather than http.) Most banks use SSL technology for *some* of their pages, but only a minority secure *all* their pages this way.

- Avoid putting contact information and security advice on insecure pages. Fifty-five percent of banks fail to enforce this standard.

  Cyber-attackers could change an address or phone number and set up their own call center to gather private data from customers who need help. The problem is that banks tend to be less cautious with information that is easy to find elsewhere. But online banking customers trust that the information on the bank's site is correct.

  Secure these pages with the standard SSL protocol.

- Safeguard the chain of trust. When a bank redirects customers to a site outside of its domain for certain transactions without warning, it immediately puts online customers at risk. This problem often arises when banks outsource some of their security functions.

  Warn users that they will be leaving your bank's site to go to a trusted new site. Or house all of its pages on the same server.

- Strengthen user ID and password security. A surprisingly large percentage of financial institutions still use Social Security numbers or e-mail addresses as user IDs. Although this information is easy for customers to remember, it is also easy for a fraudster to guess or find out.

  It is also important to implement technology that prohibits creation of usernames and passwords that are too weak to withstand modern cyber-attacks.

- Prohibit e-mailing of security-sensitive information. The e-mail data path in online banking is generally not secure. For that reason, financial statements and other sensitive documents should never be e-mailed to customers.

    A simple notification is safest. However, if the bank provides a link to statements or other sensitive information, customers become more vulnerable to phishing attacks. If the bank sends an actual statement via unencrypted e-mail, the statement is subject to eavesdropping by cyber-criminals.[40]

### Credit/Debit Card Fraud Prevention Checklist

Because so many credit card and debit card frauds result directly from theft of victims' card data and subsequent counterfeiting of credit and debit cards, many preventive measures that banks are now taking to reduce card fraud tighten technological and procedural controls over secure customer data.

However, because credit card fraud is among the fastest-growing crimes in America, it is unlikely that any combination of preventive measures will materially reduce the incidence of such fraud in the foreseeable future.

Nonetheless, issuing banks must comply with all federal and state credit card and identity theft prevention and remediation regulations.

- Work more closely with merchants to implement point-of-sale card fraud prevention measures. These include:
  - Asking for photo identification of all customers presenting credit cards for payment.
  - Examining the signature on the card. (If the signature on the credit card is smeared, it could be that the credit card is stolen and the person has changed the signature to his or her own.)
  - Comparing signatures. Besides comparing the signature on the credit card with the person's signature on the credit card slip, compare the signatures to that on a driver's license.
  - Checking the security features of the credit card. Have another look at the card's signature panel. It should show a repetitive color design of the MasterCard or Visa name. Altered signature panels (those that are discolored, glued, painted, erased, or covered with white tape) are an indication of credit card fraud.
  - Checking the credit card's embossing. Ghost images of other numbers behind the embossing are a tip-off that the card has been re-embossed. The hologram may be damaged. (Holograms on credit cards that have not been tampered with will show clear, three-dimensional images that appear to move when the card is tilted.)[41]
- Maintaining full compliance with Payment Card Industry Data Security Standards (PCI-DSS). For full details on latest compliance requirements, visit the PCI Security Standards Council Web site at www.pcisecuritystandards.org.

### Check Fraud Prevention Checklist

■ Store unprinted check stock in a locked filing cabinet under dual control, where two locks are on the cabinet and two different people hold one of the keys. Store check signature plates the same way. This helps prevent collusion with dishonest outsiders.

■ Secure boxes of unopened check stock.

■ Avoid ordering too many blank checks at a time.

■ Enforce check limits. This serves as a stop-loss control over cash disbursement, to prevent collusion with dishonest vendors.

■ Use positive pay as well as payee positive pay and even reverse positive pay if your bank offers it.

■ Use anti-counterfeiting check security features, such as copy-void pantographs, embedded fluorescent fibers, custom layer check borders, and latest-technology watermarks.

■ Conduct prompt bank reconciliations. The longer they are put off, the longer a check fraud scheme that might show up in the form of red flags in the statement can continue undetected.

■ Ensure that all disbursement checks are mailed immediately after processing to minimize the opportunity for insiders to intercept them.[42]

### ACH Fraud Prevention Checklist

■ Implement ACH blocks and filters on all accounts except those from which the institution decides to allow ACH payments to be paid.

■ Implement debit blocks and debit filters on all applicable accounts to prevent unauthorized/fraudulent ACH debits from your accounts.

■ Use ACH positive pay where advance authorization is provided for specific ACH debits that match all criteria posted to the institution's account, such as federal or state payroll tax payments.

■ Separate accounts for ACH debits from those for ACH credits.

■ Promptly return all fraudulent ACH debits.

■ Conduct more frequent bank reconciliations to screen for fraudulent electronic transactions.[43]

### Vendor Fraud Prevention Checklist

■ Conduct thorough due diligence on all suppliers and subcontractors. Treat suppliers or subcontractors as you would your own employees by screening them before establishing a business relationship. How long has the company been in business? What is its track record? Who has it worked with in the past? What do customers say about it?[44]

■ Watch out for conflicts of interest. Scrutinize potential personal relationships that might exist between the organization and a supplier or subcontractor. For example, are there common family members in responsible positions in both organizations? Although this alone is not necessarily a problem, it does suggest that the proposed relationship should be scrutinized a little more carefully.

- Require a W-9 with EIN/TIN matching for all new vendors.

- Conduct periodic vendor master file cleanup to flag duplicate/phony vendors.

- Screen new vendors against Office of Foreign Asset Control watch lists.

- Establish vendor coding standards.

- Review vendors that have the same name but are operating from multiple addresses.

- Review invoices that have been paid without a purchase order reference.

- Review consecutive invoice numbering.

- Review duplicate or similar invoices.

- Forensically examine all other pertinent vendor documents for anomalies or other irregularities.[45]

---

### LOAN FRAUD PREVENTION TECHNOLOGY

Your institution should consider these technology options for bolstering its anti-fraud efforts:

- Use a case management database. These databases can be purchased from numerous reputable vendors. At a minimum, establish an internal tracking system to track suspicious activity incidents. An internal tracking database should capture key data elements to allow for reporting and trending, such as:

  - The sources of the loan (third party, branch, etc.)
  - Borrower/co-borrower(s)
  - Property address
  - Seller name(s), to determine if duplicate problem loans exist
  - Loan officer/originator, to determine if the same person or company is responsible for the origination of delinquent or suspect loans and misrepresenting or abusing existing policy
  - Closing attorney/settlement agent, to cross-check suspicious activity or delinquency with the closing agent or company and detect unusual patterns and closing company involvement in fraud
  - Appraiser or appraisal firm, to cross-check suspicious activity or delinquency with appraisers or appraisal firms to detect unusual patterns for inflated values

- Use a front-end fraud detection vendor to screen key loan transaction information. These vendors compare loan data with national databases and verification services to identify data integrity issues and red flags.

- Use external address lists (e.g., U.S. Postal Inspection Service Hot Address File, superfund site list) to identify problematic addresses.

- Implement a software program to identify high-risk changes of address based on ZIP+4 and average incomes for that ZIP code.

## EMPLOYEES: YOUR ORGANIZATION'S EYES AND EARS AGAINST FRAUD

Well-informed and trained employees are the first line of defense against external (*and* internal) fraud.

Employees should be able to recognize loan fraud red flags and know the process for escalating suspicious activity incidents. Early detection and prevention by employees can reduce the financial institution's risk of increased operating costs and reduce financial and reputational risk. Solid employee training and awareness programs and a written code of conduct policy will greatly reduce financial losses to both the institution and its shareholders.

Loan fraud awareness should be incorporated into new employee or department orientation programs if possible.

A number of institutions use annual certification programs that are Web based or formal classroom training to ensure that all employees are up-to-date with awareness programs.

Additionally, fraud newsletters or fraud alerts distributed via the company intranet help employees to stay abreast of new fraud scams and schemes.[46]

## ▶ Review Points

- Construction fraud makes up a significant portion of nonmortgage loan fraud. Approximately 10 percent of total construction expenditures is lost to fraud every year.

- Additional forms of nonmortgage loan fraud include bid-rigging schemes, asset-based or working capital scams, floor plan/dealer frauds, and asset-shifting schemes.

- Mortgage fraud breaks down into two main categories: fraud for property and fraud for profit. Fraud for property typically is committed by prospective homeowners who falsify loan documents because they do meet bank underwriting standards. Fraud for profit is committed by outsiders, such as mortgage brokers, appraisers, attorneys, and builders, to fraudulently obtain banking financing to perpetrate illegal property purchases and sales.

- Social engineering is technically not a type of fraud. Rather it is a psychological tactic aimed at obtaining information needed to commit fraud.

- Phishing is an Internet-based—or cyber—version of conventional social engineering using e-mail to harvest victims' confidential personal data, which subsequently are used to commit identity theft and fraud.

- Unlike phishing attacks, information security breaches target the secure networks of financial institutions and other organizations, such as national retail chains, to steal very large volumes of customer data.

- Online account takeover often is performed by organized fraudsters (from virtually anywhere in the world).

- Many, if not most, external fraud against financial institutions involves some form of identity theft or fraud. Credit and debit card fraud, check fraud, ACH fraud, social engineering, and so on typically are perpetrated with theft of individuals' identities or creation of fictitious identities.

- Purchasing card (P-card) fraud hurts financial institutions in two ways: through unauthorized use by employee cardholders and through theft of P-card data by outside cyber-criminals who use it to perpetrate identity frauds of various kinds.

- Although ACH debit transactions are gradually replacing checks for settlement of business-to-business transactions, check fraud continues to grow at around 25 percent a year.

- Check fraud against financial institutions takes the form of counterfeiting, forgery, and other forms of illegal alteration. However, positive pay, payee positive pay, and other bank-provided anti-fraud services are highly effective in thwarting would-be external check fraudsters.

- Check kiting, another costly crime affecting banks, involves illegal use of deposit accounts and abuse of the check-clearing timing factors.

- With respect to internal operations, procurement is one financial institution function that is especially vulnerable to external fraud. Dishonest vendors who perpetrate a variety of billing schemes top the list, with kickback and bribery schemes between crooked vendors and dishonest insiders also posing serious threats.

## ▶ Chapter Quiz

True or False:

1. Falsely overstating property appraisal values is a form of mortgage fraud for profit.

   ❏ True ❏ False

2. Straw buyers are loan applicants who are used by fraudsters to obtain home loans and have no intention of occupying the home being purchased.

   ❏ True ❏ False

3. Straw buyer mortgage fraud schemes never involve unknowing collaboration by the buyer.

   ❏ True ❏ False

4. Although the number of insider-perpetrated information security breaches has been relatively small, the average number of records lost to insider attacks is approximately three times greater than those committed by outsiders.

   ❏ True ❏ False

5. Some sophisticated credit card frauds involve the sale of large batches of stolen credit card records to third parties, often organized crime rings located in Western Europe and Africa.

   ❏ True    ❏ False

6. Sophisticated cyber-criminals have learned how to steal not only the debit card data but also the encrypted PIN data that goes along with the cards.

   ❏ True    ❏ False

7. Prices on invoices from the same vendor that are plus or minus .3 percent of each other may indicate a billing fraud.

   ❏ True    ❏ False

8. Kickback schemes perpetrated by insiders have many of the same characteristics as those committed by external fraudsters.

   ❏ True    ❏ False

9. It is almost always just as easy for a dishonest mortgage broker or borrower's attorney to doctor the asset or employment information on a mortgage application as it is for a mortgage loan officer to do so.

   ❏ True    ❏ False

Circle the correct answer to the following questions:

10. All of the following are examples of construction fraud EXCEPT:

    a. Tools theft

    b. Product substitution

    c. Vehicle loan fraud

    d. Employee ghosting

11. One of the common ways that asset-based financing fraud is committed is by:

    a. Cutting costs to make the company's financial condition appear better than it is.

    b. Creating false invoices to document bogus receivables.

    c. Hiring additional employees to create the false appearance of growth.

    d. Submitting documentation falsely reflecting management's lack of financial interest in vendors doing business with the company.

12. Most subprime mortgage frauds involve at least one of the follow elements EXCEPT:

    a. Indicating that the borrower will occupy a property when he or she is actually buying it as an investment.

    b. Having the appraiser falsely undervalue the actual value of the property.

    c. Falsifying a borrower's employment history by having a friend or relative who owns a business say the person works there.

    d. Hiding a critical piece of information or not disclosing something about the loan and hoping the lender will not find out.

**13.** Which of the following is NOT an example of mortgage fraud for profit?

    **a.** Chunking

    **b.** Builder bailout schemes

    **c.** Equity skimming

    **d.** Falsification of personal assets, income, etc. on a mortgage application

**14.** In the area of online banking fraud, the name of the software commonly planted on a victim's hard drive to record keystrokes is:

    **a.** Spyware

    **b.** Trojan horse

    **c.** Spam

    **d.** Phishing

**15.** In enforcing the Red Flags requirements of the FACT Act, bank regulatory agencies will be monitoring institutions to determine if they are complying with the act's requirement to perform a(n):

    **a.** Covered accounts assessment

    **b.** Identity theft risk review

    **c.** Enterprise-wide risk assessment

    **d.** Change of address validation program

**16.** All of the following are possible red flags of employment-related mortgage application fraud EXCEPT:

    **a.** Employer's address is a post office box, the property address, or applicant's current residence.

    **b.** Employment verification form contains whiting out, erasures, or other signs of alteration.

    **c.** Employer cannot be contacted.

    **d.** Applicant is self-employed and has his or her tax return prepared by a professional paid preparer.

Circle *all* correct answers to the following questions:

**17.** According to the U.S. Department of Justice's Computer Crime Section, the most popular ways of perpetrating data breaches are:

    **a.** War driving, where hackers penetrate wireless networks

    **b.** Internet-based attacks

    **c.** Malicious code

    **d.** Web spoofing

**18.** Which of the following are potential red flags of appraisal fraud:

    **a.** Owner is someone other than the seller indicated on the sales contract.

    **b.** Appraisal indicates that the transaction is a refinance, but other documentation reflects a purchase.

    **c.** Appraisal is dated after the sales contract date.

    **d.** Purchase price is substantially higher than prevailing market values.

**19.** Which of the following are potential red flags of check fraud?

  **a.** Authorized signatures are missing or appear forged.

  **b.** Vendors or other payees complain about not receiving payments.

  **c.** Blank checks are missing.

  **d.** Canceled checks have fraudulent endorsements or dual endorsements.

Fill in the blank:

**20.** Mortgage fraud has been around since the early days of American banking history. It did *not* begin with the _____ crisis.

**21.** _____ is a psychological tactic aimed at obtaining information needed to commit fraud.

**22.** The crime of sending out thousands of phony e-mails to consumers urging them to click on a link that will enable them to "update" their bank account information is called _____.

**23.** Intentionally writing checks against accounts with insufficient funds and withdrawing cash before they bounce is a crime known as _____.

**24.** A builder's overanxiousness to sell a property may be a red flag of a _____."

*For the answers, please turn to Appendix A.*

# CHAPTER SEVEN

# Conducting a Successful Fraud Risk Assessment

As discussed in Chapter 5, there is a general consensus among anti-fraud experts that conducting a fraud risk assessment (FRA) is critical to the process of detecting—and ultimately designing controls to prevent—specific types of fraud threatening the organization.

FRAs do not necessarily tell you exactly what types of fraud are occurring in your organization. Instead, they are designed to focus your detection efforts on specific fraud schemes and scenarios that could occur as well as on incidents that have occurred in the past. Once these are identified, your audit team can proceed with the series of basic and specific fraud detection exercises that are presented in Chapter 8. The results of these exercises will reveal the specific fraud schemes that your organization is most exposed to. This information will enable your organization's audit team to recommend to management and support the implementation of anti-fraud controls designed for exactly those risks that have been identified.

## Remember

Fraud risk assessments are not meant to prevent fraud directly. They are exercises for identifying specific fraud schemes and scenarios that your bank is most vulnerable to. That information is in turn used to conduct fraud audit exercises that pinpoint actual frauds that have occurred or *could* occur so that the necessary controls can be put into place to prevent the at-risk illegal activity.

## ► Getting It Done

FRAs sometimes are usually conducted by the organization's external auditors. Increasingly, however, internal auditors are being pressured by senior management to conduct FRAs of their own. This can be effective when internal auditors have the tenure and experience with your organization to know better than anyone how its financial and business operations function and can understand more readily how fraud could occur in particular processes, transactions, and business procedures.

In addition, as the Federal Reserve Bank of St. Louis states:

> Audit personnel normally aren't involved in daily operations and can provide an independent check of the bank's risk management process. Audits can be considered a second channel of information on how well the bank's anti-fraud controls are functioning and whether there are any deficiencies that need to be corrected. To ensure this channel remains independent, it is important that the audit function report directly to the Audit Committee or the board of directors and not to the chief executive officer or bank president who may have responsibility for the bank's internal controls.[1]

Some anti-fraud experts claim that having internal auditors conduct FRAs is unwise since these individuals are on the organization's payroll and therefore lack the independence required to objectively analyze weaknesses that could provide opportunities for fraudsters. However, the same can be said for external auditors. Although not employees of the organization, they are paid by their clients to conduct FRAs, thus establishing the same potential compromise of independence.

Thus, if auditor independence is an issue for your institution, one solution may be to rotate members of the internal audit department so that they are not partial to a specific activity within their department. Alternatively, it may be prudent to retain an outside firm specializing in fraud risk assessments with no ambitions for a long-term business relationship and therefore no ax to grind.

The Institute of Internal Auditors has endorsed audit standards that outline the techniques and procedures for conducting an FRA—specifically those contained in *Statement of Auditing Standards 99 (SAS 99)*. In this (and other) key guidelines, an FRA is meant to assist auditors and/or fraud examiners in adjusting their audit and investigation plans and in testing to focus on gathering evidence of potential fraud schemes and scenarios identified by the FRA.

In essence, regardless of who conducts the FRA, responding to its findings requires the auditor to adjust the timing, nature, and extent of testing in such ways as:

- Performing procedures at physical locations on a surprise or unannounced basis by, for example, counting cash at different branches on a surprise basis or reviewing loan portfolios of random loan officers or divisions of the bank on a surprise basis.

- Requesting that financial performance data be evaluated at the end of the reporting period or on a date closer to period-end, in order, for example, to minimize the risk of manipulation of records in the period between the dates of loan closings and the end of the reporting period.

- Making oral inquiries of major customers and vendors in addition to sending written confirmations, or sending confirmation requests to a specific party within an organization.

- Performing substantive analytical procedures using disaggregated data by, for example, comparing gross profit or operating margins by branch, type of service, line of business, or month to auditor-developed expectations.

- Interviewing personnel involved in activities in areas where a risk of material misstatement due to fraud has been identified (such as at the country or regional level) to obtain their insights about the risk and how controls could address the risk.[2]

It is essential that most internal financial operations managers and audit professionals understand how to conduct an FRA, in order to thoroughly assess the organization's exposure to specific frauds so that they can perform the kind of direct role described here. That role must lead to management's formulation and implementation of the specific, customized controls designed to mitigate each type of fraud risk identified in the FRA. These are the measures that go beyond the basic, essential control checklists contained in previous chapters; they optimize the organization's defenses against these risks. As such, they vary from organization to organization, in accordance with the particular processes and procedures that may be vulnerable to fraud.

For example, Bank A may process invoices in such a tightly controlled way—with double or triple approvals of new vendors, manual review of all invoices, and so on—that an FRA reveals few if any areas where red flags of vendor fraud can be found. Bank B, in contrast, may process invoices simply by having the appropriate department head review and approve them. In that case, an FRA would raise red flags of potential fraud that could occur through double billing, sham company schemes, or collusion between a dishonest vendor and a bank insider.

As *SAS 99* indicates:

> Some risks are inherent in the environment of the entity, but most can be addressed with an appropriate system of internal control.
>
> Once fraud risk assessment has taken place, the entity can identify the processes, controls, and other procedures that are needed to mitigate the identified risks. Effective internal controls will include well-developed control environment, an effective and secure information system, and appropriate control and monitoring activities.
>
> Because of the importance of information technology in supporting operations and the processing of transactions, management also needs to implement and maintain appropriate controls, whether automated or manual, over computer-generated information.[3]

## ▶ Procedures for Conducting a Fraud Risk Assessment

> The heart of an effective internal controls system and the effectiveness of an anti-fraud program are . . . contingent on an effective risk management assessment.
>
> — Dr. Tommie Singleton, CPA, University of Alabama

Although conducting an FRA is not terribly difficult, it does require careful planning and methodical execution. The structure and culture of the organization dictate how the FRA is formulated. In general, however, there is a mainstream form of FRA that the audit and fraud prevention communities have agreed on. The next pages outline the essentials of that approach.

As *Managing the Business Risk of Fraud*, published by the American Institute of Certified Public Accountants, the Institute of Internal Auditors, and the Association of Certified Fraud Examiners, explains:

> Assessing the likelihood and significance of each potential fraud risk is a subjective process that should consider not only monetary significance, but also *significance to an organization's reputation* and its legal and regulatory compliance requirements.
>
> An initial assessment of fraud risk should consider the inherent risk of a particular fraud in the absence of any known controls that may address the risk. An organization can cost-effectively manage its fraud risks by assessing the likelihood and significance of fraudulent behavior.[4] (Emphasis added.)

Your FRA must be tailored to your organization's specific business functions, structure, and culture, but several basic FRA methods apply to most conventional FRAs.

## ■ Step 1: Create an FRA Team

The FRA team should include a senior internal auditor (or the chief internal auditor, if feasible) and/or an experienced outside certified fraud examiner with substantial experience in conducting FRAs for organizations in the financial services industry.

According to the Basel Committee on Banking Supervision:

> The management of the internal audit department [should] prepare a plan for all the assignments to be performed. The audit plan includes the timing and frequency of planned internal audit work. This audit plan is based on a methodical control risk assessment. A control risk assessment documents the internal auditor's understanding of the institution's significant activities and their associated risks. The management of the internal audit department should establish the principles of the risk assessment methodology in writing and regularly update them to reflect changes to the system of internal control or work process, and to incorporate new lines of business. The risk analysis examines all of the bank's activities and entities, and the complete internal control system. On the basis of the results of the risk analysis, an audit plan for several years is established, taking into account the degree of risk inherent in the activities. The plan also takes into account expected developments and innovations, the generally higher degree of risk of new activities, and the intention to audit all significant activities and entities within a reasonable time period (audit cycle principle—for example, three years). All those concerns will determine the extent, nature and frequency of the assignments to be performed.[5]

Other members of the team should include:

- Chief financial officer
- Head of purchasing or procurement

- Senior internal audit manager
- Senior risk management manager
- Senior human resources manager
- External consultant(s) with expertise in fraud detection and prevention

## ■ Step 2: Identify the Organization's Universe of Potential Risks

The FRA team's starting point is to determine what fraud schemes and scenarios typically affect financial services companies in general and the organization in particular. Next the team must assess the potential for these schemes and scenarios in the organization, based on past incidents of fraud, the culture of the organization, and its current framework of internal controls.

Employee fraud and embezzlement are most likely to occur in organizations with especially poor tone at the top, weak internal controls, and poor accounting practices. It is also widely accepted that organizations with a culture of excessive emphasis on financial performance—at the expense of employee morale, team spirit, and high-quality work results—are likeliest to be targeted by internal fraudsters. (These trends are especially pronounced during periods of economic weakness—when employees are concerned about job security or possibly even the viability of the organization they work for.)

To identify your organization's specific risks of fraud, the FRA procedure calls for the team leader to conduct brainstorming sessions with the team to develop a list of what *Managing the Business Risk of Fraud* calls the "population" of fraud schemes and scenarios likeliest to occur in the organization.[6] This is often done by evaluating an existing list of common frauds, such as the more than 150 generic fraud schemes developed by PricewaterhouseCoopers Fraud Risk and Controls Practice Leader, Jonny Frank. Frank broke down this large body of common fraud schemes into six key categories:

1. Fraudulent financial reporting
2. Misappropriation of assets
3. Expenditures and liabilities for an improper purpose
4. Revenue and assets obtained by fraud
5. Costs and expenses avoided by fraud
6. Financial misconduct by senior management[7]

To help in this exercise—and to add specific fraud schemes and scenarios to the results of the brainstorming sessions—the team should focus on each key business process in which particular types of fraud from these categories *could* occur, such as earnings manipulation (fraudulent financial reporting), theft and forgery of organization checks (misappropriation of assets), paying bribes (expenditures for an improper purpose), misrepresentation of the value of assets for sale (revenue obtained by fraud), nonpayment of taxes (costs avoided by fraud), and round-tripping transactions (financial misconduct by senior management).

In each area, the team should obtain detailed answers to these questions from managers, supervisors, and/or line employees in each function:

- What types of fraud have occurred or been suspected in the past?
- What types of fraud could be committed against the organization?
- What are the specific ways that employees or managers could commit fraud by acting alone?
- What specific ways could vendors commit fraud in your area?
- How could vendors working in collusion with your coworkers commit fraud?

### Step 3: Analyze the Likelihood of Each Scheme or Scenario Occurring

Fraud risk assessments also must consider the *likelihood* that a particular fraud will occur. International auditing standards specify four risk levels:

1. Remote
2. More than remote
3. Reasonably possible
4. Probable

### Step 4: Assess the Materiality of Risk

In this step, according to Frank, the FRA team must identify fraud risks that could have an important financial impact on the organization's shareholders, lenders, or other users of its financial reports.[8] There are three main categories of materiality:

1. Inconsequential
2. More than inconsequential
3. Material

Any risks that are more than inconsequential must be addressed by auditors to gather detailed evidence of potential fraudulent activity.

### Step 5: Assess Risks within the Context of Existing Anti-Fraud Controls

The organization's FRA team should identify the control activities for those fraud risks that have a more-than-remote likelihood of occurring and that could result in a substantial (or "material" in audit/accounting terminology) loss to the organization. This is because once the FRA and subsequent fraud-auditing work is done, the FRA team will know exactly what controls are missing or require strengthening.

Another way to get to the same result is by evaluating the effectiveness of existing controls in preventing specific fraud scenarios. This process aims to assign a numerical grade for the likelihood of a specific fraud scheme occurring with the existing control in place.

*How this process works.* Assess specific controls in place for preventing occurrence of the various fraud scenarios. Doing so enables auditors to determine how likely (or unlikely) it is—on a scale of 1 to 3—that such a scenario actually will occur based on the controls in place, with 1 representing the most effective possible risk mitigation.

For example:

1. Control design optimally minimizes the occurrence of the fraud risk *and minimizes control failures.*
2. Control design *reasonably* minimizes the occurrence of the fraud risk.
3. Control design *does not* minimize the occurrence of the fraud risk.[9]

The ultimate objective of any FRA is to guide the institution's auditors in adjusting their audit plans to incorporate specific techniques for detecting fraud and to assist management in formulating and/or adjusting its anti-fraud controls to reduce the risk of fraud.

Chapter 9 describes general fraud detection measures that most organizations must put into place but that do not involve audit practices. The latter part of Chapter 9 describes several of the specific audit procedures designed to detect frauds whose risk has been identified through conducting the FRA.

## Remember

In effective FRAs, the FRA team and the organization's internal audit department must consider whether and how anti-fraud controls can be circumvented or overridden by management and others. They also should analyze both internal and external threats to confidential electronic data and computer and network security.

## ▶ Roles of the Board and Management in Fraud Risk Assessments*

None of the steps just outlined for conducting an FRA will occur, let alone be conducted effectively, without direct guidance and buy-in from top management and the board. The board of directors has the responsibility to ensure that management designs effective fraud risk management procedures. Generally, the board delegates this oversight responsibility to the audit committee.

The board should detail these responsibilities in the audit committee's charter as well as its own. That way, there is little opportunity for board or audit committee members who feel that doing an FRA is either too costly or not worthwhile to pass the buck.

---

*This section is adapted from Nidhi Gupta, "The Roles of the Board and Management in Fraud Risk Assessments," *White-Collar Crime Fighter* (November 2008): 3.

To ensure that appropriate steps are taken to identify and prioritize the fraud risks for your organization, the audit committee should:

- Ensure that management assigns the responsibility of FRA and management of identified risks to a qualified individual. Although many individuals within the organization must be involved in the FRA, many organizations undermine their FRA processes by failing to put someone in charge of coordinating the process and reporting to the audit committee. Often a senior member of the organization's internal audit department is best qualified to take on this role. In other organizations, the CFO is best equipped to do it.

  The key is to determine which senior manager has the experience, training, and staff resources to conduct your FRA and to then make that person fully accountable for conducting and reporting on the FRA by specified deadlines.

- Evaluate the FRA process and methodology implemented by management. The audit committee must understand and question management on the methods used to conduct an FRA. The aim is to constantly improve the effectiveness and efficiency of the FRA process.

  The goal is to ensure that the organization's fraud risks are properly prioritized by using an effective ranking system, as discussed earlier.

  Because there is no single standard for conducting an FRA, the methodology and documentation of the risk assessment process must be tailored to the organization's size, complexity, industry, and goals. Again, internal audit's familiarity with these factors often proves valuable in determining whether management's risk assessment methodology is effective.

- Be aware of and concur with management's risk tolerance. It is impossible to address every fraud risk that is revealed by the risk assessment process. There are simply not enough financial and human resources to eliminate all of the vulnerabilities that exist at any given time. Internal audit or whichever team is responsible for conducting and reporting on the FRA therefore must prioritize and report to management and the audit committee on its ranking of the fraud risk it has identified.

  The audit committee then must monitor and be prepared to question management's choice to downgrade the threat of certain key fraud risks. For example, internal audit may determine through the FRA process that ACH fraud is not a serious threat to the organization because all of the available anti-fraud controls (e.g., debit blocks, debit filters, and account segregation) have been well established and are accomplishing the goal of minimizing the risk of this type of fraud.

  It is the audit committee's job to ensure that it is getting up-to-date reporting like this from internal audit and to determine if it concurs with the information. Ultimately, this critical input should help the committee to decide when to press for better internal controls where it sees the need for them.

- A fraud risk assessment is an analysis of an organization's risks of being victimized by specific types of fraud.

- Approaches to FRAs will differ from organization to organization, but most FRAs focus on identifying fraud risks in six key categories:

  1. Fraudulent financial reporting

  2. Misappropriation of assets

  3. Expenditures and liabilities for an improper purpose

  4. Revenue and assets obtained by fraud

  5. Costs and expenses avoided by fraud

  6. Financial misconduct by senior management

- A properly conducted FRA guides auditors in adjusting their audit plans and testing to focus specifically on gathering evidence of possible fraud.

- Being able to conduct an FRA is essential to effective assessment of the viability of existing anti-fraud controls and to strengthen the organization's inadequate controls, as identified by the results of your FRA.

- In addition to assessing the types of fraud for which your organization is at risk, the FRA assesses the likelihood that each of those frauds might occur.

- After the FRA and subsequent fraud auditing work is completed, the FRA team should have a good idea of the specific controls needed to minimize the organization's vulnerability to fraud.

- Auditing for fraud is a critical next step after assessing fraud risks, and this requires auditing for evidence of frauds that may exist according to the red flags turned up by your FRA.

▶ **Chapter Quiz**

True or False:

1. Fraud risk assessments typically are conducted by an organization's external auditors, not its internal auditors.

   ❑ True   ❑ False

2. FRAs often produce better results when internal auditors conduct them instead of external auditors because they are more familiar with the organization's internal workings.

   ❑ True   ❑ False

3. The board of directors in most organizations delegates oversight of the FRA process to the governance committee.

   ❑ True   ❑ False

4. An FRA is meant to guide executives in gathering evidence of potential fraud schemes and scenarios identified by the FRA.

   ❑ True ❑ False

Circle the answer to the following questions:

5. Which of the following is NOT a critical member of the FRA team?

   a. Finance manager

   b. Regional audit manager

   c. Director of procurement

   d. Information technology (IT) director

6. Which of the following is NOT a risk level of fraud that is assigned to specific fraud risks identified by an FRA?

   a. Remote

   b. Extremely likely

   c. More than remote

   d. Reasonably possible

Fill in the blank:

7. One of the key exercises in an FRA is determining the _____ of specific fraud schemes or scenarios occurring.

8. The ultimate objective of conducting an FRA is to optimize_____.

9. The appropriate exercise for identifying the organization's specific fraud risk is a _____ session.

10. The three generally accepted categories for ranking the materiality of a specific fraud risk are *inconsequential, more than inconsequential,* and _____.

*For the answers, please turn to Appendix A.*

# Legal and Regulatory Compliance for Controlling Fraud Risk

According to the Fidelity National Information Services, a provider of banking services including compliance-related guidance, there are 48 primary federal laws and regulations that directly affect banking operations and to which financial institutions must comply.

Many of these have numerous subregulations in the form of specific statutes, regulatory agency rules, or industry standards. For example, under Regulation Z, also known as the Truth in Lending Act (which alone runs 541 pages), a provision protects consumers from overcharges on finance charges. Other regulatory measures protect consumers against predatory lending or discrimination in lending practices. As succinctly explained in a report by the Congressional Research Service:

> Nearly every aspect of the operation and management of an insured institution is subject to close regulatory supervision. In an economic sense, bankers and regulators are business partners: a bank that becomes insolvent is not just a business failure; it also represents a failure of regulation.[1]

Moreover, five main federal regulatory bodies keep an eye on U.S. financial services activities, each with its own voluminous set of banking regulations. These bodies include:

1. Federal Reserve Board (FRB)
2. Federal Deposit Insurance Corporation (FDIC)
3. Office of the Comptroller of the Currency (OCC)
4. Office of Thrift Supervision (OTS)
5. National Credit Union Administration (NCUA)

In addition, if you visit the Web site www.complianceforbankers.com/ifs_cd_legislative_observer.htm at any time, you will see a list of new regulatory proposals or guidelines that are in the legislative or regulatory process or are about to go into effect.

U.S. banks bear a regulatory and legal compliance burden unparalleled in any other American industry. Of course, most financial institution rules and regulations are unrelated to fraud. They are designed to protect customers against losses, prevent the use of banks as conduits for terrorist financing, ensure fairness in lending practices, and other key objectives. However, plenty of regulations are designed to mitigate banks' vulnerability to fraudsters, information thieves, or money launderers. Some examples from the United States Code (U.S.C.) include:

18 U.S.C. § 215: Bank bribery

18 U.S.C. § 656: Theft or embezzlement of bank funds

18 U.S.C. § 709: False advertising or misuse of federal terms, such as "federal deposit insurance"

18 U.S.C. § 1005: False entries by bank employees or false statements to regulators

18 U.S.C. § 1014: False statements on a loan or credit application

18 U.S.C. § 1029: Access device fraud

18 U.S.C. § 1344: Bank fraud[2]

There are two problems with these regulations:

1. Many of the laws and regulations do not accomplish what their legislative or regulatory authors intended. Many industry experts will tell you that because Congress and many regulatory bodies are populated by individuals who have no experience in the banking industry, they are fundamentally incapable of writing laws and regulations that work well. The dilemma lies in the banking industry's rich history of being both perpetrator and victim of misconduct, unfair business practices, deception, greed, and, yes, fraud. Even the most outspoken advocates of less government involvement in the banking industry would agree that some rules of fair play and for the protection of investors, customers, and the general public are appropriate.

2. Achieving and sustaining compliance with all of the existing rules is a herculean task, to put it mildly. According to some observers, many of these rules lose their effectiveness simply due to the sheer burden of achieving and sustaining compliance. In other words, say these experts, banks spend so much time dotting the *i*'s and crossing the *t*'s to comply with laws and regulations that they lose sight of the actual purpose of the measures, and their effectiveness is lost in the process.

Although it would be impossible to detail the many anti-fraud provisions of laws and regulations applicable to the financial services industry, this chapter addresses the most important laws designed to reduce the exposure of banks to internal and external financial crime.

Despite the understandable griping by bank executives about the excessive burden of regulation, the costly fraud problem discussed in previous chapters will not go away of its own accord. It is therefore in banks' own self-interest to devote sufficient human and financial resources to comply with and implement the provisions of certain laws that *can* have a meaningful impact in reducing exposure to fraud. Some key examples follow.

## ■ Sarbanes-Oxley Act

Known as SOX, this law was passed in 2002 in the wake of the string of massive corporate scandals, such as those that destroyed Enron and WorldCom and caused serious financial and reputational damage at Tyco, Adelphia, and Xerox.

The primary objective of SOX was to establish preventive measures against fraudulent financial reporting in public companies. SOX requires implementation and monitoring of internal controls over financial reporting as well as top executive certification of the accuracy—including the absence of fraud—of all financial reports.

Although banks, along with most other publicly traded companies, initially strained under the onerous financial burden of implementing the necessary controls, testing procedures, and other compliance measures associated with SOX, studies prove that the cost of compliance has steadily declined since the law's enactment. Although in recent years there have been attempts to repeal SOX or to "lighten" its compliance standards, these initiatives have proven unsuccessful. Yet attempts by special interest groups to have SOX declared unconstitutional continue to make their way through the legislative and legal systems.

Meanwhile, many executives now admit that having implemented SOX has had a beneficial impact on the accuracy and reliability of financial statements and on investors' confidence in the financial reporting of their organizations.

Regardless of management's feelings about SOX, there is no getting around complying with its provisions, at least for the foreseeable future. Doing so boils down to how then–Federal Reserve board member Susan Bies explained SOX in 2003 to the American Banker's Association Regulatory Compliance Committee:

- The message for boards of directors is: uphold your responsibility for ensuring the effectiveness of the company's overall governance process.

- The message for audit committees is: uphold your responsibility for ensuring that the company's internal and external audit processes are rigorous and effective.

- The message for chief executive and chief financial officers and senior management is: uphold your responsibility to maintain effective financial reporting and disclosure controls and adhere to high ethical standards. This requires meaningful certifications, codes of ethics, and conduct for insiders that, if violated, will result in fines and criminal penalties, including imprisonment.

- The message for external auditors is: focus your efforts solely on auditing financial statements and leave the add-on services to other consultants.

- The message for internal auditors is: you are uniquely positioned within the company to ensure that its corporate governance, financial reporting and disclosure controls, and risk management practices are functioning effectively. Although internal auditors are not specifically mentioned in the Sarbanes-Oxley Act, they have within their purview of internal control the responsibility to examine and evaluate all of an entity's systems, processes, operations, functions, and activities.[3]

More relevant to the potential damage that can be caused by lax or poorly designed internal controls, the Federal Reserve Bank of New York (FRBNY), in a report on sound practices for bank internal controls, stated:

> An institution may be subjected to both financial and reputational risk if accounting data is inaccurate. An adverse impact on share prices and reputation has been noted in prior instances involving major financial restatements by publicly traded corporations.
> Some of the most notable accounting missteps by corporations have resulted in legal penalties, fines, prison terms, and the downsizing and/or dissolution of the entity. . . . To date, the majority of known accounting frauds have occurred at non-financial companies, though some financial institutions have had adverse publicity and in some cases restated financial statements due to problems with certain transactions such as securitized assets. The specific financial controls appropriate for financial institutions depend on the organization's size, complexity, and operations. However, as a result of a recent study of financial controls at a number of large, complex banking institutions in the Second Federal Reserve District, we have identified a number of industry sound practices for financial controls that may have a broader relevance for the industry.[4]

Details of the "sound practices" that the FRBNY refers to can be found in the full document. A summary of the practices appears in Exhibit 8.1.

SOX, together with additional guidelines developed by regulators since its enactment in 2002, contains some valuable guidelines for key anti-fraud issues, such as:

- Implementation of a code of ethics for senior executives and accounting officers

- Preparation and certification of financial reports

- Implementation of clear policies prohibiting conflicts of interest

- Loans to bank officers and directors

- Implementation and monitoring of internal controls over financial reporting

- Protection of whistleblowers against retaliation for reporting fraud or misconduct they detect in their day-to-day activities

- Industry-developed practices for optimizing the effectiveness of internal controls

## ■ FDIC Improvement Act Section 112

Since 2005, FDIC-insured financial institutions with assets in excess of $1 billion have been subject to Section 112 of the FDIC Improvement Act (FDICIA 112),

| 1. | Institutions establish clear accountability for the development, implementation, and review of financial controls. |
|---|---|
| 2. | Accounting and finanace staff are knowledgeable and independent. |
| 3. | Institutions develop and periodically update their corporate accounting policies and procedures framework. |
| 4. | Institutions have processes and competent staff in place to ensure that relevant accounting standards are reviewed and implemented throughout the organization. |
| 5. | Institutions have comprehensive global general ledger (G/L) frameworks and a detailed chart of accounts. |
| 6. | Institutions have formal processes for account openings and closings and monitoring of inactive accounts. |
| 7. | Institutions have formal account ownership processes and periodically confirm account ownership responsibilities. |
| 8. | Institutions have appropriate account reconciliation frameworks based on risk. |
| 9. | Institutions establish account aging processes and develop defined write-off guidelines. |
| 10. | Institutions have processes to facilitate timely, complete, and accurate financial closings. |
| 11. | Boards/audit committees and senior management exercise effective oversight of financial controls. |

**Exhibit 8.1:** Summary of Industry Sound Practices for Financial Institutions
Source: Federal Reserve Bank of New York.

which requires annual audited financial statements and an attestation on internal controls over financial reporting by management with a sign-off by the bank's external audit firm. As a result of these rules, impacted institutions are required to implement an effective control framework.

The only problem, according to the Federal Reserve Bank of New York, is that "neither FDICIA 112 nor its implementing regulations or accompanying guidance, however, provides details as to what constitutes adequate or sufficient controls over financial reporting."[5] Filling this gap was one of the intended purposes of the authors of Section 404, which adds considerable detail to the rules governing implementation and monitoring of internal controls.

## ■ Information Security Laws, Rules, and Guidelines

As described in Chapter 4, because a large proportion of fraud committed against banks today involves the illegal use of stolen customer or bank data, some of the newest and most important laws and regulations that management must be aware of and comply with relate to the safeguarding of confidential data both from internal theft and from breaches of the bank's information security defenses by outside criminals.

In fact, due to the increased frequency of breaches of bank information security systems, many financial institutions are allocating increased monetary and human resources to minimize the risk that they will be victimized by internal or outside info-thieves.

Chapter 4 listed several of the key preventive measures for securing confidential information. Unfortunately, there is no silver bullet for fully protecting the organization from the growing threat of information theft. Yet implementing the measures listed in Chapter 4 as well as some of the *required* provisions of federal banking regulators can at least lower the risk of a costly breach occurring. This is particularly true since federal enforcement agencies are becoming increasingly active in monitoring compliance with the critical rules governing the safeguarding of customer credit card data, bank account information, Social Security numbers, and other personal identifying information.

Among these key rules are the Federal Reserve Board's critical *Interagency Guidelines Establishing Information Security Standards,* which defines "customer information" as:

> any record containing nonpublic personal information about an individual who has obtained a financial product or service from the institution that is to be used primarily for personal, family, or household purposes and who has an ongoing relationship with the institution.[6]

Under the *Interagency Guidelines,* "customer information" refers not only to information pertaining to people who do business with the bank (i.e., consumers). It also encompasses, for example, information about:

> (1) an individual who applies for but does not obtain a loan; (2) an individual who guarantees a loan; (3) an employee; or (4) a prospective employee. A financial institution must [also] require, by contract, its service providers that have access to consumer information to develop appropriate measures for the proper disposal of the information.[7]

The FRB's *Guidelines* are to a large extent drawn from the information protection provisions of the Gramm Leach Bliley Act (GLBA) of 1999, which repealed the Depression-era Glass-Steagall Act that substantially restricted banking activities. However, GLBA is best known for its formalization of legal standards for the protection of private customer information and for rules and requirements of organizations to safeguard such information. Since its enactment, numerous additional rules and standards have been put into place to fine-tune the measures that banks and other organizations must take to protect consumers from the identity-related crimes that information theft inevitably leads to. The Red Flags Rules of the FACT Act, discussed in Chapter 6, represent some of the most detailed and onerous measures for customer information protection and identity theft prevention to be passed into law in several years. To audit for a bank's compliance with the Red Flags Rules, download the free, useful audit guidelines at www.bankersonline. com/tools/redflagaudit_lg.pdf.

Among GLBA's most important information security provisions affecting financial institutions is the so-called Financial Privacy Rule. It requires banks to provide consumers with a privacy notice at the time the consumer relationship is established and every year after that.

The notice must provide details collected about the consumer, where that information is shared, how that information is used, and how it is protected.

Each time the privacy notice is renewed, the consumer must be given the choice to opt out of the organization's right to share the information with third-party entities. That means that if bank customers do *not* want their information sold to another company that will in all likelihood use it for marketing purposes, they must indicate that preference to the financial institution.

Most pro-privacy advocacy groups strongly object to this and other privacy-related elements of GLBA because, in their view, these provisions do not provide substantive protection of consumer privacy. For example, the influential Electronic Privacy Information Center states:

> GLBA does not protect consumers. It unfairly places the burden on the individual to protect privacy with an opt-out standard. By placing the burden on the customer to protect their data, GLBA weakens customer power to control their financial information. The agreement's opt-out provisions do not require institutions to provide a standard of protection for their customers regardless of whether they opt-out of the agreement. This provision is based on the assumption that financial companies will share information unless expressly told not to by their customers and if customers neglect to respond, it gives institutions that freedom to disclose customer nonpublic personal information.
>
> Second, the GLBA notices are confusing and limit the transparency of information practices. GLBA assumes a company will explain a complex set of legal definitions added to numerous exceptions to the law in a way that will allow for an informed choice and in transparent language. There are reservations about a company's desire to do this.[8]

For banks, regardless of how effective—or not—GLBA may be in protecting customer information, noncompliance is not an option. However, because of the earlier-discussed explosion in breaches of bank information security systems, the privacy issue has to some degree been overshadowed by the urgency to *physically* protect customer data.

As such, compliance with the *Interagency Guidelines* concerning information security is more critical than ever. The basic elements partially overlap with the preventive measures against employee abuse of the bank's computer systems. However, they go quite a bit further by requiring banks to:

- Design an information security program to control the risks identified through a security risk assessment, commensurate with the sensitivity of the information and the complexity and scope of its activities.

- Evaluate a variety of policies, procedures, and technical controls and adopt those measures that are found to most effectively minimize the identified risks. Some of these are listed in the Confidential Information Theft Prevention Checklist in Chapter 4. However, these are insufficient to be in compliance with the *Interagency Guidelines,* which provide an additional list of measures that an institution must consider and, if appropriate, adopt. These are:

  - Application and enforcement of access controls on customer information systems, including controls to authenticate and permit access only to authorized individuals and to prevent employees from providing customer information to unauthorized individuals who may seek to obtain this information through fraudulent means.

- Access restrictions at physical locations containing customer information, such as buildings, computer facilities, and records storage facilities to permit access only to authorized individuals.

- Encryption of electronic customer information, including while in transit or in storage on networks or systems to which unauthorized individuals may have access.

- Procedures designed to ensure that customer information system modifications are consistent with the institution's information security program.

- Dual control procedures, segregation of duties, and employee background checks for employees with responsibilities for or access to customer information.

- Monitoring systems and procedures to detect actual and attempted attacks on or intrusions into customer information systems.

- Response programs that specify actions to be taken when the institution suspects or detects that unauthorized individuals have gained access to customer information systems, including appropriate reports to regulatory and law enforcement agencies.

- Measures to protect against destruction, loss, or damage of customer information due to potential environmental hazards, such as fire and water damage or technological failures.

## ▶ Hypothetical Case: Compliance and InfoSecurity

The *Interagency Guidelines* require a financial institution to determine whether to adopt controls to authenticate and permit only authorized individuals access to certain forms of customer information.

Under this control, a financial institution also should consider the need for a firewall to safeguard confidential electronic records. If the institution maintains Internet or other external connectivity, its systems may require multiple firewalls with adequate capacity, proper placement, and appropriate configurations.

Similarly, the institution must consider whether its risk assessment warrants encryption of electronic customer information. If it does, the institution must adopt necessary encryption measures that protect information in transit, in storage, or both. (The *Interagency Guidelines* do not impose specific authentication or encryption standards, so it is advisable to consult your outside expert on the technical details applicable to your institution's security requirements.)

The financial institution also must consider the use of an intrusion detection system to alert it to attacks on computer systems that store customer information. In assessing the need for such a system, the institution should evaluate the ability—or lack thereof—of its staff to rapidly and accurately identify an intrusion. It also should assess the damage that could occur between the time an intrusion occurs and the time the intrusion is recognized and action is taken.

Although the *Interagency Guidelines* do not prescribe a specific method of information disposal, the banking regulatory agencies "expect institutions to have appropriate risk-based disposal procedures for their records."

For example, banks should:

- Ensure that paper records containing customer information are rendered unreadable as indicated by its risk assessment, such as by shredding or any other means.

- Recognize that computer-based records present unique disposal problems. Residual data frequently remain on media after erasure. Since these data can be recovered, additional disposal techniques should be applied to sensitive electronic data.

As mentioned, in addition to considering the measures required by the *Interagency Guidelines*, each institution may need to implement additional procedures or controls specific to the nature of its operations. An institution may implement safeguards designed to provide the same level of protection to all customer information, provided that the level is appropriate for the most sensitive classes of information.

## ▶ Develop and Implement a Response Program

The regulatory agencies also have provided requirements for responding to information breaches. These are contained in a related document entitled *Interagency Guidance on Response Programs for Unauthorized Access to Customer Information and Customer Notice* (Incident Response Guidance). According to the *Incident Response Guidance*, a financial institution should develop and implement a response program as part of its information security program. The response program should address unauthorized access to or use of customer information that could result in substantial harm or inconvenience to a customer.

The components of an effective response program include:

- Assessment of the nature and scope of the incident and identification of what customer information has been accessed or misused.

- Prompt notification to its primary federal regulator once the institution becomes aware of an incident involving unauthorized access to or use of sensitive customer information.

- Notification to appropriate law enforcement authorities, in addition to filing a timely Suspicious Activity Report, in situations involving federal criminal violations requiring immediate attention.

- Measures to contain and control the incident to prevent further unauthorized access to or misuse of customer information, while preserving records and other evidence.

- Notification to customers when warranted by the breach. Specific steps include:
  - Once the institution becomes aware of an incident of unauthorized access to sensitive customer information, it should conduct a reasonable investigation to determine promptly the likelihood that the information has been or will be misused.
  - If the institution determines that misuse of customer information has occurred or is reasonably possible, it should notify any affected customer as soon as possible.

## ■ Training Staff

The *Interagency Guidelines* require financial institutions to train staff to prepare and implement their information security programs. The institution should consider providing specialized training to ensure that personnel sufficiently protect customer information in accordance with its information security program.

For example, an institution should:

- Train staff to recognize and respond to schemes to commit fraud or identity theft, such as guarding against pretext calling.

- Provide staff members responsible for building or maintaining computer systems and local and wide area networks with adequate training, including instruction about computer security.

- Train staff to properly dispose of customer information.[9]

### Remember

The threat of identity theft and fraud resulting from breaches of a financial institution's information security systems is potentially costly and time consuming. Although the threat continues to worsen, there are steps that institutions can—and must—take to at least reduce their risk of being victimized by both dishonest employees with access to confidential customer information and outsiders who are adept at hacking into bank information systems and stealing large volumes of such data.

## ■ FACT Act Red Flags Rules

As mentioned briefly in Chapter 6, banks (as well as other organizations that provide what the Federal Trade Commission terms "covered accounts"[10]) were subject to this set of anti–identity theft measures starting November 1, 2009.

The Federal Trade Commission (FTC), along with the OCC, OTS, FDIC, NCUA, and FRB, are responsible for enforcing the Red Flags Rules, which are intended to protect consumers by having tested measures in place at financial institutions that screen for unusual activity in covered accounts, such as address changes to credit card accounts and similar triggers that must be followed up by bank staff to validate their legitimacy.

Under the Red Flags Rules, there are five main categories of red flags:

1. Alerts, notifications, and warnings from a credit reporting company. Here are some examples of changes in a credit report or a consumer's credit activity that may signal identity theft:

   - A fraud or active duty alert on a credit report
   - A notice of a credit freeze in response to a request for a credit report
   - A notice of address discrepancy provided by a credit reporting agency
   - A credit report indicating a pattern of activity inconsistent with the person's history—for example, a big increase in the volume of inquiries or in the use of credit, especially on new accounts
   - An unusual number of recently established credit relationships or an account that was closed because of an abuse of account privileges

2. Suspicious documents. Sometimes paperwork has the telltale signs of identity theft. Here are examples of red flags involving documents:

   - Identification that looks altered or forged
   - The person presenting the identification does not resemble the photo or match the physical description
   - Information on the identification that differs from what the person presenting the identification is telling you or does not match with other information, such as a signature card or recent check
   - An application that looks like it has been altered, forged, or torn up and reassembled

3. Suspicious personal identifying information. Identity thieves may use personally identifying information that does not ring true. Here are some red flags involving identifying information:

   - Inconsistencies with what else you know—for example:
     - An address that does not match the credit report
     - Use of a Social Security number listed on the Social Security Administration Death Master File
     - Use of a number that has not been issued, according to the monthly issuance tables available from the Social Security Administration
   - Inconsistencies in the information the customer has given—say, a date of birth that does not correlate to the number range on the Social Security Administration's issuance tables
   - An address, phone number, or other personal information that has been used on an account known by the financial institution to be fraudulent
   - A bogus address, an address for a mail drop or prison, a phone number that is invalid, or one that is associated with a pager or answering service

- A Social Security number that has been used by someone else opening an account

- An address or telephone number that has been used by many other people opening accounts

- A person who omits required information on an application and does not respond to notices that the application is incomplete

- A person who cannot provide authenticating information beyond what is generally available from a wallet or credit report—for example, a person who cannot answer a challenge question

4. Suspicious account activity. Sometimes the tip-off is how the account is being used. Here are some red flags related to account activity:

- Requests soon after the organization is notified of a change of address for new or additional credit cards, cell phones, and so on, or to add users to the account

- A new account that is used in ways associated with fraud—for example, the customer does not make the first payment or makes only an initial payment, or most of the available credit is used for cash advances or for jewelry, electronics, or other merchandise easily convertible to cash

- An account that is used in a way that is inconsistent with established patterns—for example:

  - Nonpayment when there is no history of missed payments

  - A substantial increase in the use of available credit

  - A major change in buying or spending patterns or electronic fund transfers

  - A noticeable change in calling patterns for a cell phone account

- An account that has been inactive for a long time is suddenly used again

- Mail sent to the customer that is returned repeatedly as undeliverable although transactions continue to be conducted on the account

- Information that customers are not receiving their account statements in the mail

- Information about unauthorized charges on the account

5. Notice from other sources. Sometimes a red flag that an account has been opened or used fraudulently can come from a customer, a victim of identity theft, a law enforcement authority, or someone else.[11]

This is a partial list of potential red flags of identity theft. Each financial institution is required to make its own assessment of potential red flags of identity theft in its particular processes and procedures. Having done that, organizations are required to put into place methods for detecting these red flags, to enforce methods of mitigating the *risk* of identity theft, and to continually update their Red Flags program.

As mentioned in Chapter 6, there is considerable doubt on the part of industry analysts as to whether this program will in fact make a dent in the rapidly growing crime of identity theft. Nonetheless, financial institutions that fail to comply with the rules are subject to potential civil monetary penalties.

A useful guide for complying with the Red Flags Rules is available from the FTC at www.ftc.gov/bcp/edu/pubs/business/idtheft/bus23.pdf.

## ▶ Future Regulation: A Prediction

Following the worst months of the 2007 to 2008 financial industry crisis, fraud against *all* businesses—including financial services—increased significantly. Cases of embezzlement, mortgage fraud, identity theft, and credit card fraud were reported to be on the increase as a result of enhanced desperation on the part of employees fearing loss of their jobs as companies slashed costs to weather the worst economic downturn in 75 years.

Moreover, the collapse of Bernard Madoff's $65 billion Ponzi scheme pushed federal agencies, such as the Securities and Exchange Commission, to proclaim their commitment to more rigorous scrutiny of financial conduct and to ramp up their enforcement efforts.

Following the regulatory pendulum's swing toward deregulation in the 1990s, many leading experts expected the political fallout from the economic crisis of 2007 to 2008 to cause a rapid swing in the opposite direction. The powerful banking industry lobbying groups can be expected to apply their considerable weight to resisting a knee-jerk flood of new rules intended to prevent another mortgage fraud–related financial crisis. How far the pendulum ultimately moves remains to be seen. Yet the history of the financial services industry provides us with a clear warning: Whatever we do now to prevent a repeat of the latest debacle will prove only temporarily effective, if that. The banking industry seems hard-wired for periodic crisis, and it will be difficult for even the most astute politicians to argue that they have come up with the silver bullet to end this pattern for good.

## ▶ Review Points

- The financial services industry is the most heavily regulated of any. However, although many, if not most, of the laws, regulations, and industry standards requiring financial institution compliance are *not* related to fraud prevention, plenty are.

- U.S. banks bear a regulatory and legal compliance burden unparalleled in any other American industry. Although many financial institution rules and regulations are unrelated to fraud, many are designed to minimize banks' vulnerability to fraudsters, information thieves, or money launderers.

- The primary objective of the Sarbanes-Oxley Act is to establish preventive measures against fraudulent financial reporting in public companies. It requires implementation and monitoring of internal controls over financial reporting as well as top executive certification of the accuracy—including the absence of fraud—of all financial reports.

- Because many frauds committed against banks today involve the illegal use of stolen customer or bank data, some of the newest and most important laws and regulations that management must be aware of and comply with relate to the safeguarding of confidential customer data.

- There is no silver bullet for protecting the organization against the rising tide of information security attacks. However, implementing required provisions of federal banking regulations can at least lower the risk of a costly breach occurring.

- In the context of theft of confidential information, "customer information" is defined as "any record containing nonpublic personal information about an individual who has obtained a financial product or service from the institution that is to be used primarily for personal, family, or household purposes and who has an ongoing relationship with the institution."

- The Federal Reserve Board's *Interagency Guidelines Establishing Information Security Standards* provide a detailed set of guidelines aimed at helping banks protect themselves against increasingly frequent attempts to steal electronic customer information.

- Under the FACT Act Red Flags Rule, financial institutions are required to make their own assessments of potential red flags of identity theft in their particular processes and procedures. Having done that, organizations are required to put into place methods for detecting these red flags, to enforce methods of mitigating the *risk* of identity theft, and to continually update their Red Flags program.

## ▶ Chapter Quiz

True or False:

1. Most financial institution rules and regulations are unrelated to fraud.

   ❏ True     ❏ False

2. One of the key provisions of the Sarbanes-Oxley Act is to protect whistleblowers against retaliation for reporting fraud or misconduct they detect in their day-to-day activities.

   ❏ True     ❏ False

3. The Glass-Steagall Act is a law protecting against unfair lending practices.

   ❏ True     ❏ False

Circle the correct answer to the following questions:

4. There are five major federal bank regulatory agencies. All of the following are among the five EXCEPT:

   a. Office of Comptroller of the Currency

   b. Federal Reserve Board

    c. Office of Bank Superintendent

    d. Office of Thrift Supervision

    e. Federal Deposit Insurance Corp.

5. The following are critical anti-fraud laws and regulations that, when complied with, can benefit banks' anti-fraud efforts:

    a. Sarbanes-Oxley (SOX)

    b. FACT Act Red Flags Rules

    c. Regulation Z

    d. Interagency Guidelines Establishing Information Security Standards

    1. a, b, c

    2. a, b, d

    3. b, c, d

    4. a, b, c, d

6. Under the *Interagency Guidelines,* "customer information" does not refer only to information pertaining to people who do business with the bank. It also encompasses all of the following EXCEPT:

    a. An individual who applies for but does not obtain a loan

    b. An individual who guarantees a loan

    c. A vendor

    d. A prospective employee

Fill in the blank:

7. Among the most devastating forms of theft of customer data is an information _____.

8. The potentially costly result of a bank information breach is _____.

9. Under the Red Flags Rules, one of the five main categories of red flags is suspicious _____.

*For the answers, please turn to Appendix A.*

◄ CHAPTER NINE ►

# Fraud Detection in Financial Services Companies

By now you have a good familiarity with the many types of fraud at both the employee level and the management level. You also have learned about the red flags of specific types of fraud as well as the internal anti-fraud controls and risk assessment methods that must be in place as the foundation of an effective anti-fraud program.

Now it is time to dig a little deeper and learn how to ensure that the red flags of fraud (or potential fraud) are not missed by internal financial managers or by employees throughout the organization.

Although fraud *prevention* is always more effective and less costly than fraud *detection* (and subsequent investigation), unfortunately prevention is not always possible. That is why all employees must be trained in how to identify the major red flags of fraud that they may encounter in their daily activities. It is also why mastering key detection techniques is essential for your organization's audit and financial professionals. This is why we spent considerable time in earlier chapters learning about the red flags of employee-level and management-level fraud and how to assess the risks of specific types of fraud at your financial institution.

Once internal auditors and financial managers know what to look for, there is a good chance that fraud or suspicious activity will be detected one way or another, *but only if the organization has the proper monitoring, reporting, and auditing procedures in place.*

Many banks require audits of specific business units only once every two or three years. In an age when so much can change so quickly in the financial services world, this approach is not the most effective insofar as fraud detection and prevention are concerned. This is especially so because conventional audits are not designed to detect fraud in the first place. They are meant only to ensure compliance with existing laws and regulations.

That is why today, anti-fraud experts often recommend that a fraud risk assessment (FRA) be conducted annually and that the fraud-auditing procedures designed to detect red flags in the high-risk areas identified by the FRA be incorporated into internal audit plans immediately.[1]

Some of the fraud detection techniques discussed in the pages to come may sound similar to the anti-fraud controls discussed in earlier chapters. This is because there is often a fine line between detection and prevention. In fact, some detection steps *overlap* with prevention methods, as in the case of conflict of interest, where enforcing a management financial disclosure policy may both detect conflicting financial interests and prevent frauds resulting from them by virtue of the actual detection of the relationships.

In most financial institutions, however, carefully assessing the descriptions of prevention and detection methods demonstrates that there is usually a clear distinction between the two.

There are numerous procedures and techniques for detecting actual or potential fraud. In the interest of simplicity, we will divide them into two segments: basic and advanced.

The financial services industry is unique compared to most others in that many of the fraud detection and reporting rules that are *recommended* for nonfinancial companies by professional standards, such as those from the American Institute of Certified Public Accountants (AICPA), the Institute of Internal Auditors (IIA), and the Association of Certified Fraud Examiners (ACFE), are *required* for banks by one or more of the five regulatory agencies.

As such, some of the detection methods described in this chapter are based on regulatory or legal requirements. For example, while delicately avoiding use of the "f" word, the Federal Deposit Insurance Corporation (FDIC) states:

> The internal audit function is a critical element in assessing the effectiveness of an institution's internal control system. The internal audit consists of procedures to prevent or identify significant inaccurate, incomplete, or unauthorized transactions; deficiencies in safeguarding assets; unreliable financial reporting; and deviations from laws, regulations, and institution policies. When properly designed and implemented, internal audits provide directors and senior management with timely information about weaknesses in the internal control system, facilitating prompt remedial action. Each institution should have an internal audit function appropriate to its size and the nature and scope of its activities.[2]

This is a complex way of saying that a bank's internal audit function should focus on monitoring the institution's internal controls—which, although not mentioned explicitly, include controls specifically designed to prevent fraud.

As discussed earlier, however, in order to design effective anti-fraud controls, auditors first must exercise detection techniques and procedures that confirm the existence of red flags or actual evidence of potential fraud in the risk areas identified by the FRA. This too is required by FDIC rules, although the word "fraud" is again noticeably absent:

> The internal audit manager is responsible for the following:

> ■ A control risk assessment documenting the internal auditor's understanding of significant business activities and associated risks. These assessments typically analyze the risks inherent in a given business line, the mitigating control processes, and the resulting residual risk exposure.

- An internal audit plan responsive to results of the control risk assessment. This plan typically specifies key internal control summaries within each business activity, timing and frequency of internal audit work, and the resource budget.

- An internal audit program that describes audit objectives and specifies procedures performed during each internal audit review.

- An audit report presenting the purpose, scope, and results of the audit. Work papers should be maintained to document the work performed and support audit findings.[3]

When fraud is suspected or detected in a bank, often management does not have the choice of calling in investigative or enforcement entities. Banks that are hit by fraud are virtually guaranteed to draw the involvement of the enforcement arm of the applicable regulatory agency, whether they like it or not. Whereas a nonfinancial organization often can choose not to investigate (or to investigate privately, without the involvement of pubic law enforcement agencies) in order to avoid negative publicity, banks do not enjoy this option. This, according to some anti-fraud experts, is all the more reason why banks should be extra aggressive in preventing fraud.

## ▶ Basic Detection Methods

Basic fraud detection methods typically involve screening for operational fraud—as opposed to loan fraud—and involve manual, nonauditing measures.

By contrast, detailed detection is designed for spotting frauds such as those whose red flags are found in the banks' lending procedures and financial reporting.

Detection therefore depends heavily on specific anti-fraud auditing techniques designed to measure the organization's specific risks of fraud. These techniques always must be applied with an attitude of professional skepticism, as described in key fraud detection guidelines (such as those beginning on page 212).

This section addresses the basic detection tools and procedures that all employees in the organization should be familiar with. The next section addresses the advanced, audit-related techniques that must be used in response to the findings of your FRA in order to identify red flags of fraud in the organization's lending and financial records and to collect supporting evidence so that management can determine whether a full-fledged fraud investigation is warranted.

---

### Remember

Internal auditors and financial managers are increasingly expected to detect fraud. However, it is everyone's responsibility to play a role in preventing, detecting, and reporting fraud.

---

As PricewaterhouseCoopers points out in a major report on forensic accounting: "Internal auditors should improve their fraud detection skills and should program fraud detection into their work plans. Internal auditors should also be ready to exercise integrity and courage when the situation calls for it."[4]

The place to start is in the area of basic detection of fraud in operational activities, such as embezzlement, collusion, cash theft, check fraud, and information theft.

Financial institutions should have in place at all times these important basic detection measures:

- Surprise audits
- Surveillance
- Regular internal audits
- Manual review of travel and entertainment (T&E) claims
- Manual assessment of payroll information
- Manual review of vendors
- Confidential fraud hotline

## ■ Surprise Audits

When dishonest employees are aware of scheduled audits, it is easy for them to conceal their fraudulent activities. For example, unscrupulous managers can have corporate or branch tours prearranged to guide external auditors to areas where signs of cash theft, collusion, or loan document manipulation (or other schemes) are not evident. Or they can conceal documentation that might lead the auditors to suspect misconduct.

The solution is to set up unannounced audits by external auditors or fraud examiners.

Organizations that conduct these exercises once or twice a year and tell employees only that they can expect such an audit at any time not only are likely to detect fraud that is not concealed when employees are caught off guard, but also put a powerful anti-fraud deterrent into place. Employees who, though dishonest, are smart enough not to get caught will be less likely to perpetrate financial crimes if they know that they may be investigated at any time.

## ■ Surveillance

Most banks need no advice on the use of sophisticated closed-surveillance camera systems for such purposes as:

- Crime investigation in robbery and fraud cases.
- Check fraud prevention. (Internet Protocol [IP] surveillance systems with advanced video analytics such as facial recognition are helping to fight the problem of check fraud at banks by recording transaction data and capturing images of offenders. This information can be used to identify criminals and helps in protecting customer accounts.)
- Detecting phantom automated teller machine (ATM) withdrawals. It is not uncommon for customers to report suspicious ATM withdrawals in which money has been fraudulently withdrawn from their accounts. Security cameras that record every ATM transaction often can provide answers to the incidents in question.

- Coordinating information from multiple locations. IP video surveillance allows footage from multiple branches to be transmitted to a central monitoring room or viewed over the Internet.

- Digital storage. With digital technology, storage and management of surveillance footage is more efficient, convenient, and accessible, allowing for advanced search techniques that help in pinpointing specific incidents and identifying suspects with greater ease and speed.

- Data recognition. Surveillance systems that use digital technology are capable of advanced forms of data recognition that prove useful for searching video footage for specific bank transactions and images of particular individuals.

To set up security cameras at a branch:

- Place cameras at entrances and exits in order to capture images of each bank customer coming and going.

- Situate security cameras at all ATMs to gather clear pictures of individual customer faces.

- Capture video footage of all bank transactions by closely monitoring teller areas.

- Use surveillance cameras to provide an overall view of the bank lobby.

- Make sure the safe is thoroughly monitored by security cameras.

- Consider investing in advanced video analytics, such as motion sensing and behavioral recognition, to assist in spotting suspicious activity.[5]

Implementing these detection techniques requires careful planning by an experienced fraud examiner, information technology security specialist, or investigator. If your organization does not employ such an individual, you can retain one of the many qualified independent fraud examiners. For help in locating one in your area, contact the Association of Certified Fraud Examiners at www.acfe.com.

## ■ Regular Internal Audits

Although, as mentioned earlier, auditors are not expected to be fraud prevention specialists, there is growing pressure on internal auditors to focus on the detection of illegal activity. Later in this chapter, you will learn the detailed audit-related procedures for following up on the results of an FRA.

As for the basic fraud detection measures, internal auditors should start by adopting a mind-set of professional skepticism in determining the existence and seriousness of fraud risks in their regular internal audits. This intellectual approach to auditing assumes that evidence of fraud exists in the organization's books and records and that proper attention to the details of such documentation—within the context of existing internal controls against fraud—will inevitably result in discovery of such evidence.

As PricewaterhouseCoopers states, "Professional skepticism is a key attribute of an effective auditor."[6]

In addition, according to *Statement of Auditing Standards* (SAS) 99 and similarly reflected in *International Standard of Auditing* (ISA) 240, professional skepticism calls for the auditor to:

> [t]horoughly probe the issues, acquire additional evidence as necessary, and consult with other team members and, if appropriate, experts in the [organization], rather than rationalize or dismiss information or other conditions that indicate [that] fraud may have occurred.[7]

This approach serves auditors well in the fraud detection process as it applies to the specific types of fraud you learned about earlier. Examples of how auditors can use these procedures in some of the key areas of major fraud risk are presented next.

## ■ Manual Review of T&E Claims

Manual reviews of T&E claims often are challenging when an organization has many employees taking frequent business trips or making business-related purchases. However, detecting the red flags of fraud in T&E (which you learned about in Chapter 3) does not require manual review of *every* receipt or airline boarding pass. Random but frequent manual review of individual reimbursement claims is often enough to detect specific incidents of fraud and to establish a strong deterrent for employees who might be tempted to fudge their expenses if the organization did no manual review of reimbursement claims.

Moreover, although properly designed T&E fraud automation detection software is helpful in reducing audit fees, it is risky to rely too much on these applications. As Ari Schonbrun, director of administration and expense management at Cantor Fitzgerald's Debt Capital Markets Group, says, "Although automation is important, it should not be solely relied upon. No system is foolproof. Manual spot checking is a must! There is nothing like having Columbo going through T&E reports."[8]

## ■ Manual Assessment of Payroll Information

One highly effective way to detect the red flags of payroll fraud—such as creation of ghost employees by payroll managers—is to conduct a periodic, unannounced manual distribution of paychecks, requiring all employees to show ID to receive their checks. Any unclaimed paychecks should be compared against the master payroll file. If unclaimed checks have addresses matching those of legitimate employees, chances are that legitimate employees are perpetrating a ghost employee scheme.

It is also important to look for cashed paychecks with dual endorsements. This may be evidence of a legitimate payroll manager colluding with a live ghost who is endorsing the paycheck over to the manager who also endorses it before cashing or depositing it.

Management should also be suspicious of any employee who takes no holiday or sick leave. A ghost employee would obviously take neither—unless the payroll or human resources manager is perpetrating the fraud and creates fictitious records of the ghost's time off.

## ■ Manual Review of Vendors

As you learned, fraudsters try to perpetrate countless varieties of vendor or billing schemes against organizations whose anti-fraud controls are weak. Detecting these crimes can be challenging. Here are some of the important basic fraud auditing techniques that financial institutions should follow on a regular basis:

- Look for situations where payments to a vendor substantially exceed the budgeted amount, especially when the disbursed amount is exactly double the budgeted amount. This is a sign of possible double billing either by a phony vendor or by a dishonest legitimate vendor who receives the first check while a dishonest conspirator in the accounts payable department takes the second.

- Periodically (at least twice a year) examine details and patterns in the organization's largest accounts. Those are typically where fraudsters attempt to hide billing schemes, in the hope that the stolen amounts will not raise red flags in large-dollar accounts.

- Regularly test to confirm that vendors are legitimate. It may not be necessary to investigate every vendor in every business unit, but at least those added since the last audit should be checked. To confirm their legitimacy, simply call them up and interview them, search for them on the Internet, check local or national business databases for licenses, or contact others who have used them.

- Print out each business unit's entire vendor list alphabetically and examine any two (or more) vendors with the same or similar addresses.

## ■ Confidential Fraud Hotline

In publicly traded financial institutions, confidential (and anonymous) fraud hotlines give employees at all levels a way to report to management indicators of embezzlement, kickbacks, collusion, and other frauds without fear of retribution or retaliation.

For this reason, a hotline is one of the most important basic fraud detection tools any organization can have.

Research has shown that employees who have a confidential hotline at their disposal and who are trained in the red flags of fraud are likely to report such red flags that they notice. In fact, as discussed earlier, employee tips represent the most common way that fraud is detected. Although hotlines are not the only mechanism used to communicate those tips (many whistleblowers prefer direct contact with a supervisor), they play a critical role in enabling employees who detect signs of fraud to come forward.

Further supporting the argument for implementing a hotline is that doing so is quite inexpensive. Even if an organization uses a third-party independent hotline service, the cost is insignificant compared to the losses from fraud that would otherwise go unreported.

A hotline is only as effective as the people who run it. The most productive hotline systems are those operated by outside vendors whose employees are trained in how to field calls from employees, vendors, donors, and others. They know how to filter out frivolous calls and how to converse with legitimate whistleblowers in order to obtain as much evidence of fraud as possible to enable management to decide how to pursue each case.

Martin Biegelman, director of the Financial Integrity Unit at Microsoft Corp., and Joel Bartow, director of fraud prevention at ClientLogic, addressed the common problem of employee reluctance to blow the whistle:

> Because whistle-blowers are often reluctant and nervous about making hotline calls, the operators who answer these calls must be extremely careful to avoid causing undue anxiety or stress that might cause the caller to get "cold feet" and abruptly end the call.[9]

They must be skilled in coaxing answers from callers without intimidating them. From the very first moments of the call they must convey an encouraging and supportive tone, respect for the caller, and patience in understanding what the caller is trying to communicate. Specific guidelines for handling whistleblower calls include:

- Assure the caller that the call is confidential and advise him or her that there is no obligation to be identified at any time unless the caller specifically asks to be identified.

- Record the time and date of the call.

- Record the operator's name, identification number, and location.

- Assign a caller ID code or number.

- Ask if the caller is an employee, vendor, contractor, customer, or other.

- Ask for as many details as the caller can provide regarding the specific fraud incident. Try to find out how the caller became aware of the incident.

- Ask which individuals are involved in the incident, including names, titles, addresses, and any other contact information the caller may have.

- Determine when the incident occurred and if it is still ongoing.

- Ask for any physical or electronic evidence that the caller may have that is directly related to the incident.

- Inform the caller that while he or she may have the opportunity to provide additional information at a later date, it is advisable to share as much detail as possible now to enable the organization to follow up on the call effectively.

For additional detailed information on how to establish and manage a hotline, download Deloitte's very useful report, *2006 Corporate Governance and Compliance Hotline Benchmarking Report,* at www.tnwinc.com/downloads/2006BenchmarkingReport.pdf.

## ▶ Advanced Fraud Detection Tools and Techniques

The fraud risk assessment described in Chapter 7 is not the only option available to you for identifying fraud risks in your bank. There are, in fact, many varieties of FRAs that organizations of all kinds use. Some are more effective than others. The one described in this workbook, however, has been used by large numbers of organizations with considerable documented success.

Regardless of the type of FRA used, if properly executed, it will provide your organization with a list of fraud schemes and scenarios that are likeliest to occur in different operational sectors. If it is determined through an FRA that there are specific areas where a particular fraud scheme or scenario is likely to occur, your organization's auditors must adjust their audit procedures to screen for the red flags of those frauds listed in Chapters 3 through 6 and then dig deeper for hard evidence of potential incidents of those frauds.

## Remember

These procedures augment the basic fraud detection procedures discussed earlier in this chapter and must be conducted to determine if sufficient evidence exists to persuade management to initiate a full-fledged fraud investigation.

## ■ Critical FRA Perspective

Keep in mind that it is impossible to prevent all fraud, which, as discussed earlier, is why we must devote substantial resources to detection. This point provides an important additional perspective to the FRA. Not only is the FRA conducted for the purposes of identifying the specific risks of fraud so management can formulate and implement better preventive controls, it also serves to guide auditors in detecting the detailed signs of fraud so that investigative or other action can be taken at management's discretion.

For example, as Stephen Pedneault, an independent forensic accountant and fraud investigator, says:

> A regular banking audit isn't designed to detect fraud. It is designed to determine the bank's compliance with essential laws, regulations and operating standards. It also includes auditing to ensure that the amounts and results reflected in the institution's financial statements are reasonably presented and free of material misstatement. However, when auditing for *fraud,* the auditor uses the findings of the fraud risk assessment to pinpoint specific functions and procedures that are vulnerable to fraud and audits specifically for the red flags of fraud schemes and scenarios that could be occurring in these particular "high-risk" areas.[10]

The next pages describe several of the key advanced audit methods. Auditors can use them when adjusting their audits in response to the findings of the FRA. These methods are designed for digging out the indicators of fraud at financial insitutions in the way Pedneault describes.

---

### THE FED ON BASIC FRAUD CONTROLS

According to Federal Reserve Bank of St. Louis:

> Bank processes usually contain multiple controls. This layering strengthens overall control. In some instances, controls reinforce one another (e.g., internal and external door locks, vaults, and alarm systems). In some cases, layering

*(Continued)*

helps compensate for a missing control. For example, rotation of duties might compensate for lack of sufficient personnel to implement segregation of duties.

Because internal controls represent a process—typically managed by the bank's internal audit department—the process must be monitored to determine its level of effectiveness. Often this is done through ongoing monitoring and separate evaluations.

Many ongoing monitoring procedures are built into the normal, recurring activities of the bank. They typically include routine management reviews, comparisons, reconciliations, exception reports, and other actions taken by personnel as part of their job responsibilities. Ongoing monitoring procedures generally are performed while work is being done or soon after it is completed.

For example, at the end of each day, tellers may be required to reconcile the balance in their drawers against receipts and payments made during business hours. The tellers' supervisor reviews their reports, looking for large overages and shortages, and compares reports over time for noticeable patterns. When the supervisor believes there is a problem, he or she will look into possible causes and determine what action should be taken. A possible cause might be one where a teller does not follow policy and leaves a drawer open and unattended when leaving the work area.

Separate evaluations often result from management's request to look into a matter or from risk assessments performed by the bank's internal auditors. Closer examinations generally occur after a potential fraud is detected.

## ■ Internal Audit and the Audit Plan

The ACFE-IIA-AICPA's document *The Business Risk of Fraud* provides additional clarity about the internal auditor's role in detecting fraud in organizational operations and financial statements. Specifically, the document states that internal auditors should consider the organization's assessment of fraud risk when developing their annual audit plan and periodically assess management's fraud detection capabilities. They should also interview and regularly communicate with those conducting the assessments, as well as others in key positions throughout the bank, to help them assess whether all fraud risks have been considered.

Moreover, according to the document, when performing audits, the bank's internal auditors should devote sufficient time and attention to evaluating the "design and operation" of internal controls related to preventing and detecting significant fraud risks. They should exercise professional skepticism when reviewing activities to be on guard for the signs of potential fraud. Potential frauds uncovered during an engagement should be treated in accordance with a well-defined response plan consistent with professional and legal standards.[11]

## Remember

There are distinct basic fraud detection measures that should be used by a financial institution's internal auditors and financial managers to apply the findings of their FRA in order to adjust their audit procedures to detect specific red flags of fraud. However, to truly screen for fraud hidden in the organization's operations, books, and records, management must adopt rigorous *detailed* fraud auditing practices and techniques.

Among the most helpful guides for planning a detailed audit to detect fraud is the all-important *SAS 99*, described in Chapter 7 as containing key fraud detection techniques including performing certain analyses of financial ratios. For perspective on why doing these analyses is important but insufficient for getting the full picture of fraud risks, *SAS99* tells us:

> Analytical procedures performed during planning may be helpful in identifying the risks of material misstatement due to fraud. However, because such analytical procedures generally use data aggregated at a high level, the results of those analytical procedures provide only a broad initial indication about whether a material misstatement of the financial statements may exist. Accordingly, the results of analytical procedures performed during planning should be considered *along with other information gathered by the auditor in identifying the risks of material misstatement due to fraud.*[12] (Emphasis added.)

*SAS 99* was formulated with the aim of detecting fraud that has a direct impact on "material misstatement." Essentially this means that anything in the organization's financial activities that could result in fraud-related misstatements in its financial records should be audited for by using *SAS 99* as a guide. *SAS 99* breaks down the potential fraudulent causes of material misstatement into two categories:

1. Misstatement due to fraudulent financial reporting (i.e., "book cooking")
2. Misstatement due to misappropriation of assets (i.e., theft)

The specific types of fraud that fall into these two categories—at both the employee and management level—have been discussed in previous chapters.

The fraud auditing procedures of *SAS 99*—or of any other reputable audit guidance—can greatly assist bank internal auditors in distinguishing between actual fraud and error. Often the two have similar characteristics, with the key difference being that of the existence or absence of *intent*.

Toward this end, *SAS 99* and other key fraud auditing guidelines provide detailed procedures for gathering evidence of potential fraud based on the lists of fraud risks resulting from your FRA. As *SAS 99* states:

> *SAS 99* . . . strongly recommend[s] direct involvement by internal auditors in the organization's fraud-auditing efforts: Internal auditors may conduct proactive auditing to search for corruption, misappropriation of assets, and financial statement fraud.

This may include the use of computer-assisted audit techniques to detect particular types of fraud. Internal auditors also can employ analytical and other procedures to isolate anomalies and perform detailed reviews of high-risk accounts and transactions to identify potential financial statement fraud. The internal auditors should have an independent reporting line directly to the audit committee, enabling them to express any concerns about management's commitment to appropriate internal controls or to report suspicions or allegations of fraud involving senior management.[13]

Specifically, *SAS 99* provides a set of audit responses designed to gather hard evidence of potential fraud that could exist based on what you learned from your FRA. These responses are critical to the auditor's success in identifying clear red flags of potential fraud in the bank's operations. The responses are wide ranging and include anything from the application of appropriate ratio analytics, to thorough and detailed testing of controls governing specific lending procedures, to the analysis of anomalies in customer deposit account activity. Listed next are the three broad categories into which such detailed fraud auditing responses fall.

1. The *nature* of auditing procedures performed may need to be changed to obtain evidence that is more reliable or to obtain additional corroborative information.

2. The *timing* of substantive tests may need to be modified. The auditor might conclude that substantive testing should be performed at or near the end of the reporting period to best address an identified risk of material misstatement due to fraud.

3. The *extent* of the procedures applied should reflect the assessment of the risks of material misstatement due to fraud. For example, increasing sample sizes or performing analytical procedures at a more detailed level may be appropriate.[14]

## ▶ Essentials of Fraud Auditing in Financial Institutions

*SAS 99* provides some useful examples of how a detailed fraud-related response to specific risks determined by your FRA should be handled. For example, in the case of fraudulent revenue recognition (one of the predominant frauds resulting in misstatement due to fraudulent financial reporting), *SAS 99* recommends these detailed audit steps:

- Increase sample sizes or perform analytical procedures at a more detailed level.

- Conduct computer-assisted audit techniques for more extensive testing of electronic transactions and account files. Such techniques can be used to select sample transactions from key electronic files, to sort transactions with specific characteristics, or to test an entire population instead of a sample. (See the section "Essentials of Automated Auditing" later in the chapter for details.)

- Make oral inquiries of major customers and suppliers and send written confirmations, or send confirmation requests to a specific party within an organization.

- Perform substantive analytical procedures using disaggregated data, such as comparing gross profit or operating margins by location, line of business, or month to auditor-developed expectations.

- Interview personnel involved in activities in areas where a specific risk of material misstatement due to fraud has been identified. The aim is to obtain their insights about the risk and how controls address the fraud risk identified by your FRA.

## Additional Audit Procedures Relating to Risks of Fraudulent Financial Statements

Naturally, in any fraud auditing engagement, the deeper the auditor digs, the likelier it is he or she will find signs of wrongdoing. The line must be drawn somewhere, but many forensic accountants recommend taking at least these additional measures before doing so:

Industry-specific fraud auditing procedures, according to *SAS 99*:

> Because revenue recognition is dependent on the particular facts and circumstances, as well as accounting principles and practices that can vary by industry, the auditor ordinarily will develop auditing procedures based on [his or her] understanding of the entity and its environment, including the composition of revenues, specific attributes of the revenue transactions, and unique industry considerations. If [the FRA has identified a risk] of material misstatement due to fraudulent revenue recognition, the auditor also may want to consider:
>
> - Performing substantive analytical procedures relating to revenue using disaggregated data, for example, comparing revenue reported by month and by product line or business segment during the current reporting period with comparable prior periods.
>
> - Using computer-assisted audit techniques in identifying unusual or unexpected revenue relationships or transactions.
>
> - Confirming with customers . . . relevant contract (i.e., loan) terms and the absence of side agreements, because the appropriate accounting often is influenced by such terms or agreements. For example, acceptance criteria, payment terms, cancellation or refinancing provisions often are relevant in such circumstances.
>
> - Inquiring of [the bank's] sales and marketing personnel or in-house legal counsel regarding loans or deposits near the end of the period and their knowledge of any unusual terms or conditions associated with these transactions.
>
> - Performing other appropriate closing and transaction cutoff procedures.
>
> - For those situations for which revenue transactions are electronically initiated, processed, and recorded, testing controls to determine whether they provide assurance that recorded revenue transactions occurred and are properly recorded.
>
> - Obtain an understanding of the entity's financial reporting process and the controls over journal entries and other adjustments.

- Identify and select journal entries and other adjustments for testing.

- Determine the timing of the testing.

- Inquire of individuals involved in the financial reporting process about inappropriate or unusual activity relating to the processing of journal entries and other adjustments.[15]

## ■ Fraud Audit Procedures Relating to Misappropriation of Assets

As discussed in Chapters 4 and 5, the methods by which employees and senior managers can divert customer or bank funds to their own accounts are numerous. The risks of specific types of such theft, together with stealing physical assets such as laptop computers, confidential information, and other valuable property, should be revealed by your fraud risk assessment. Once the risks of particular theft-related scenarios have been identified, the auditor's response again is to incorporate fraud auditing procedures into the audit plan.

For example, the auditor may determine that the risk of theft at a particular branch or operating location is significant because controls preventing access to cash maintained at that location are weak, or there are inventory items, such as laptop computers at that location, that can be moved and sold easily.

According to *SAS 99*, the auditor's response to a risk of material misstatement due to fraud relating to misappropriation of assets usually should be directed toward certain account balances.

The scope of a fraud audit should be linked to the specific information about the misappropriation risk that has been identified. For example, if a particular asset is especially susceptible to theft and a resulting misstatement would be material to the financial statements, understanding the controls related to the prevention and detection of such theft and *testing the operating effectiveness of such controls* is essential.[16]

In response to other fraud risks, physical inspection of such assets (e.g., counting cash or securities) at or near the end of the reporting period may be appropriate. In addition, the use of substantive analytical procedures, such as the development of an expected dollar amount at a high level of precision, to be compared with a recorded amount—and/or with industry standards—may be appropriate.

These lists and examples of audit procedures represent a partial sampling of specific fraud auditing procedures that may apply to your financial institution, based on the findings of your FRA. Every institution's structure and business processes are unique. Internal fraud audit procedures must be designed carefully using not only the guidelines provided in this chapter but also those formulated independently among your own audit team in cooperation, if appropriate, with a forensic accountant.

In addition, *SAS 99* is not the only source of guidance in formulating fraud auditing procedures in response to the findings of your FRA. The five bank regulatory agencies have developed some techniques, as have banking trade associations, the audit and accounting professional associations, as well as individual banks themselves.

Many auditors feel most comfortable conducting key transaction analyses manually or with Excel spreadsheets, but highly effective and affordable audit software programs are available that enable you to perform most of these key fraud analyses much more efficiently. These programs perform what is called *audit analytics*, or data analysis designed for audit and fraud detection.

A major reason that many financial organizations use audit analytics today is that no system of internal anti-fraud controls is perfect. For that reason, fraudsters always find the loopholes to enable them to commit crimes. Audit analytics software monitors internal controls to help pinpoint deviations from normal financial operations that can be evidence of fraud.

Using such popular audit analytics software tools as ACL and IDEA, auditors can convert data from an organization's databases to information that is useful in gathering evidence of fraud.

For example, let us say that an FRA indicated a risk of, among other things, procurement fraud. As discussed in Chapter 4, one of the brightest red flags of this crime is setting up sham corporations. Using ACL or IDEA, the auditor can specifically search for two contractors having common names, with the first two letters of the names always the same. This duplication points to the possible existence of sham corporations, which can be determined by:

- Finding two or more suppliers with the same telephone number or address.

- Matching of vendors paid with the vendor master file revealing vendors that do not exist.

- Determining that an employee and a "vendor" have the same demographics (address or phone number).

- Noting that checks paid to the "vendor" are always for even amounts, such as $2,000, $3,000, $8,000.

- Noting that there are employees in the payroll master file with no Social Security number, the same Social Security numbers, or the same demographics (address or phone number).

Custom-built programming scripts that run on the organization's servers are even better. They usually cost more than off-the-shelf products, such as ACL and IDEA. However, they usually are much more effective in identifying accounting anomalies and patterns that support suspicions of fraud based on the red flags that the FRA directed the auditor's attention to.

## ► Conclusion

It is not the auditor's or fraud examiner's decision to launch a full-scale fraud investigation. Although the fraud audit procedures described in this chapter may provide management with an abundant supply of evidence to go after suspected fraudsters, the decision to do so depends on more than just the results of the fraud audit. It often involves judgments about the cost, repercussions from publicity regarding the investigation and possible prosecution of suspect(s), and the availability of experienced and qualified investigators to conduct such a probe.

Many anti-fraud experts argue that management should never let a suspected fraud go unaddressed. They suggest that not only does this send a message to other employees that management does not take fraud seriously enough to investigate and prosecute, it also perpetuates the widely held misconception that fraud is a victimless crime. Even though the theft of a few thousand dollars by an employee with serious personal financial problems may not make a significant difference in the organization's financial performance, letting the perpetrator off the hook simply by terminating employment conveys the attitude that fraud is simply a cost of doing business or that it does not pay to prosecute.

Others agree, adding that companies, law enforcement, and the judicial system have been comparatively lenient on white-collar criminals and that this is a key reason we are seeing more and more fraud in our corporate, financial, governmental, and nonprofit institutions.

It is hoped that the information contained in this workbook has provided you with a foundation of knowledge from which to draw your own conclusions about the seriousness of the fraud problem in our economy and whether more should be done to detect and prevent it.

### Remember

It is management's job to determine if a fraud investigation is required—not the auditor's, financial manager's, or controller's.

### ▶ Review Points

- Although fraud *prevention* is always more effective and less costly than fraud *detection* (and subsequent investigation), prevention is unfortunately not always possible.

- Many of the red flags of fraud mentioned in earlier chapters of this book are readily identifiable by any employee with a bit of fraud awareness training. Other more financially complex indicators of fraud must be sought out by trained auditors, using the findings of their FRA as a guideline.

- Once internal auditors and financial managers know what to look for, there is a good chance that fraud or suspicious activity will be detected—*but only if the organization has the proper monitoring, reporting, and auditing procedures in place.*

- Conventional audits are not designed to detect fraud in the first place. They are meant only to ensure compliance with existing laws and regulations. Many anti-fraud experts therefore recommend that a fraud risk assessment be conducted annually and that the fraud auditing procedures designed to detect red flags in the specific high-risk areas identified by the FRA be incorporated into internal audit plans immediately.

- Whereas a nonbank corporation often can choose not to investigate (or to investigate privately, without the involvement of pubic law enforcement agencies) to avoid negative publicity, banks do not enjoy this option.

- Fraud detection depends heavily on specific anti-fraud auditing techniques designed to measure the organization's specific risks of fraud. These techniques always must be applied with an attitude of professional skepticism.

- With computer technology, storage and management of surveillance footage is more efficient, convenient, and accessible, allowing for advanced search techniques that help in pinpointing specific incidents and identifying suspects with greater ease and speed.

- Random but frequent manual review of individual reimbursement claims is usually enough to detect incidents of T&E fraud and to establish a strong deterrent for employees with travel and expenses privileges who might be tempted to fudge their expenses if the organization did no manual review of reimbursement claims.

- Be suspicious of any employee who takes no holiday or sick leave. A ghost employee would obviously take neither—unless the payroll or human resources manager is perpetrating the fraud and creates fictitious records of the ghost's time off.

- To confirm that new vendors are not shams, simply call up and interview them, search for them on the Internet, check local or national business databases for licenses, or contact others who have used them.

- The most productive hotline systems are those operated by outside vendors whose employees are trained in how to field calls from employees, vendors, donors, and others.

- An FRA is conducted not only to identify the specific risks of fraud so that management can formulate and implement better preventive controls; it also serves to guide auditors in detecting the detailed signs of fraud so that investigative or other action can be taken at management's discretion.

- Among the most helpful guides for planning a detailed audit to detect fraud is the all-important *SAS 99*, which contains key fraud detection techniques, including performing certain analyses of financial ratios.

- Anything in the organization's financial activities that could result in fraud-related misstatements in its financial records should be audited for by using *SAS 99* as a guide. To facilitate this, *SAS 99* breaks down the potential fraudulent causes of material misstatement to (1) misstatement due to fraudulent financial reporting (i.e., "book cooking") and (2) misstatement due to misappropriation of assets (i.e., theft).

- A major reason that many financial organizations use audit analytics today is that no system of internal anti-fraud controls is perfect; fraudsters always will find the loopholes to enable them to commit crimes. Audit analytics software monitors internal controls to help pinpoint deviations from normal financial operations that can be evidence of fraud.

True or False:

1. The financial services industry is unique compared to most others in that many of the fraud detection and reporting rules that are recommended for nonfinancial companies by professional standards, such as those from the AICPA, the IIA, and the ACFE, are *required* by one or more of the major banking regulator agencies.

   ❏ True     ❏ False

2. Just like nonbanks, financial institutions often can choose not to investigate (or to investigate privately, without the involvement of pubic law enforcement agencies) in order to avoid negative publicity.

   ❏ True     ❏ False

3. Periodically examining the details and patterns in your organization's largest accounts often can turn up red flags of fraud because these are the accounts where fraudsters frequently attempt to hide billing schemes, hoping that the stolen amounts will not raise red flags in large-dollar accounts.

   ❏ True     ❏ False

4. A confidential fraud hotline is usually most effective in gathering employee tips when it is managed in house.

   ❏ True     ❏ False

Circle the correct answer to the following questions:

5. According to the FDIC, all of the following are required of internal auditors EXCEPT:

   **a.** Control risk assessment

   **b.** Internal audit plan

   **c.** Fraud detection program

   **d.** Internal audit program

6. It is generally agreed that protecting against fraud in financial institutions cannot be assigned to a single anti-fraud manager or department. Instead, experts agree that EVERYONE in the organization has the responsibility to:

   **a.** Detect fraud

   **b.** Prevent fraud

   **c.** Report fraud

   **d.** Investigate fraud

   **1.** a, b, c

   **2.** a, b, d

   **3.** a, c, d

   **4.** a, b, c, d

**7.** All of the following are BASIC fraud detection measures EXCEPT:

    **a.** Surveillance

    **b.** Surprise audit

    **c.** Fraud risk assessment

    **d.** Manual review of T&E claims

**8.** According to all-important fraud auditing standard *SAS 99*, the three broad categories into which detailed fraud auditing responses fall include:

    **a.** The *nature* of auditing procedures performed

    **b.** The *timing* of substantive tests

    **c.** The *frequency* with which audit procedures are performed

    **d.** The *extent* of the procedures applied

    **1.** a, b, c,

    **2.** a, b, d

    **3.** a, c, d

    **4.** a, b, c, d

Fill in the blank:

**9.** *SAS 99* was formulated with the aim of detecting fraud that has a direct impact on _____.

**10.** Conducting surprise audits puts a powerful anti-fraud _____ into place.

**11.** Not only is the FRA conducted for the purposes of identifying the specific risks of fraud so management can formulate and implement better *preventive* controls, it also serves to guide auditors in _____ the detailed signs of fraud.

**12.** It is _____ job to determine if a fraud investigation is required—not the auditor's, financial manager's, or controller's.

*For the answers, please turn to Appendix A.*

# Answers to Chapter Quizzes

## ▶ Chapter 1: Why No Financial Services Institution Is Immune to Fraud

1. T
2. F
3. F
4. T
5. c
6. b
7. c
8. d
9. Deception
10. ACH
11. billing schemes

## ▶ Chapter 2: The Human Element of Fraud

1. T
2. F
3. T
4. b
5. b
6. c
7. a
8. greed
9. unindicted coconspirator
10. inverse ratio
11. subprime lender

## ▶ Chapter 3: Internal Fraud: Loan and Mortgage Fraud

1. F
2. F
3. T
4. F
5. c
6. a
7. d
8. a
9. phantom
10. suspense
11. straw buyers
12. segregation of duties

## ▶ Chapter 4: Employee-Level Embezzlement

1. T
2. T
3. T
4. F
5. T
6. T
7. b
8. c
9. b
10. c
11. skimming
12. consignment items
13. vendor master file
14. bid splitting
15. identity theft

## ▶ Chapter 5: Internal Fraud: Management Level

1. F
2. T
3. T
4. c
5. a
6. c

7. d
8. d
9. c
10. insider trading
11. complaints
12. self-dealing

## ► Chapter 6: External Fraud against Financial Services Companies

1. T
2. T
3. F
4. T
5. F
6. T
7. F
8. T
9. T
10. c
11. b
12. b
13. d
14. b
15. c
16. d
17. a,b,c
18. a,b,d
19. a,b,c,d
20. subprime mortgage
21. social engineering
22. phishing
23. kiting
24. builder bailout scheme

## ► Chapter 7: Conducting a Successful Fraud Risk Assessment

1. T
2. F
3. F
4. F

5. b
6. c
7. risk
8. internal controls
9. brainstorming
10. material

## ► Chapter 8: Legal and Regulatory Compliance for Controlling Fraud Risk

1. T
2. T
3. F
4. c
5. a,b,d
6. c
7. breach
8. identity theft
9. documents

## ► Chapter 9: Fraud Detection in Financial Services Companies

1. T
2. F
3. T
4. F
5. c
6. a,b,c
7. c
8. a,c,d
9. material misstatement
10. deterrent
11. detecting
12. management's

# Answer Key for Case Studies

## ▶ Case Study #1: Alleged Mortgage Fraud of Massive Proportions

- Proper tone at the top.
- Procedures for monitoring compliance with the bank's code of conduct.
- Audit committee oversight: The board should have stepped in and taken action well before the fraud became so widespread.
- Board oversight of the bank's adherence to responsible credit risk standards.
- Written policies prohibiting specific lending fraud practices.
- Enforcement and monitoring by senior management of compliance with anti-fraud policies.
- Termination of policy violators.
- Proactive oversight by the audit committee.
- Employee fraud awareness training and encouragement to use confidential hotline to report questionable activities.
- More stringent scrutiny by internal and external auditors of questionable financial activities.
- Surprise internal audits.
- Implementation of stringent loan review function independent of the credit and underwriting functions and use of technology to "score" applications.
- Confidential hotline and regular employee communication on how and when to use it.
- Prosecution of perpetrators as a deterrent to potential frauds.

## ▶ Case Study #2: The Amazing Tale of How Arson Tipped Off Investigators to Massive Financial Statement Fraud

- Tougher internal controls over financial reporting.
- Proactive audit committee oversight.
- Physical inspection by bank officials of the company's inventory and examination of sales records and documentation.

- Physical inspection by outside auditors of the company's operations and inventory and scrutiny of suspicious sales records.

- Regular (annual) review of borrowing executives' personal financial condition, especially unusual accumulation of assets.

- Employee training to detect red flags of accounts payable fraud and other internal operations frauds.

- Bank review of borrower's internal audit procedures—to identify possible weaknesses that would allow fraudulent financial reporting to go unnoticed.

- Conduct regular fraud risk assessments

### ▶ Case Study #3: Lapping All the Way from the Bank

- Segregation of duties, prohibiting approval of loans and making payments on loans by the same person.

- Spot audits of loan documentation.

- Surprise audits of all lending processes.

- Employee training to detect red flags of possible financial misconduct.

- Audit all loan officer payment transactions from in-house accounts and investigate unusual patterns.

- Confidential hotline and regular employee communication on how and when to use it.

- Monitor compliance with all of the bank's FACT Act Red Flags program components.

### ▶ Case Study #4: "It Was the Bank's Fault"

- Segregation of duties: Cynthia should not have been able to write checks to herself and make entries to the general ledger.

- Delegation of authority: Cynthia was obviously a fairly low-level employee (since her father tells us that she was hired as a temp and had no training in banking). She should not have had authorization to access the bank's accounting records.

- Much better internal controls over (1) funds transfer procedures; (2) suspense accounts; and (3) accounting processes and procedures.

- Fraud risk assessment and subsequent implementation of controls over areas where fraud could occur.

- Better background checks or a policy requiring a minimum amount of experience in banking plus contacting references from previous bank employers.

- Application of professional skepticism by internal auditors in reviewing accounting records.

- Audit plans should include examination of suspense accounts and other loans in progress as well as all wire transfers initiated by employees.
- Confidential hotline and regular employee communication on how and when to use it.

## ▶ Case Study #5: When Bank Employees Have Too Much Control over Customer Accounts

- Surprise audit of funds transfers might have revealed red flags of unusual patterns in accounts being looted by Pereira and unusually high number of credits to an account he controlled.
- Sampling by auditors or regional manager of suppressed statements should point to the perpetrator as the one requesting that the statements be held.
- Communicate with retail customers: On the bank's Web site and included in bank statements, encourage customers to carefully review their statements for unusual or suspicious activity and to report questionable items to the bank.
- Use one of the many available automated fraud pattern detection applications. Ensure that an information technology (IT) professional capable of programming the software to flag suspicious branch manager activity is assigned to the task.
- Thorough background checks on branch managers and periodic examination of activity in any manager-controlled bank accounts.
- Require mandatory vacation. Examining Pereira's computer hard drive while he was away might have revealed the suspicious transfers.
- Confidential hotline and regular employee communication on how and when to use it.

## ▶ Case Study #6: The Case of the Phony CD Sales Scheme Using Forged Bank Documentation

- Periodically examine branch manager financial records, including bank accounts, for signs of suspicious activity. (Pickhinke had deposited much of the stolen CD money into an account she maintained at MetaBank.) Because the accounts were set up using the Social Security numbers of deceased individuals, an automated fraud program might have flagged this anomaly and led bank managers to investigate.
- Make random "customer satisfaction" calls to retail customers—including CD customers—to determine if there have been any problems with the bank's service. Chances are that at some point during the seven-year fraud, Pickhinke would have made a late interest payment to a customer; this might be revealed in such a survey and lead to further investigation.

- Investigate signs of a bank employee's change in lifestyle. Having stolen $4 million, chances are that Pickhinke would have shown signs of a lifestyle more lavish than her salary would have suggested.

- Examine all branch manager personal financial background, including credit report and unusual acquisition of assets beyond pay level. Ensure that all legal rules are followed in gathering this information.

- Require mandatory vacation and examine employee's computer and paper files for indicators of potential theft, embezzlement, or, in this case, document forgery.

- Confidential hotline and regular employee communication on how and when to use it.

### ▶ Case Study #7: Teller's $1 Million Six-Year Theft Scheme Shows How Easy It Can Be to Rob a Bank

- Conduct an annual fraud risk assessment to pinpoint possible vulnerabilities to fraud. This might have identified weaknesses in PNC's teller processes and procedures, specifically the ability to make unusually large numbers of credits and debits compared to other tellers.

- Implement automated fraud detection software specifically programmed to flag unusual patterns of transactions by tellers. This would have led bank managers to suspect Baer's activity well before the six years that she was able to perpetuate this fraud.

- Tighter reconciliation procedures for cash transfers to and from the Federal Reserve Bank.

- Ensure that cash counts are scheduled for times when the teller has balanced to the general ledger.

- Ensure that cash counts are conducted on all branch cash supplies on at least a quarterly basis.

- Employee awareness training aimed at helping coworkers detect suspicious activity early in the game.

- Confidential hotline and regular employee communication on how and when to use it.

- Surprise audits of teller credit and debit activity.

### ▶ Case Study #8: Industrial-Strength Copier Toner Ends Up on eBay

- Require supervisor approval of all purchase requests over a specified amount (billing fraud, shell company schemes, kickback schemes, vendor master file fraud, check fraud).

- More rigorous employee background checks and conduct regular background checks *during* employment.

- Be alert to changes in lifestyle—especially acquisition of expensive items beyond employee's pay scale.

- Install video surveillance of delivery and shipment areas.

- Conduct detailed reviews of purchasing/procurement records to detect unusual pricing for certain vendors *before* payment is made (kickback/bribery schemes, billing schemes, shell companies).

- Regular audits of entire procure-to-pay process.

- Segregation of duties: Employee ordering merchandise should not be same person processing deliveries.

- Implement tighter invoice processing controls—screening for unusual or erroneous vendor address, departures from normal order processing, product or service ordering, matching of purchase orders with invoices, and so on.

## ▶ Case Study #9: Multibank Collusion Victimizes Taxpayers

This case is one involving fraud perpetrated by bands rather than against banks. As such, controls would be the responsibility of the bank customer(s), in this case the municipal agencies purchasing bank products.

## ▶ Case Study #10: Illegal Loans, Greed, and a Culture of Fear

The only way to stop the fraud in this case was to remove the chief executive. In situations involving banks controlled by the CEO, fraud is very difficult to stop. It is not that hard to detect, since CEOs like Allbritton usually are not very discreet in their illegal activities. As such, it often requires discovery by a bank examiner or whistle-blowing by a demoralized employee to expose the illegal conduct of the CEO.

## ▶ Case Study #11: The Vault Was His Personal Piggy Bank

- Conduct surprise *manual* cash counts on a monthly basis if feasible, or as frequently as bank operations reasonably allow. Include vault teller cash, such as loose bills; samples of strapped $20s, $10s, $5s, and $1s; open sample "Fed-wrapped" packages and fan bills to screen for counterfeits.

- Ensure that cash counts are scheduled for times when the teller has balanced to the general ledger.

- Ensure that cash counts are conducted on all branch cash supplies on at least a quarterly basis. (Include all returned checks, food stamps, and other teller-assigned cash equivalents.)

- Review all documentation related to cash movements for signs of alteration or forgery.

- Reconcile all cash counts to teller records.
- Balance cash counted with the general ledger.
- Increase the frequency of branch audits.
- Beware of employee lifestyle changes, especially acquisition of assets beyond pay scale.
- Require mandatory vacation to provide opportunity to examine employee computer and paper files and to reveal changes in patterns of transactions.
- Confidential hotline and regular employee communication on how and when to use it.

## ▶ Case Study #12: The Banker's Hand Was in the Cookie Jar for Five Years

- Investigate signs of loan officers' change in lifestyle. Although Whitelock allegedly stole only $101,000, there might nonetheless have been signs of a lifestyle more lavish than her salary would have suggested.

- Examine all loan officers' personal financial backgrounds, including bank account activity and unusual acquisition of assets beyond pay level.

- Require mandatory vacation, and examine loan officers' computer and paper files for indicators of potential theft, embezzlement, or, in this case, document forgery. In Whitelock's case, such an examination while she was on vacation would have provided easy access to computer records showing signs of the funds transfers she was accused of making.

- Surprise audits of the general ledger. This probably would have indicated suspicious entries by Whitelock.

- Conduct a fraud risk assessment to determine weaknesses, such as poor segregation of duties or inadequate delegation of authority for loan officers with regard to accessing accounts and approving funds transfers.

- Examine all held statements. In all likelihood, Whitelock would have had the credit line customer's statements held back to prevent discovery of the phony entries. Regularly reviewing such statements can act as both a fraud deterrent and a detection method.

## ▶ Case Study #13: Trusted Trust Officer Abuses Trust for Five Full Years

- Segregation of duties and/or dual authorization of trust transactions over a specified amount. Turner should not have been able to oversee incoming payments to client accounts and initiate disbursement checks—even if they were for amounts below the authorized $5,000.

- Regular unscheduled audits of all trust accounts to screen for suspicious transactions or lack of transactions. If Turner's trust clients were receiving regular payments from mutual funds and these payments suddenly stopped, an audit should have been able to flag this anomaly.

- Review of officers' bank accounts to screen for unusually frequent or large deposits.

- Review of suspected employee lifestyle changes and review of their assets. Turner admitted to stealing $1.1 million from his employers, so acquisitions of expensive possessions probably would have been noticed by anyone looking for them.

- Job rotation. If Turner had been required to rotate with another bank employee, the latter may have discovered Turner's wrongdoing. Alternatively, a job rotation requirement acts as a deterrent to many would-be fraudsters. Turner may not have committed the fraud had such a protocol been in place.

### ▶ Case Study #14: The Banker's Bidding Bust

- Segregation of duties. Because he possessed confidential information pertinent to the bidding process, O'Keefe should not have been permitted to determine who could bid and who could not. Doing so provided the opportunity to exploit a conflict of interest.

- Due diligence of all bidding companies should have been conducted prior to the bidding process. This would have revealed the shell companies.

- Use automated software programs to screen for unusual patterns in bidding—bids that are unusually low based on past history may indicate a fraudulent scheme in progress.

- Conduct a risk assessment to determine risks in the bank's loan management processes.

- Regular review of executives' personal financial accounts for unusual transactions or patterns.

- Confidential hotline and regular employee communication on how and when to use it.

### ▶ Case Study #15: The Greatest Corruption Story of All Time

This particular bribery scheme would have been difficult to prevent because it had the authorization of the company's highest executives. However, a whistleblower tip to regulatory or law enforcement authorities might have put an early stop to it. Generally, though, many overseas bribery schemes in violation of the Foreign Corrupt Practices Act (FCPA) can be prevented by implementing these measures:

- Develop internal policies that are effective geographically and that strictly prohibit violations of anti-fraud–based regulations.

- Train all employees who will be interfacing with overseas business entities about the FCPA rules.

- Implement thorough investigative due diligence procedures covering all prospective overseas business partners, employees, vendors, and so on.
- Modify your internal controls framework and legal resources in a way that incorporates anti-fraud measures that can be applied in new types of business relationships in new areas and jurisdictions.
- Include audit rights in all contracts with third parties, including agents and consultants, *wherever they are located.*

If initial due diligence indicates potential violation of the FCPA, consider retaining an attorney with FCPA experience to investigate potential ways around the legal obstacles.

### ► Case Study #16: The Case of the $2.7 Million "Segregated Cash"

- Investigate circumstances of unusually high amounts of cash recorded as stored in the vault. (The $2.7 million supposedly stored in the CNB banks was extremely high for a bank of its size.)
- Segregation of duties. The CEO should not have had sole authority to store excessive sums of cash in the vault. A board member should have had a third key for events like the one involved.
- Surprise audits. Such an audit would have revealed the absence of thorough documentation for the corresponding liability on the $2.7 million customer's cash out.
- Tighter internal controls on transaction documentation.
- Application of professional skepticism by internal auditors in reviewing accounting records.
- Confidential hotline and regular employee communication on how and when to use it.
- Review of executives' financial account activity.
- Conduct a fraud risk assessment to determine weaknesses in cash transaction processes.

### ► Case Study #17: New Yankee Stadium Construction Shows Red Flags of Concrete Crime

- Conduct thorough due diligence on all suppliers and subcontractors. Treat a supplier or subcontractor as you would your own employees by screening them before establishing a business relationship. How long has the company been in business? What is their track record? Whom have they worked with in the past? What do customers say about them?
- Watch out for conflicts of interest. Scrutinize potential personal relationships that might exist between your organization and a supplier or subcontractor.

For example, are there common family members in responsible positions in both organizations? Although this alone is not necessarily a problem, it does suggest that the proposed relationship should be scrutinized a little more carefully.

- Examine all incoming shipments or purchased product for quality, quantity, and other pertinent specifications.

- Conduct due diligence on all new vendors—to screen for complaints or legal actions against them.

- Ask for references of prospective new vendors, and contact them for feedback on their experience in doing business with the vendor.

- Forensically examine all other pertinent vendor documents for anomalies or other irregularities.

## ▶ Case Study #18: How to Use Social Engineering to Defraud Just about Any Organization

The only truly effective way to prevent this kind of social engineering scheme is to train all employees—especially those who have regular contact with vendors, clients, or other visitors or customers—in the specifics of social engineering. Provide them with numerous actual or potential case studies of how social engineering is (or could be) attempted in order to (1) obtain confidential information that should not be dispensed; (2) have funds fraudulently transferred to accounts that should not be receiving the funds; and (3) gain unauthorized access to your facilities.

If your bank lacks the in-house facilities to develop and implement such training, seek an outside provider with experience in social engineering training at banks. Such vendors can be found on the Internet or through trade associations.

## ▶ Case Study #19: International Card Gang Went to Town to the Tune of $75 Million

This case is about protecting the bank against a data breach that could result in the theft of customer credit card information by thieves who then use it to initiate fraudulent purchases. The technological and policy-related preventive measures designed to prevent such information loss are numerous and should be reviewed and adjusted at least twice per year. These measures include:

- Formulating and enforcing a strict policy of information security, including training on all aspects of the policy. Require all employees to read and sign a document indicating that they understand and will comply with all elements of the policy.

- Monitoring compliance with all regulatory standards governing bank information security.

- Conducting thorough background checks on all IT security personnel prior *and subsequent* to hiring.
- Benchmarking the bank's information security systems and protocols against industry standards and correcting any deficiencies.

## ▶ Case Study #20: "Cardbusters"

This is a basic identity fraud that can be prevented only by:

- Validating all personal identifying information of applicants for new credit card accounts.
- Conducting due diligence on all individuals or corporate entities seeking to set up new merchant credit card accounts.
- Utilizing state-of-the-art credit card fraud prevention technology to screen for unusual transaction patterns. These include volume and frequency of transactions, geolocation, card processor fraud prevention technology, and Suspicious Activity Report (SAR) data mining.

## ▶ Case Study #21: Student Learns Tricks of the Check Fraud Trade

- Store unprinted check stock in a locked filing cabinet under dual control—where two locks are on the cabinet and two different people hold one of the keys. Store check signature plates the same way. This helps prevent collusion with dishonest outsiders.
- Secure boxes of unopened check stock.
- Use positive pay, as well as payee positive pay, and even reverse positive pay if your bank offers it.
- Use anticounterfeiting check security features, such as copy-void pantographs, embedded fluorescent fibers, custom layer check borders, and latest-technology watermarks.
- Conduct prompt bank reconciliations. The longer you put off completing them, the longer a check fraud scheme that might show up in the form of red flags in the statement can continue undetected.

## ▶ Case Study #22: Even Fraud Fighters Can Get Bitten by the Bad Guys

To prevent many forms of ACH fraud, including the one initiated against the West Virginia Auditor's Office:

- Never make changes to ACH payment accounts based on letter or e-mail requests from the vendor. Only make such changes by validating the request by phone with a vendor contact you know to be legitimate.

- Implement debit blocks and debit filters on all applicable accounts to prevent unauthorized/fraudulent ACH debits from your accounts.

- Implement ACH blocks and filters on all accounts except those from which you do want to allow ACH payments to be paid.

- Use ACH positive pay where you provide advance authorization for specific ACH debits that match all criteria posted to your account, such as federal or state payroll tax payments.

- Separate accounts for ACH debits from those for ACH credits.

- Promptly return all fraudulent ACH debits. Conduct more frequent bank reconciliations to screen for fraudulent electronic transactions.

▶ **Case Study #23: Kite Soars to $1.3 Million in a Week before Crashing**

- Consider implementing restricted policies regarding depositors' use of uncollected funds.

- Place holds on deposits for the maximum time limit allowed by federal regulations. (When doing so, ensure compliance with applicable banking regulations to avoid violations.)

- Consider using automated check-kiting detection software tools that screen for unusually frequent NSF problems, suspicious checking account transaction patterns, and other anomalies.

# Notes

## ► Introduction

1. Murray N. Rothbard, *A History of Money and Banking in the United States* (Auburn, AL: Ludwig von Mises Institute, 2002), p. 63.
2. Ibid., pp. 86–87.
3. Edward S. Kaplan, *The Bank of the United States and the American Economy* (Santa Barbara, CA, Greenwood Publishing Group, 1999), p. 63.
4. Research by Hugh Rockoff, cited in Gerald P. Dwyer Jr., "Wildcat Banking, Banking Panics, and Free Banking in the United States," *Economic Review* (Federal Reserve Bank of Atlanta) (December 1996): 11.
5. Rothbart, *History of Money and Banking*, pp. 112–113.
6. The Hon. Eldbridge Gerry Spaulding, "One Hundred Years of Progress in the Business of Banking," address at the meeting of the Bankers Association at the International Exposition (May 1876), p. 26.
7. Jeremy Markham, *A Financial History of the United States*, vol. 1 (Armonk, NY: M.E. Sharpe, 2001), p. 296.
8. Charles R. Morris, *Money, Greed and Risk, Why Financial Crises and Crashes Happen* (New York: Times Books, 1999), p. 53.
9. Scott MacDonald and Jane Hughes, *Separating Fools from Their Money* (Edison, NJ: Transaction Publishers, 2007), p. 248.
10. Morris, *Money, Greed and Risk*, p. 62.
11. Ibid., p. 68.
12. Ibid., p. 76.
13. Kitty Calavita, Henry N. Pontell, and Robert Tillman, *Big Money Crime* (Berkeley: University of California Press, 1997), p. 9.
14. Bert Ely, "Savings and Loan Crisis," *The Concise Encyclopedia of Economics*, www.econlib.org/library/Enc/SavingsandLoanCrisis.html.
15. General Accounting Office Report, *Thrift Failures. Costly Failures Resulted from Regulatory Violation and Unsafe Practices* (June 1989), p. 3. Government Accountability Office (formerly General Accounting Office), Washington, DC, www.gao.gov.
16. Ibid., p. 51.
17. Ibid., p. 23.
18. William K. Black, *The Best Way to Rob a Bank Is to Own One* (Austin, TX: University of Texas Press, 2005), p. 1.
19. Ibid., p. 51.

20. N.R. Kleinfeld, "He Had Money, Women, and S. & L. Now Don Dixon Has Jail," *New York Times*, March 17, 1991.

21. Black, *The Best Way to Rob a Bank*, pp. 107–108.

22. MacDonald and Hughes, *Separating Fools from their Money*, p. 248.

## ▶ Chapter 1

1. Association of Certified Fraud Examiners, *2008 Report to the Nation on Occupational Fraud and Abuse*, p. 4

2. Ibid., p. 18.

3. Ibid., p. 14.

4. Ibid., p. 37.

5. KPMG *Forensic Integrity Survey 2008–2009*, p. iii, http://us.kpmg.com/services/content.asp?lıid=10&l2id=30.

6. ACFE, *2008 Report to the Nation on Occupational Fraud and Abuse*, p.15

7. Deloitte Forensic Center, *Ten Things about the Consequences of Financial Statement Fraud: A Look at Some of the Adverse Consequences Companies Have Experienced* (December 2008), p. 6, www.deloitte.com/dtt/cda/doc/content/us_dfc_ttafsfconsequences_26112008(2).pdf.

8. ACFE, *2008 Report to the Nation on Occupational Fraud and Abuse*.

9. Ken Yormark and Pam Verick Stone, "The Current State of Corporate Fraud Risk Management (FRM)" (March 2008), p. 28.

10. Ibid.

11. Federal Deposit Insurance Corporation, *Statistics on Depository Institutions Report*, December 31, 2008, p. 1, www.donfishback.com/donblogs/images/FDIC.pdf.

12. Association for Financial Professionals, *2007 AFP Payments Fraud Survey Report of Survey Results*, p. 2, www.afponline.com.

13. Ibid.

14. Ibid.

15. Ibid.

16. ACFE, *2008 Report to the Nation on Occupational Fraud and Abuse*, p. 28.

17. Ibid., p. 29.

18. Stanford Law School's Securities Class Action Clearinghouse and Cornerstone Research, Securities Class Action Filings, *2008: A Year in Review*, research by http://securities.stanford.edu/clearinghouse_research/2008_YIR/20090106_YIR08_Full_Report.pdf, p. 2.

19. Ibid., p. 7.

20. Mortgage Asset Research Institute, *Quarterly Fraud Report*, 2Q, 2008, p. 2, www.marisolutions.com.

21. Ibid., p. 3.

22. Institute of Internal Auditors, www.theiia.org.

23. American Institute of Certified Public Accountants, www.aicpa.org.

24. *Preventing Fraud: Assessing the Fraud Risk Management Capabilities of Today's Largest Organizations*, www.protiviti.com.

25. Deloitte Forensic, "Ten Things about Fraud: How Executives View the 'Fraud Control Gap,'" www.deloitte.com/us/forensiccenter.

26. *In re: Washington Mutual, Inc.* Securities Litigation, No. 2:08-Md-1919 MJP, Lead Case No. C08–387 MJP, filed October 21, 2008, pp. 343–344.

## ► Chapter 2

1. PricewaterhouseCoopers, *Economic Crime: People, Culture and Controls—The 4th Biennial Global Economic Crime Survey*, 2007, p. 8, www.pwc.com/gx/en/economic-crime-survey/download-economic-crime-people-culture-controls.jhtml.

2. Association of Certified Fraud Examiners, *2008 Report to the Nation on Occupational Fraud and Abuse*, p. 48.

3. Donald R. Cressey, *Other People's Money* (New York: Free Press, 1953).

4. Alice Gomstyn, "Bleeding Green: The Fall of Fuld Money, Respect and the Corner Office: What Lehman's 'Gorilla' CEO Has Lost," ABC News Business Unit, October 8, 2008, www.abcnews.com.

5. Richard Girgenti, commenting on KPMG *Forensic Integrity Survey 2008–2009*, p. iv, http://us.kpmg.com/services/content.asp?l1id=10&l2id=30.

6. "If You Had a Pulse We Gave You a Loan," by producer Richard Greenberg and correspondent Chris Hansen, Dateline NBC, March 22, 2009.

## ► Chapter 3

1. Association of Certified Fraud Examiners, *Fraud Examiners Manual* (2009), p. 1.903.

2. E. Michael Thomas, "Effective Solutions for Combating Employee Theft; Combating Internal Fraud in the Banking Industry," presentation at the *ACFE 15th Annual Fraud Conference*, July 2004, Las Vegas, NV.

3  *United States v. Abellon*, 2:02-CR-01139-JSL (C.D. Cal. 2003).

4. Federal Financial Institutions Examination Council (FFIEC) White Paper, *The Detection, Investigation and Prevention of Insider Loan Fraud* (2002), p. 2, www.ffiec.gov/pdf/ilf050703_guidance.pdf.

5. Kitty Calavita, Henry N. Pontell, and Robert H. Tillman, *Big Money Crime: Fraud and Politics in the Savings and Loan Crisis* (Berkeley: University of California Press, 1997), p. 54.

6. Ibid.

7. Hearing before the House Subcommittee on Commerce, Consumer, and Monetary Affairs of the Committee on Government Operations, *Adequacy of Federal Efforts to Combat Fraud, Abuse and Misconduct in Federally Insured Financial Institutions*, November 19, 1987, p. 79.

8. Federal Deposit Insurance Corporation, *Risk Management Manual of Examination Policies*, Section 9.1, www.fdic.gov/regulations/safety/manual/Section9-1.html.

9. BITS Fraud Reduction Steering Committee, *Fraud Prevention Strategies for Consumer, Commercial and Mortgage Loan Departments* (Washington DC: Author, 2005), p. 8

10. Ibid.

11. Thomas, "Effective Solutions for Combating Employee Theft."

12. ACFE, *Fraud Examiners Manual*, p. 1.909.

13. Jane Moss Snow, "Uncovering Mortgage Fraud," *Mortgage Banking* 55, no. 7 (April 1995): 38–44.

14. Thomas, "Effective Solutions for Combating Employee Theft."

15. FFIEC White Paper, p. 4.

16. BITS Fraud Reduction Steering Committee, *Fraud Prevention Strategies*, p. 43.

17. Ibid., p. 46.

18. Ibid., p. 10.

19. Ibid., pp. 36–37.

20. Freddie Mac, *How to Read a Credit Report*, www.freddiemac.com/learn/lo/creditreport/lo_credrpt.html.

21. BITS Fraud Reduction Steering Committee, *Fraud Prevention Strategies*, pp. 35–39.

22. Ibid., pp. 36–37.

23. Ibid., p. 44.

24. Ibid., p. 46.

25. Thomas, "Effective Solutions for Combating Employee Theft."

26. Ibid.

27. FFIEC White Paper, p. 20.

28. Ibid., p. 21.

## ▶ Chapter 4

1. Association of Certified Fraud Examiners, *Report to the Nation on Occupational Fraud* (2008), p. 29.

2. E. Michael Thomas, "Effective Solutions for Combating Employee Theft; Combating Internal Fraud in the Banking Industry," *Fraud Magazine* (July 2004).

3. Joseph T. Wells, *Corporate Fraud Handbook* (Hoboken, NJ: John Wiley & Sons, 2006), p. 196.

4. *White-Collar Crime Fighter* (newsletter), 10, No. 3 (March 2008): 8.

5. Peter D. Goldmann, *Detecting and Preventing Fraud in Accounts Payable* (Orlando, FL: International Accounts Payable Professionals, 2009), p. 16.

6. Ibid., p. 34.

7. Wells, *Corporate Fraud Handbook*, pp. 292–296.

8. U.S. Department of Transportation, Federal Highway Administration, www.fhwa.dot.gov/programadmin/contracts/fraud.cfm.

9. Wells, *Corporate Fraud Handbook*, p. 296.

10. Association for Financial Professionals, *2009 Payments Fraud and Control Survey*, p. 19, www.afponline.org/pub/pdf/2009_Payments_Fraud_Survey.pdf.

11. Ibid..
12. Ibid., p. 6.
13. Ibid., p. 7.
14. Ibid., p. 9.
15. Ibid., p. 13.
16. Office of the Comptroller of the Currency, *Check Fraud: A Guide to Avoiding Losses* (2005), p. 4, www.occ.treas.gov/chckfrd/chckfrd.pdf.
17. "Riggs Probe Includes Recordings," *Washington Post*, September 17, 2004.
18. National Automated Clearing House, *Risk to Financial Institutions of Using the Automated Clearing House for Large-Value Payments*, p. 4, http://nacha.org/OtherResources/riskmgmt/FIRisk.pdf.
19. Association of Certified Fraud Examiners, *2008 Report to the Nation on Occupational Fraud and Abuse*, p. 13.
20. Goldmann, *Detecting and Preventing Fraud in Accounts Payable*, p. 40.
21. Ibid.
22. Ibid., p. 41.
23. Verizon Business RISK Team, *2009 Data Breach Investigation Report*, p. 9, www.verizonbusiness.com/resources/security/reports/2009_databreach_rp.pdf.
24. Ibid., p. 13.
25. Ibid., p. 7.
26. Ibid., p. 33.
27. U.S. Secret Service and CERT Coordination Center, Software Engineering Institute, Carnegie Mellon University, *Insider Threat Study: Illicit Cyber Activity in the Banking and Finance Sector*, p. 5, www.cert.org/archive/pdf/insiderthreat_gov2008.pdf.
28. Ibid.
29. Thomas, "Effective Solutions for Combating Employee Theft."
30. Chris Doxey, "Fraud Prevention Essential: Segregation of Duties," *White-Collar Crime Fighter* (newsletter), 11, No. 4 (April, 2009): 4.
31. Goldmann, *Detecting and Preventing Fraud in Accounts Payable*, p. 107.
32. Ibid., p. 115.
33. Ibid., p. 116.

## ▶ Chapter 5

1. Joseph T. Wells, *Corporate Fraud Handbook* (Hoboken, NJ: John Wiley & Sons, 2006), p. 141.
2. Ronald R. Volkmer, 1992, "Breach of Fiduciary Duty for Self-Dealing," *Estate Planning* 19 (September–October), http://law.jrank.org/pages/10125/Self-Dealing.html#ixzzoQNZdEwOK.
3. Association of Certified Fraud Examiners, *Report to the Nation on Occupational Fraud* (2008), p. 29.
4. Office of the U.S. Attorney, Hartford, CT, July 24, 2008, www.usdoj.gov/usao/ct/Press2008/20080724-1.html.

5. William Jacobson, Richard Smith, Kim Walker, and Anne Elkins Murray, "FCPA Enforcement Trends: More International Cooperation and Forfeiture Actions?" *Fulbright Briefing,* Fulbright & Jaworski L.L.P., www.fulbright.com/index. cfm?fuseaction=publications.detail&pub_id=3713&site_id=494&detail=yes.

6. U.S. Department of Justice, www.usdoj.gov. Securities and Exchange Commission, www.sec.gov. *Statement of Offense in United States v. Siemens Aktiengesellschaft,,* www.usdoj. gov/opa/documents/siemens-ag-stmtoffense.pdf. *United States v. Siemens Aktiengesellschaft* No. 08-367 (D.D.C.), Dec. 12, 2008.

7. William K. Black, *The Best Way to Rob a Bank Is to Own* One (Austin, TX: University of Texas Press, 2005), pp. 253–254.

8. Frank Partnoy, *F.I.A.S.C.O. Blood in the Water on Wall Street* (New York: W.W. Norton & Company, 2009), pp. 248–249.

9. ACFE, *Report to the Nation on Occupational Fraud and Abuse 2008* (2008), p. 29.

10. Brian Patrick Green and Alan Reinstein, "Banking Industry Financial Statement Fraud and the Effects of Regulation Enforcement and Increased Public Scrutiny," *Research in Accounting Regulation* 17, pp. 87–106, 2004.

11. Ibid., p. 101.

12. *Securities and Exchange Commission v. Federal Home Loan Mortgage Corporation, et al.,* United States District Court, District of Columbia, September 27, 2007.

13. Securities and Exchange Commission, *Accounting and Auditing Enforcement Release No. 458,* June 28, 1993.

14. Michael C. Knapp and Loreen Knapp, *Contemporary Auditing,* 5th rev. ed. (Florence, KY: Cengage Learning South-Western, Division of Thomson Learning Edition, 2003), pp. 197–200.

15. William K. Black, "The Two Documents Everyone Should Read to Better Understand the Crisis," *Huffington Post,* March 28, 2009, www.huffington post.com/william-k-black/the-two-documents-everyon_b_169813.html.

16. Rep. Elijah Cummings, speaking at hearing, "Credit Rating Agencies and the Financial Crisis," October 22, 2008, House of Representatives, Committee on Oversight and Government Reform, Washington, D.C.

17. Investopedia, www.investopedia.com/terms/s/shortswingprofitrule.asp.

18. Thomas C. Newkirk, "Insider Trading: A U.S. Perspective," speech *16th International Symposium on Economic Crime,* Jesus College, Cambridge, England, September 19, 1998, September 19, 1998, www.sec.gov/news/ speech/speecharchive/1998/spch221.htm#FOOTNOTE_22.

19. Federal Defense Cases, www.federaldefensecases.com/treatisearticle2.php.

20. Vicky B. Heiman-Hoffman, Kimberly P. Morgan, and James M. Patton, "The Warning Signs of Fraudulent Financial Reporting," *Journal of Accountancy* 182 (1996).

21. Sun Microsystems, www.sun.com.

22. Robert Heim, "How to Win an Insider Trading Case," www.meyersandheim. com/insider_trading.html.

23. Association of Certified Fraud Examiners, American Institute of Certified Public Accountants, and Institute of Internal Auditors, *Managing the Business Risk of Fraud: A Practical Guide* (2008), p. 15.

24. Ellen Zimiles and Joseph Spinelli, *White-Collar Crime Fighter* (September 2007): 3–5.

25. Brian A. Ochs, "The SEC's Enforcement of Procedures to Prevent Insider Trading," *Journal of Investment Compliance* 8, no. 3 (Fall 2007): p. 5.

26. Division Report, SEC's Division of Market Regulation, 1990.

27. Ochs, ibid., p. 5.

28. Ibid.

29. Wells, ibid., p. 141.

## ► Chapter 6

1. Blake Coppotelli, "Audits, Screening, and Expertise Help to Build Integrity," *Kroll Global Fraud Report, 2007–2008*, p. 24, http://www.kroll.com/about/library/fraud/.

2. Clifton Gunderson LLP, *Combating Construction Fraud*, pp. 6–7, www.cliftoncpa.com, 2008.

3. BITS Fraud Reduction Steering Committee, *Fraud Prevention Strategies for Consumer, Commercial and Mortgage Loan Departments* (Washington DC: Author, 2005), p. 8.

4. Ibid.

5. E. Michael Thomas, "Effective Solutions for Combating Employee Theft; Combating Internal Fraud in the Banking Industry," presented at the ACFE's *15th Annual Fraud Conference*, Las Vegas, NV; July 2004.

6. BITS Fraud Reduction Steering Committee, *Fraud Prevention Strategies*, pp. 20, 21, 34.

7. Peter Goldmann, "Subprime Fraud: The Real Story," *White-Collar Crime Fighter* (April 2009): 6, no. 11.

8. Ibid.

9. MortgageFraudBlog, www.mortgagefraudblog.com/index.php/weblog/permalink/ten_charged_in_florida_chunking_scheme.

10. Association of Certified Fraud Examiners, *2009 Fraud Examiners Manual* (Austin, TX: Author, 2009), p. 1.928.

11. Mortgage Asset Research Institute, *Understanding Mortgage Fraud*, www.marisolutions.com/mortgage-fraud.asp.

12. Ibid.

13. Brad R. Jacobsen and Michael Barnhill, "Drawing the Short Straw—Mortgage Fraud and Straw Buyers," *Utah Bar Journal*, July 16, 2008, http://webster.utahbar.org/barjournal/2008/07/drawing_the_short_straw_mortga.html.

14. Business Software Alliance, www.bsacybersafety.com/threat/social-engineering.cfm.

15. "applekid" post, "The Life of a Social Engineer," www.protokulture.com. *White-Collar Crime Fighter* 9, no. 7 (July 2007): 4.

16. Anti-Phishing Work Group, www.apwg.org.

17. Tom Mahoney, www.merchant911.org.

18. Verizon Business RISK Team, 2009 *Data Breach Investigations Report,* www.verizonbusiness.com/resources/security/reports/2009_databreach_rp.pdf.

19. Shirley Inscoe, "Top 10 Fraud Threats That Won't Go Away," www.mementosecurity.com/bankfraudforum/index.php/about.

20. Michael Mulholand, "Fraudsters Unite! A Look at the Rise of Collusive Fraud Networks," www.mementosecurity.com/bankfraudforum/index.php/comments/classifying_internal_fraud/.

21. Ibid.

22. Tony Hayes, quoted in Julia S. Cheney, "An Update on Trends in the Debit Card Market," Federal Reserve Bank of Philadelphia (June 2007): 9–10.

23. "Identity Theft/Red Flags Industry Guidance and Compliance Procedures," Office of Thrift Supervision, August, Industry Conference Call, August 11, 2008.

24. Kevin Null, "One Bank's Fraud Fight," *Security Management* (February 2000): 37.

25. Office of the Comptroller of the Currency, *Check Fraud: A Guide to Avoiding Losses* (2005), p. 3, www.occ.treas.gov/chckfrd/chckfrd.pdf.

26. Inscoe, "Top 10 Fraud Threats That Won't Go Away."

27. Frank Abagnale, "Combating ACH Fraud," Bankers Information Service, www.sheshunoff.nghet/content/view/786/81/.

28. KPMG Financial Risk and Advisory Services, "Preventing Deposit Fraud: Effective Strategies for Banks" (2002), p. 5.

29. Grace Leong, "Provo Man Accused of $1M Credit-Union Fraud," *Daily Herald,* April 10, 2009, www.heraldextra.com/content/view/305595/18.

30. BITS ibid., p. 23.

31. Fannie Mae Mortgage Resources, www.efanniemae.com/utility/legal/antifraud.jsp.

32. Bruce Dubinsky and Christine Warner, "Uncovering Accounts Payable Fraud Using Fuzzy Matching Logic," *Business Credit* (March 2008).

33. ACFE, 2009 *Fraud Examiners Manual,* p. 37.

34. ACFE, 2008 *Report to the Nation on Occupational Fraud and Abuse,* p. 5.

35. Mike Noyes, "Combating Construction Fraud," ENR.com, http://enr.construction.com/opinions/viewPoint/archives/080910.asp.

36. Ibid.

37. BITS ibid., p. 39.

38. Mark Edmead, "New Guidance on Strong-Factor Authentication for Internet Banking," *IT Compliance Journal* 2 (Winter 2006): 23.

39. Federal Financial Institutions Examination Council, *Authentication in an Internet Banking Environment,* p. 12, www.ffiec.gov/pdf/authentication_guidance.pdf.

40. Atul Prakash, with Laura Falk and Kevin Borders, "Analyzing Websites for User-Visible Security Design Flaws," University of Michigan, Ann Arbor (July 2008): 1, 8, 9, http://cups.cs.cmu.edu/soups/2008/proceedings/p117Falk.pdf.

41. Susan Ward, "Steps to Prevent Credit Card Fraud: A Credit Card Fraud Prevention Checklist for Businesses," About.com, http://sbinfocanada.about .com/od/insurancelegalissues/a/creditcardfraud.htm.

42. Peter D. Goldmann, *Detecting and Preventing Fraud in Accounts Payable* (Orlando, FL: International Accounts Payable Professionals, 2009), pp. 155–156.

43. Ibid., p. 156.

44. Noyes, "Combating Construction Fraud."

45. Ibid., p. 154.

46. BITS ibid., p. 43.

## ► Chapter 7

1. Federal Reserve Bank of St. Louis, *Insights for Bank Directors: A Basic Course on Evaluating Financial Performance and Portfolio Risk,* 2004, www.stlouisfed .org/col/director/bankfraud/whatyouneedtoknow.htm.

2. American Institute of Certified Public Accountants, *Statement on Auditing Standards (SAS) 99, Consideration of Fraud in a Financial Statement Audit,* p. 25. 2002.

3. Ibid.

4. American Institute of Certified Public Accountants, Institute of Internal Auditors, Association of Certified Fraud Examiners, *Managing the Business Risk of Fraud: A Practical Guide* (2008), p. 6.

5. Basel Committee on Banking Supervision, Bank for International Settlements, "Internal Audit in Banks and the Supervisor's Relationship with Auditors," p. 9, http://www.bis.org/publ/bcbs84.pdf?noframes=1.

6. Ibid., p. 22.

7. Jonny Frank, *Deeper & Broader: Performing Fraud & Reputation Risk Assessments* (Altamonte Springs, FL: Institute of Internal Auditors, 2004).

8. Ibid.

9. Leonard Vona, *Fraud Risk Assessment, Building a Fraud Audit Program* (Hoboken, NJ: John Wiley & Sons, 2008).

## ► Chapter 8

1. William D. Jackson, Mark Jickling, Gary Shorter, M. Maureen Murphy, and Michael V. Seitzinger, "Banking and Securities Regulation and Agency Enforcement Authorities," Congressional Research Service, Library of Congress, 2006, pp. 5–6, digital.library.unt .edu/govdocs/crs/permalink/meta-crs-10810:1.

2. Ibid., p. 8.

3. Susan S. Bies, "Strengthening Compliance through Effective Corporate Governance," speech before the American Bankers Association, *Annual Regulatory Compliance Conference*, Washington DC, June 11, 2003.

4. Federal Reserve Bank of New York, "Industry Sound Practices for Financial and Accounting Controls at Financial Institutions" (2006): 3.

5. Ibid., p. 4.

6. Federal Reserve Board, *Interagency Guidelines Establishing Information Security Standards*, p. 4, www.federalreserve.gov/boarddocs/press/bcreg/2005/20051214/attachment.pdf.

7. Ibid., p. 3.

8. Electronic Privacy Information Center, "The Gramm Leach Bliley Act," http://epic.org/privacy/glba/.

9. Federal Reserve Board, *Interagency Guidelines Establishing Information Security Standards*, pp. 8–12.

10. "Covered accounts" include any account that is "used mostly for personal, family, or household purposes, and that involves multiple payments or transactions. Covered accounts include credit card accounts, mortgage loans, automobile loans, margin accounts, cell phone accounts, utility accounts, checking accounts, and savings accounts." See Federal Trade Commission, "New 'Red Flag' Requirements for Financial Institutions and Creditors Will Help Fight Identity Theft," www.ftc.gov/bcp/edu/pubs/business/alerts/alt050.shtm.

11. FTC, *Fighting Fraud with the Red Flags Rule: A How-To Guide*, www.ftc.gov/bcp/edu/pubs/business/idtheft/bus23.pdf.

▶ **Chapter 9**

1. *Insights for Bank Directors: A Basic Course on Evaluating Financial Performance and Portfolio Risk*, http://www.stlouisfed.org/col/director/bankfraud/whatyouneedtoknow.htm.

2. Federal Deposit Insurance Corporation, "Supervisory Insights," www.fdic.gov/regulations/examinations/supervisory/insights/siwin05/article03_enforcement.html.

3. Ibid.

4. Thomas W. Golden, Steven L. Skalak, and Mona M. Clayton, *A Guide to Forensic Accounting Investigation* (New York: PricewaterhouseCoopers LLP, 2006), p. 179.

5. videosurveillance.com, www.videosurveillance.com/banks.asp.

6. Golden, Skalak, and Clayton, *Guide to Forensic Accounting Investigation*, p. 129.

7. American Institute of Certified Public Accountants, *Statement on Auditing Standards (SAS) 99, Consideration of Fraud in a Financial Statement Audit*,

2002, www.aicpa.org and International Auditing and Assurance Standards Board of the International Federal of Accountants, *International Standard on Auditing (ISA) 240*, 2002, d.org/cos/cos_021001b.htm.

8. "Travel and Entertainment Fraud," Ari Schonbrun, speech before the *2009 Anti-Fraud/Anti-Money Laundering Conference*, Foundation for Accounting Education, New York, June 10, 2009.

9. Martin T. Biegelman and Joel T. Bartow, *Executive Roadmap to Fraud Prevention and Internal Control: Creating a Culture of Compliance* (Hoboken: NJ: John Wiley & Sons, 2006).

10. Stephen Pedneault, CPA, CFE, Forensic Accounting Services, LLC, Glastonbury, CT, 06033, www.forensicaccountingservices.com.

11. Association of Certified Fraud Examiners, American Institute of Certified Public Accountants, and Institute of Internal Auditors, *Managing the Business Risk of Fraud: A Practical Guide*, p. 15.

12. AICPA, *Statement of Auditing Standards 99*, p. 16.

13. Ibid., p. 75.

14. Ibid., pp. 24–25.

15. Ibid., pp. 26–27.

16. Ibid., pp. 26–30.

# Glossary

## A

**accounts payable fraud** Any fraud that impacts an organization's payments or disbursements, processes, and procedures. Such frauds may include check theft, check forgery, setting up sham vendors, vendor-perpetrated fraud, a variety of billing schemes, and automated clearinghouse frauds.

**asset-backed security (ABS)** A bond backed by loans, leases, credit card debt, a company's receivables, royalties and so on, but *not* mortgages.

**asset misappropriation** This type of fraud includes skimming revenues, stealing confidential customer data from company computers, check forgery, and payroll fraud.

## B

**bid rigging** The illegal act of manipulating the competitive bidding process to ensure that a preferred vendor or contractor receives a contract, usually in exchange for a kickback or bribe.

**bribery** Money, a favor, or something else of value is promised to, given to, or taken from an individual or organization in an attempt to sway decisions, such as the choice of vendor.

**builder bailout scheme** Loan fraud where a straw buyer or a legitimate buyer is led to believe that he or she is getting a great deal by being able to buy a new home with no money down but is actually duped into taking on a mortgage he or she cannot afford.

## C

**check fraud** A category of schemes including theft of blank organization checks, forging endorsements, forging signatures, counterfeiting, intercepting mailed checks, and the like.

**chunking** Loan fraud in which the victim is a gullible investor who is recruited to purchase a home, site-unseen, with no money down and with no risk because, according to the perpetrator, the property is either currently or soon to be occupied by a tenant whose payments will be made to the "investor" and will be more than adequate to cover the mortgage payments.

**collateralized debt obligation (CDO)** A bond backed by other bonds of varying degrees of risk, divided accordingly into separate segments or *tranches*. Each tranche receives the cash flow from the underlying bonds, with the riskiest tranche most exposed to loss due to the low quality of the underlying bonds.

**collusion** Fraud committed by two perpetrators—usually one who works for the target organization and the other a dishonest outsider such as a vendor or customer.

**computer fraud** The deliberate unauthorized access, distribution, abuse, or alteration of electronic data, usually for financial gain.

**conflict of interest** A situation in which an employee or manager with influence to affect business decisions has a direct or indirect interest in an entity that is in a position to receive business from the organization. For example, a purchasing manager of an organization has a duty to perform her work with loyalty to that employer, thus choosing sellers who offer the best products at the lowest prices, but might be tempted to have the organization buy products from, for example, the manager's sibling that are not as good or as cheap.

**corruption** This type of fraud occurs when an employee—usually a manager—abuses power in a business transaction to get money or favors illegally. Bribery and kickbacks are common forms of corruption.

**credit default swap (CDS)** An insurance-like agreement representing a bet by the insurance buyer that a specific bond won't default, and the insurance seller bets that it will. The seller collects a fee or "premium" from the buyer in exchange for a promise to pay the full amount of the buyer's loss in the event of a default or loss of value of the bond.

**cyber-extortion** Hacking into an organization's database(s) of confidential customer or employee information, stealing it, and threatening to release it on the Internet if the organization does not do what the extortionist demands.

## D

**detection** Methods used by fraud examiners, employees, auditors, or law enforcement officials to discover red flags or hard evidence of potential or actual fraud. Detection can range from management's learning about fraud from an employee tip, to using a confidential informant to detect evidence of fraud, to auditors conducting a full-scale fraud audit to discover signs of fraud.

**double billing** A form of accounts payable fraud where a dishonest vendor or insider submits a duplicate bill after submitting a legitimate one in the hope that the accounts payable controls will not notice the duplicate invoice and simply pay it.

## E

**employee-level fraud** Any fraud committed against an organization by someone who works for that organization and who is not a supervisor, manager, or executive.

**equity skimming** A fraud in which an individual or group buys one or more single-family homes with mortgages in amounts equal to 80 to 90 percent of the property value, with the rest of the purchase amount invested by the buyer(s) as equity. The properties are then rented, but the owner/perpetrators fail to make the mortgage payments. They collect rent until they have recouped their equity investment and continue to collect until the mortgage is foreclosed. Any rental payments they receive in excess of the equity "investment" are proverbial gravy—until the bank forecloses. The lending bank is left holding the bag.

**extortion** The illegal use of legitimate or criminally obtained authority or influence to demand money, information, property, or other concessions from the targeted victim.

**F**

**FACT Act Red Flag Rules** The Fair and Accurate Credit Transactions Act was amended to include anti–identity theft rules for financial institutions. The Red Flags requirements have specific rules for credit and debit card issuers. Most important, issuers are required to have in place procedures for authenticating card-holders' requests for changes of address. Bank examiners will assess financial institutions' policies in this regard based on four tests:

1. Can the card issuer assess the validity of a change of address?
2. Do the institution's policies and procedures prohibit issuance of a card until it verifies the change of address?
3. Are electronic notices sent for verification clear and conspicuous?
4. Is sampling performed, if needed?

**firewall** A system that can detect and prevent unauthorized access to or from an individual personal computer or computer network. Private or sensitive information is kept inside the firewall, which can stop certain messages (such as those containing viruses) from entering a network if they do not meet the organization's security standards.

**floor plan loan fraud** Fraud involving pledging high-value in-stock merchandise, such as automobiles, boats, or furniture, as collateral for a loan. In a legitimate transaction, the loan is repaid as the merchandise is sold. In a loan fraud, the merchant sells an asset but fails to use the proceeds to repay the loan. Instead, a kickback is paid to the loan officer or manager who ensures that the appropriate due diligence procedures to verify the value of the merchandise are ignored and that any documentation falsification required to conceal the loan is taken care of.

**Foreign Corrupt Practices Act (FCPA)** A law on the books since 1997 which prohibits offering or giving bribes or other corrupt payments to foreign officials for the purpose of obtaining or retaining business. The FCPA also requires companies to keep accurate books and records and to maintain internal accounting controls for preventing and detecting FCPA violations.

**forgery** Falsely and fraudulently making or altering a document (as a check).

**fraud risk assessment** The procedure conducted by auditors to identify types of fraudulent schemes or scenarios that could occur at the organization due to inadequate internal controls or to specific motives of fraudsters.

**fraudulent financial reporting** The category of frauds involving intentional misrepresentation of the organization's financial performance or condition. These frauds typically include creating fictitious sales, concealing liabilities, falsifying inventory values, and the like.

**financial statement fraud** Remember Enron? Financial numbers games destroyed the company and cost thousands of employees their jobs and life savings.

## G

**ghost employee** An employee in name only. A name fraudulently added to the organization's payroll records in order to generate fraudulent paychecks to the perpetrator, usually an internal payroll staffer or senior manager.

**Gramm Leach Bliley Act (GLBA)** Gramm Leach Bliley Act (GLBA), passed in 1999, repealed the Glass-Steagall Act. It is also known for its formalization of legal standards for the protection of private customer information and for rules and requirements of organizations to safeguard such information.

**government-sponsored entity (GSE)** An investment company, such as Fannie Mae and Freddie Mac, chartered by the federal government to purchase residential mortgages from mortgage loan originators as a way to add liquidity to the mortgage business. The GSE's typically purchase only "prime" loans and issue bonds secured by these loans to the open market.

## H

**hacker** An unauthorized computer system user who attempts to or gains access to an information system.

## I

**identity fraud** Use of someone else's identity to facilitate fraud. This usually involves the use of stolen or forged identity documents such as a driver's license or Social Security number, to obtain goods or services by deception. Such frauds include fraudulently opening bank accounts, applying for loans, and applying for credit cards.

**identity theft** Theft of the identity of another person by stealing personal identifying information (PII), which includes Social Security number, driver's license number, date of birth, and bank account information.

**internal controls** Measures designed to prevent fraud. These can be numerous in large organizations where the opportunities for employees or outsiders to commit fraud are numerous. Internal controls are formulated to foil specific types of fraud at all levels of the organization: entity level, department level, and process level.

## K

**kickback** An illegal payment by a seller to a purchasing agent as compensation for awarding the seller a piece of business.

## L

**linked financing** Offers of large deposits in return for favorable treatment on loans to out-of-area borrowers or to other borrowers previously unknown to the institution.

Where the brokered deposits are not pledged to secure the associated loans, the institution is exposed to substantial risk since it must refund the deposits regardless of the collectability of the loans.

**loan lapping** A loan scheme in which the fraudster steals payments from one or more loans and makes loan payments on those loans from funds received from subsequently closed loans.

## M

**mortgage backed security (MBS)** A bond secured by a pool of residential mortgages, usually "prime" rated mortgages rather than subprime loans.

**mortgage broker** An independent mortgage specialist who offers various types of residential mortgages to prospective borrowers on behalf of specific lenders. Brokers are supposed to serve borrowers by offering the best mortgage for their specific financial situation. When the broker sells a loan to a borrower, he or she collects a commission from the lender that has agreed to provide the loan.

**mortgage fraud** Any attempt by an applicant to obtain a mortgage by submitting false details about income, employment, or any bogus information supplied in support of a mortgage by mortgage brokers, appraisers, attorneys, or underwriters.

## N

**nominee loan** A loan provided to a "straw buyer," or someone recruited to take on a mortgage based solely on the strength of their credit history. The borrower may or may not be part of this fraudulent scheme but in either case receives payment in exchange for allowing a fraudster to use his or her credit details to falsely secure a loan.

## P

**phishing** Pronounced "fishing," the act of sending e-mail messages to multiple computer users, falsely claiming to be a legitimate enterprise, in an attempt to scam users into surrendering private information that will be used for identity theft. The e-mail directs users to visit a fraudulent Web site, where they are asked to update personal information, such as passwords and credit card number, Social Security number, and bank account numbers, that the legitimate organization already has.

**property flipping** Fraud in which a home is purchased using an initial mortgage. The property is then fraudulently appraised by an unscrupulous appraiser. The home is then quickly resold for maximum profit. Often this is a one-time event. But in many instances, the same process is initiated again and again by a group of co-conspirators who buy and sell the same property to each other or to new straw buyers at progressively higher prices, and applying for bigger and bigger mortgages each time.

## R

**reciprocal loan** A loan authorized by a dishonest loan officer or bank manager to one or more crooked bank colleagues or to dishonest counterparts in *other* financial institutions.

During the savings and loan (S&L) crisis of the 1980s, bank owners lent to each other in order to avoid drawing regulators' attention by issuing loans to themselves. Each loan made to an accomplice was made with the understanding that a comparable, reciprocal loan would be made in return.

## S

**Sarbanes-Oxley Act** A law signed by President George W. Bush in 2002 in response to the Enron debacle and other major corporate frauds. It put into place tough rules and regulations about what company auditors and top executives can and cannot do when it comes to managing the company's financial statements and reports. One of the act's main requirements is that all public company chief executive officers and chief financial officers must now certify all financial statements, taking responsibility for the accuracy of these statements. If it is later found that the statements covered up illegal financial activity, these executives can be charged with criminal activity.

**shell company fraud** A form of billing fraud involving setting up phony vendors and generating false invoices to be paid by the organization. The payees are not companies at all but rather businesses in name only. They are created by employees with the intention of generating bogus invoices in the "vendor's" name and submitting them to the bank for payment.

**social engineering** In the context of confidential, secure computer information, the practice of persuading or "conning" a targeted individual who has access to such information to either provide the information or access to it to the perpetrator.

**stated income mortgage** Also known as a "liar loan," a mortgage that is applied for without having to divulge or document personal income by providing pay stubs, income tax returns or other proof of earnings.

**subprime mortgage** A mortgage provided by a lender to a borrower with below "A" quality credit, that is, with blemishes on their credit histories such as missed mortgage or consumer loan payments.

**suspense account fraud** Also known as "pass-through" account fraud involving special accounts held by the bank in which funds are temporarily held for various reasons, such as insufficient loan documentation, pending closing of a loan, or interdepartmental transfers or wire transfers. It is easy for bank employees with authority to credit and debit these accounts to move funds from such accounts to one that they control (such as a personal checking account).

## T

**Trojan horse** A piece of software that, when loaded onto your computer via e-mail or downloading Internet files, allows a hacker to take control of your computer behind your back. A Trojan infection can allow a cyber-criminal to have total remote access to your computer.

# About the Author

**Peter Goldmann** is president of White-Collar Crime 101 LLC, the publisher of *White-Collar Crime Fighter,* a monthly newsletter for internal auditors, controllers, corporate counsel, financial operations managers, and fraud investigators.

Peter has published *White-Collar Crime Fighter* since 1998 and has interviewed hundreds of fraud investigators, forensic accountants, white-collar crime attorneys, ex-convicts, and auditors.

In addition, White-Collar Crime 101 has developed the leading employee fraud awareness training program, *FraudAware.* The program is a user-friendly workshop and e-learning training tool designed to educate employees at all levels in how to detect, prevent, and report incidents of fraud or suspicious conduct.

The course, which is customized for individual corporate, nonprofit, and government agency clients, reinforces companies' whistleblowing programs by enabling employees to detect fraudulent activity that can then be reported to supervisors or managers or by using the organization's confidential hotline.

Peter has 25 years of experience as a business journalist and trainer, having launched, edited, and published numerous business trade periodicals covering small business, international trade, management strategy, banking, and personal finance. He is a member of the Editorial Advisory Committee of the Association of Certified Fraud Examiners (ACFE) as well as an active member of the Institute of Internal Auditors, the High-Tech Crime Investigation Association, and InfraGard.

He is a regular columnist for the ACFE's newsletter, *The Fraud Examiner,* and is a frequent contributor to other leading industry publications on anti-fraud topics. He has appeared on *The Wall Street Journal This Morning, Fox Business News,* and in *The New York Times* and *Internal Auditor* magazine. He can be reached at pgoldmann@wccfighter.com.

# Index